A DANCER IN DEPTH

Paragraphs From A Theatrical Life

Stanley Howard Mazin

ARPress
45 Dan Road Suite 5
Canton MA 02021
Hotline: 1(888) 821-0229
Fax: 1(508) 545-7580

Ordering Information:

Quantity sales. Special discounts are available on quantity purchases by corporations, associations, and others. For details, contact the publisher at the address above.

Printed in the United States of America.

ISBN-13:   Paperback   979-8-89356-427-3
                eBook   979-8-89356-426-6
                Hardcover   979-8-89356-428-0

Library of Congress Control Number: 2024904625

A DANCER IN DEPTH

Paragraphs From A Theatrical Life

Stanley Howard Mazin

ARPress
ILLUMINATING IDEAS
EMPOWERING VOICES

PREFACE

I've had a life in show business. Often, whenever I meet someone new, the conversation turns to my telling special stories about this person or that. "You should write a book!", the listener will tell me. "Everyone tells me that", I'll retort, "but it won't happen. I can never remember facts..."

Several months ago a new acquaintance pushed the issue about my writing a book. "Listen! My wife is a ghost writer and she has helped many celebrities write their own autobiographies." I responded with my familiar thought about how I am never able to remember specific incidents factually. "And besides", I added, "I'm sure if I did write a memoir, with my memory it would be finished by page 10!" My new friend said, "Just start writing one paragraph and see where it leads you." And so this book was begun...

I do want the reader to know that every story told here is real to my recollection and never exaggerated. That is important to me. I realize some situations are perhaps graphically explained and not for the demure reader, but I believe for the reader to truly get to know me, all content must be truthful and honest. To that objective perhaps I have bent over backwards ... for the reader to decide. By the way, this is all my own writing and the ghost writer mentioned above never worked on this memoir. At any rate, without writing a 'britannica' of my life, here is the Stanley Howard Mazin lowdown I am eager to share with you! Let's get started!

A DANCER IN DEPTH

Paragraphs From A Theatre Life

By Stanley Howard Mazin

Mother was a lesbian. Well, she may not have been an 'all-out' lesbian. In my mind she was merely taking advantage of any situation which would protect her and her children from anything less than financial security. You see, she and my father were married for 16 years before they divorced right after my bar mitzvah. My father was always very possessive of my mother ... apparently by loving her so much. He accused her of fooling around with Stogie, a man both my mother and father were friendly with, along with Stogie's wife. I remember the night it happened...

I was awakened by the sound of shouting, which had happened many times before. But this time there was a gunshot, and my sister and I both came running into their bedroom. My mother had been hit, not by the gun, but by his fist. Then my father said to us coldly, "Okay, you have to decide if you are staying here or going with your mother". My sister was too young and afraid to leave the house, but I said I would go with Mom. So off we went, my mother and I in the middle of the night to God knows where. She got a room at the Clinton Hotel in Philadelphia for 1 night, and I stayed in the room with her... and in the same bed. I remember now how 'cheap' I felt, having heard the rumors about Mom, and possibly partially believing them. I felt like I was being 'used'... I don't think I have ever felt that low. The following morning my mother told me I had to return to my father because she had no idea what she was going to do. So I returned to our row house in South Philadelphia the following morning. My mother had some friends who lived in Atlantic City, so she went there. She told me she would send for me once she got settled.

I stayed with my dad and sister for 1 year, and was sort of 'brain washed' during that year, beginning to actually believe my father's accusations. My mother came to visit every other week for one day at a time. On each visit, I got colder and colder to her, which must have been so hurtful to her since I was her fair-haired golden boy. But during the last visits with her, I remember beginning to feel so sorry for her, as my sister wouldn't even talk to her. By the end of that first year I was 14 and she was settled into an apartment and a job at Kornblau's Deli Restaurant as their cashier. I didn't know it then but she was quite friendly with Freda, her childhood girlfriend, and I felt nothing strange about the relationship, so when she asked me to move to Atlantic City, I accepted, and began attending Atlantic City High. Now I knew from childhood that Mom was very friendly with my cousin Alan's mother, Rose, and this childhood friend of theirs called Freda Brandow. When they were young they kept telling me they were like the Three Musketeers. I do know whenever I saw the three of them together they did nothing but laugh, and laugh so hard that all three of

them were peeing themselves. I loved knowing that. It was after I moved in with my mother that I realized how much time she was spending with Freda, even having Freda sleep overnight many many times. I didn't think anything unusual about it at the time. In the interim, my father began dating this wonderful woman named Alice. After a while they were married and lived in the house in South Philly along with my younger sister.

Here is the interesting part. My father would bring Marsha, my sister, down to the shore for her visit, and of course Freda was never around during those times. Eventually, he began sleeping with her again, with my mother of course. I assume he was giving her some money each time, so she allowed herself to be used. Alice had no idea

2

of what was going on, but Freda eventually suspected. This went on for quite a while, and Freda showed up sometimes surprising my mother and my father but not during their 'lying down' periods. I felt good about the relationship of my parents... what child wants his parents to be apart? I do remember feeling so sorry for Alice, as she was such a wonderful woman... and also Freda, because it was so evident to me how much she loved my mother. Eventually Alice became aware of the situation and finally gave my father an ultimatum. So when he stopped romancing my mother again, Freda took over.

Some time after this, Freda and Mom made the arrangements for all of us to move to Florida. By this time Marsha also forgave our mother and wanted to live with us. Somehow after about two and a half years after entering high school in Atlantic City, we all got into a station wagon and drove to Hollywood Florida, where Freda and my mother bought a home which was being built in Miami Gardens, West Hollywood, Florida. Because the house wouldn't be ready for at least another month, we all lived in an 18 foot trailer. .. my mother, Freda, Sandra (Freda's daughter), and my sister Marsha. It was very strange for me during that time living with all the women and me being the only boy-man. But I felt it was an adventure. Needless to say once the house was ready it was like moving into a palace... I even had my own bedroom and bathroom ... Hallelujah!!! Speaking of my bathroom, I remember every single morning I would get up, go into the bathroom, and begin sneezing. Not knowing what was causing it, and not knowing what caused allergies, I honestly thought I was allergic to porcelain... DUH!?! How stupid could I be. It wasn't until working in Hollywood that someone explained that I probably had pollen allergies, and I do remember those jalousied windows in my bathroom. Porcelain allergies, PLEASE...

When Alice became pregnant with my half sister Denise, my father was of course ecstatic. I remember one time that I went to a dance in Atlantic City during one of my visits to Philadelphia and Dad allowed me to take his car... a blue Nash Rambler. The night was very long and the drive back to Philly seemed endless. My father said to me, "Drive safely, but try to get back tonight and we will all go to the hospital to see Alice and your new sister." All I remember was seeing the sign, 'Entering Berlin... Philadelphia 18 miles'. The next thing I felt was the car shaking and I opened my eyes to see the car knocking down signs in front of me. Apparently I fell asleep and the road curved but I didn't. I jammed on the breaks and the car stopped on an island between two streets. I jumped out of the car as quickly as I could and when I looked in the car, it was like a miracle. There was broken glass everywhere on the seat except where I was sitting. I now realize that when I jumped out of the car, the broken glass that fell on my body was shaken off onto the street, but at the time I thought, "Wow! This is a true miracle! Look how God saved me." My father was so relieved that I was not hurt that he never got the least bit angry. We did go to see Alice later that day and Denise was and still is beautiful.

I continued attending high school at South Broward in Hollywood, Florida. It took me quite a while to make friends as, believe it or not, I feel like I am quite shy. An obvious gay student befriended me and asked me to join them for lunch, which I did, and immediately was accepted into their group. They convinced me to join the Glee Club as they needed male singers (don't they always???). It was at this time that our school was going to do "Carousel" and they needed male dancers (don't they always???). I joined the cast and it was then that I realized that with my minimal dance training (I'll explain this at another time), I was better than the few male dancers who had studied a lot of dance. So I was then hit by 'THE BUG'. Now I had never had what I call a true homosexual experience by this time. In enough time, that would change. But it was during this time that I had very strong feelings for Maureen Pederson, one of the girls in our 'group'. As a matter of fact, during this time Maureen and I would make out in the back of my '53 Ford, and one particular time, we were both de-virginized. Wow!!! That felt terrific!!! We saw each other sexually as often as we could be alone. On one occasion, she was not feeling well, and she stayed home. Her mother was out and I went to see her. Love conquers all. I took a condom and got into bed with her, and while we were 'doing the deed', we heard the front door and her mother called to her. I grabbed my clothes and rushed into the bathroom. Her mom went to the doorway and Maureen told her I was in the john. Her mother immediately said, "Maureen, I hope you know what you are doing!" She then paused, and went back into the kitchen. When I returned to the bedroom, I looked down and right where her mom was standing was the wrapper of the condom lying on the floor of the doorway. Her mother never really looked at me the same ever since.

e

There was an event that took place which I must mention since it left me with a rather insecure feeling. One of the girls whom I did not know well was dating Walter Watson, this short very muscularly built football player. The girl seemed nice enough, and I really don't think she meant to harm me, but she told her boyfriend that while we were onstage, I gave her 'the finger'. It never happened! I would never hurt a girl in that way... it's just not in my nature. Anyway, at one of the cast parties, Walter comes up to me and tells me what the hell was I thinking giving his girl 'the finger'. I denied it of course, and he said, "Are you accusing my girlfriend of lying?" I said, "NO!" but he was so hot headed that he started hitting me. I remember it was in the kitchen of someone's house, and I was really afraid of hitting back because I thought he could slaughter me, so I tried protecting myself but didn't return any punches. I felt ashamed for months after that, and my only true feeling at that point was that Walter would have killed me if I hit back. This was the lowest point I had in high school.

After the show closed, our group decided to find some dance classes, and we found this dance teacher named Chance Conklin. He gave us what was called 'free style jazz' classes that we all chipped in to pay for. At this point in history it was not called 'modern jazz' yet. I believe that expression came about after Jack Cole, who specialized in East Indian dance choreography, was hired for the Latin Quarter in NYC. His show was a failure until he changed the music and did the same movements to 'Jazz' music, and then he became a huge success. (I've always loved that story and have heard it's basically true.) After Chance's lessons we began taking folk dance lessons of different countries, but we were all doing it for a lark. I was the only one of them who became a professional dancer later on ... and I believe it was this moment in my life that inadvertently gave me a basis for 'The Dance'.

e

While attending high school there was an array of jobs that I worked at part time so I could pay my way through college. I particularly remember one summer when I worked as a maintenance man in a motel. I thought it was the heat but for some reason I was getting these horrendous migraine headaches, and I don't get headaches. The pain was excruciating and I genuinely thought it was because I was in the sun so much while working there. I hated what I was doing... that just could be the reason I am not so neat today. I'm clean, just not too neat. At any rate, just when I thought I was going to have to go to the hospital, I quit my job and what do you know? The pain left immediately. Apparently my body was telling my brain, "Get the hell out of here!" And to this day I never did have another migraine.

I did become a 'pool boy' at the Colonial Inn Motel on Sunny Isles shortly after they opened for business. That was fun because besides putting out the lounge chairs and towels for the visitors of the motel, there was a trampoline on the premises not far from the pool and since we had a good deal of time where there were not many things to do, I got to play on the trampoline. And what fun I had. I never claimed to be a gymnast, but I loved doing forward and backward somersaults on it, and I think I was getting pretty good, except that may have been when my fear of heights began. I was fearful in springing too high in the air, but since I wasn't being judged, I felt very good about my trampoline accomplishments.

Another of my odd jobs while in school was one that I always wanted to relay in the TV show at the time, "What's My Line". You know the one... with John Daly as the host, and Arlene Francis on the panel along with Dorothy Kilgallen, Bennett Cerf, and one more position on the panel that would change occasionally. The show I mean is the one that ran in the 50's. And the reason I wanted to be on it is because I was an 'Extrusion Polisher'. Now what the hell is an extrusion polisher, you ask? You know those metal pieces that contain the glass or plastic pane in a shower door? Well those and other additional metal 'holders' and such are what are called extrusions. And when they are cut to size, they must be covered in a wax product or they might melt in the cutting process. Of course this was in the 50's and things no doubt are different today. Well in order to be used once the extrusions are cut, they must be polished to eliminate the wax residue. And so, I was an Extrusion Polisher. I was sure the panel would never have guessed that. Honestly I didn't even know what they were. But, alas, my starring spot on "What's My Line" never happened. And so I had to find something else.

Ultimately I began working at restaurants as a busboy. So afterwards I was trained as a waiter, which pleased me because there was a sense of class to the job. And the tips were a lot better. I remember one job I had at a luncheonette at the beginning of Venetian Causeway on the Biscayne Boulevard side. I was a waiter in this restaurant and the owner of the place was intrigued by the way I walked around. By the way, it was here that I was working behind the counter and a woman asked for a tea and I put her teabag into a cup and without thinking poured fresh coffee over it. Realizing my mistake I quickly made her a proper cup of tea and gave it to her. A little later on I thought, "Why not try this 'coffee-tea' combo, so I put some cream in it and tried it. An interested thing happened. If I thought of coffee, it tasted like coffee, but if I thought of tea, it tasted like tea. I wondered why no one ever thought of putting those two flavors together before. Just give it a try, it's worth an experiment. Well, I honestly don't think I was swishy, but the owner thought I carried an air of confidence when I walked, as if I owned the place. So she asked if I would mind being the maitre d' to her little restaurant. She did explain that I probably wouldn't be getting tips, but she would pay me a little more and I felt like it was a raise in position. It only lasted there for another month as I had to leave because of my schedule at school, but I loved being a maitre d' even at this little luncheonette. My first real taste of pride in a job!

During my last year of high school, I was thinking about taking up theatre arts in college. Both my mother and Freda said I should take up something more practical, which would guarantee me a more secure future. And they discouraged anything I would do that would have anything to do with a gay (at that time 'homosexual') world. I remember that while they were away for an overnight somewhere, I decided to have a party for our group. We were only a group of about 9 people, and only one was openly gay, and another man, Brian Taylor, was very gay acting, but he later wound up marrying Maureen my high school sweetheart ... and they have been married for well over 55 years, with three children and several grandchildren. It taught me a lesson to not judge a book by it's gay cover. At any rate, toward the end of the party, my mother and Freda came home and the first one that greeted them at the door was Charles, the proud ultra gay queen. Mom and Freda were so upset with me that we didn't speak for 4 months. My mother told me that if I didn't do the 'right' thing in relation to choosing a college direction, she would charge me housing, which she knew would prevent my attending college. I was so angry that ultimately I applied to Drexel Institute in Philadelphia, and since I was working my way through college myself, and couldn't afford housing, I chose Philly so I could live with my grandparents.

e

A little side story about my grandparents. As it happened my grandmother who was a short very slight bit of a woman and my grandfather, a strapping large man, and very Russian, both speaking very little English (he fought in the Russian Revolution in 1917) had only one child, my father. Rumor has it that my Bubba almost died giving birth to my father who they say was a 17 pound baby. And from that time on it is rumored that my grandmother never let my grandfather near her sexually, explaining why she only had one baby, my father. Years before I went to college, my grandmother came down with Tuberculosis, and spent several years at the Deborah Sanitarium. Before I came to Philly to live with them, she came home, but was so traumatized by being back at the house and having to take care of her husband, that she threw herself out of the bedroom window from the second floor, onto the marble steps in front of his Frank Mizen and Son Sewing Machine store on 8th Street in South Philly. The police said she may have tried stopping her fall as there were scratch marks on the inside of the window sill on the second story. But really, why would she have been cleaning or wiping the windows at 3 o'clock in the morning. So the police are the ones who said she committed suicide. I know my Zada truly loved her so much and he was so heartbroken after she left him. It was difficult for him to live alone, but that was his only recourse. At any rate, during my one year at Drexel it was very strange living in the second story bedroom where my Bubba threw herself out of my bedroom window. Zada always lived and slept downstairs after she died. It was a very difficult year at the house living with my grandfather.

Another little interesting note is that if you noticed my grandfather spelled his name Mizen, but my father and I spell ours as Mazin. When my grandparents came through Ellis Island, they could not read or write English ... so when asked his name, in Russian, they pronounced it Mazen (short 'a' as in 'ah'). So the man who did the papers spelled it M I Z E N, as that is how it sounded to him. By the time my father was born, the rest of the Mazins were in town and they corrected my father's last name. It was always strange that my father and my grandfather spelled their names differently.

e

Before leaving Florida for Philadelphia, another very curious event during that 4 months of silence in the family occurred. A male friend of Freda's, her age, not mine, asked her if she could put him up at our house for one night. She told me he would be sleeping in my bed with me... very strange indeed! So we all went to bed, and he kept bothering me, wanting to fondle and suck me the entire night, which I fought off until morning finally came. I was exhausted, having not slept, but he did not succeed. It was difficult for me to imagine, but the thought of her 'testing' me was on my mind, and it wasn't until a week afterwards that I confronted her with what had happened. She denied putting him up to it, and was shocked at him for his behavior. My mother became quite angry with Freda and they had quite a fight over that. But I survived untouched, almost.

When I did finally arrive to attend Drexel, they had no Theatre Arts department, so the first year I took up Business Administration and Hotel Management as a major. The business part of the courses didn't enthuse me very much but the thought of running a hotel in Hotel Management was intriguing to me. Nevertheless my first and only year at Drexel in Philly was sexless, as I now recall. I didn't even think about it... too much. I couldn't bring anyone home with me as I was staying

9

at my grandfather's, but honestly, I never got the opportunity to even ask. Classes were pretty easy, but I had no idea where to go for any 'action' ... so I remained a nun that year.

e

While at Drexel I still had to work so I had a little spending money, even though I was on a scholarship loan to help pay for my college. The job I had was a women's shoe salesman at Snellenberg's Department Store on Market Street. I was not on commission so I was not as frantic when a prospective buyer came into our department. The other salesmen jumped at the walk in clients. I do remember when they had ads in the Philadelphia Daily Inquirer for 'Easy Walkers' for $4.99 a pair and the ladies would swarm in. Many would ask for a certain size not realizing that in any shoe the last of the shoe might make them take a different size. I recall on several occasions that a woman would take 10 minutes to squeeze her foot into the shoe, then stand (in great pain) and finally say "I really don't care for the color". When I suggested a half size larger they would insist "I know my size! I've worn this size for the last 10 years", or words to that effect. The customer is always right! Amen.

It was also during this first year of college that I got myself my first pair of contact lenses. I remember thinking the first time I wore them, "What a fantastic invention this is to allow people to see without the use of regular glasses". Since my first pair of hard contact lenses, I've had soft lenses, then a couple of procedures on my eyes. One of them involved getting a different pair of hard lenses every month or 3 weeks and each pair would be tighter and reshape the eyeball so sight was better. Eventually you would only need to wear the lenses once a week and our eyeballs would stay in the shape to allow you to see without them the rest of the time. My eyes were different apparently. Once in a while I would wake up and see clearly without any lenses, but the effect didn't last long. Then after that procedure I tried Radial Keratotomy, which is a refractive surgical procedure involving making tiny cuts in the cornea which flatten and reduce nearsightedness. Again this lasted for some time but then again I found I needed something else. My later procedure was Lasik Laser Eye Surgery where with the use of a laser a thin flap in the cornea is created using a microkeratome blade. The surgeon folds back the flap, then removes some corneal tissue underneath using an excimer laser. My final procedure was cataract surgery, in which I had what they call monovision, one eye is for nearsightedness and one for farsightedness, but your eyes do automatically adjust. At this point I'm surprised I can see at all considering all the procedures I've had done to my eyes. But I am a trusting soul and of all my senses, I hope the loss of my eyesight is the last one I lose.

e

But after accepting that I was not studying theatre at Drexel (even though they had no theatre courses) my mother was happy and finally said that since I was doing 'the right thing', I could return to Florida and continue my education at the University of Miami in Coral Gables, to which I was also accepted, the year before.

And so I returned to Florida and continued my studies at the University of Miami, Coral Gables. But after my first 6 months I was getting bored with my courses. I was cramming for my tests and getting good grades, but I was afraid that I was not retaining any of my education if I ever needed it in the future. You see, to this day I've always had a 'television mentality' … easy in and easier out. After seeing a guidance counselor I was told to take a series of guidance tests which would help me decide what courses to take in college in the future. Understand

I was still not 'allowed' to take theatre course, although I did take several beginning theatre courses that I never told my mother or Freda about. After taking the tests, I was told to do something more social that would benefit me working directly with people.. .like teaching. So I changed from Business Administration to the school of Arts and Sciences, majoring in Mathematics (can you picture me as a Mathematics teacher … I cannot, but Mathematics, Geometry, etc. was easy for me… don't ask me what any of those courses do for me today). I still resent spending my hard earned money for college and not using the money toward my show biz career.

And so I had little money to spend on luxuries like food, dates, movies, etc, since I was putting all my hard earned cash into college. I had several good friends, one in particular who took care of me at lunch. Brenda Berg would always buy a hamburger or cheeseburger and she was always on a kind of diet, so she would take the burger out of the bun and give it to me, whereupon I would fill it with relish, mustard, catsup, and whatever free condiments they had in the commissary. And I lived on those lunches for a very long time thanks to Brenda. And I appreciate and love her to this day. I was lucky on another front as well. One of my girlfriends in college was Leslie Coven, whose father was paying for her education. She knew how 'college poor' I was, so quite often she would take me to restaurants like the Pub Restaurant and others of that ilk, all on his money. She made sure I ate well. And Leslie was also a member of The Ring Theatre at the U. of Miami. And that was my first introduction to something that would lead to my future career. The Ring Theatre had no one else, so even with my extremely limited experience, I was often asked to choreograph shows there as well as even dancing there sometimes.

I remember a specific show where I was asked to dance as well as choreograph a ballet to one of the duets in Tchaikovsky's 'Swan Lake', and I chose a partner from the ballet school I attended... but that is another story. It was quite different for me to choreograph a ballet, but I did it and since the girl was the star, I allowed her all the freedom within the number. After performing the number at the show itself, several people came up to us and asked how long we were going together. Apparently both of us were quite good at the acting part of the dance, so we 'sold' the fact that we loved each other. This was the first time that I realized that acting was a part of the dance itself, but I honestly thought it was a natural thing to do.

e

I'd like to regress to my childhood and any sexuality which may have been born without my knowledge. I attended Taggart Elementary School in South Philly while still living at 2550 S. Sheridan Street, just north of Shunk Street and 1 block east of 7th Street, for those who are familiar with the area. I was pals with 3 other children ... Joel, David, and Jerry. We did everything together from going to school, sometimes coming home for lunch, and playing games after school. At this point I must interject that my mother must have been having a bad relationship with my father. .. remember he was so very possessive of her so she felt like she was in a prison. Oftentimes When I came

12

home from school for lunch, she was still in bed. The woman who really raised me during that time was a black cleaning woman we had whose name was Frances, a lovely strong woman with her front teeth missing, but a loving person and someone I think of to this very day. She worked at our house about 7 hours a day, 3 times a week, and I loved being with her. Anyway, one of the games the boys and I would play was our version of 'strip poker'... it wasn't strip poker, but 'blow poker'. The loser in any game had to go into our tiny row house back yard, probably 10' by 8', and put his mouth on his players' penis and keep it there for 10 seconds. It wasn't even sexual, but more forbidden than anything truly pleasurable. I can tell you now that of the four of us, I am the only one who learned to enjoy that, but of course, not at that time. We were so young and I remember thinking how intelligent we all were. Ah, youth... it teaches us to accept such falsities as truths. As a footnote to this last statement, I returned to Philadelphia in my first Broadway show for a pre Broadway run, and looked up my old elementary school friend Joel. I made plans to meet him for lunch. When I arrived I saw his fingers were all scarred and some had band-aids on them. He said he was a butcher, and honestly spoke like a hick from the deepest part of the Ozarks ... lots of "Daaahs, Dems, and Do's". I couldn't believe it was the same person as the rest of us when we were so young... we all seemed so smart... such a disappointment, which I never repeated afterwards. He never married, but it was obvious why a woman wouldn't want to get involved with him. My heart bled.

e

There was another kid named Samuel Griffith, who went by the nickname of 'Sluggo'. He was like a juvenile delinquent who had no friends, and would often scare me into going down to the 'dumps' with him, and walking through the wooded area below Oregon Avenue. I always felt threatened for my life, but he never did anything to me... just wanted company since he had no friends, and probably thought I could always be afraid enough not to say 'no', even though I often tried. I remember one time we were doing our walk and came upon 3 other juvenile types who had a kitten with a string around her neck, and they kept dropping her from a railroad trestle, probably only 6 feet above the ground. When Sluggo asked why they were doing that to the kitten they said they wanted to know if she indeed had nine lives. Children can be cruel. They claimed the kitten had no future and would have probably died there anyway. Sluggo insisted I take the kitten and bring her home with me, after convincing those young thugs that I would give her a good home. BTW I had no idea if the kitten was a girl or boy, but in those early years to me, dogs were male and cats were female. When I did get home, I was locked with the cat in our backyard, and knocking on the window to get in, I broke the glass to our back door and cut my right wrist almost through the artery, and bled all the way through the house, to the corner store, to the doctor who lived in the next block who stitched it up for me. When I got home the kitten was gone and I never saw her again. At least I saved her from those juveniles. I still carry that scar on my right wrist with pride. I often wonder what became of Sluggo.

e

I then attended Thomas Junior High School, and during that time we moved to a larger house at 2540 S. 8th Street. Nothing really exciting happened during that time except I had two teachers I just adored. One was Miss Cohee who taught Art, and loved my ability in the field and told me I should continue in art because of it. Another wonderful teacher was Adele Layton who taught Latin. I remember how embarrassed we all were when she had to teach us the words, "Facio, Facere, Feci, Factus"... it did sound so much like the "F" word. She even tried to prepare us for the similarities. She was probably the best teacher I ever remember having. At least she was the only teacher I remember having a crush on. But it was during this time that I had my Bar Mitzvah, my parents split up, and I moved to Atlantic City to be with my mother and Freda. It's too bad we can't take our best teachers with us throughout life.

e

In Atlantic City High School I met several girls and 'dated'. But the only girl I wanted to date was one who treated me like her brother. Her name was Anita Murray, and she was different from any other girl I had ever met. Anita's mother used to be a stripper, so I thought, at the Globe Theatre in Atlantic City, and her father was a comedian there also. So the word 'jaded' does not come even close to the type of lingo her mother and father shared. Consequently Anita always talked with an edge of 'show biz savvy', which I found so appetizing to me. Eventually her mother married her father and gave up stripping and began managing his career. Anita ruined my life!!! Or should I say I allowed her to ruin my life. I suppose I fell in love with her because she wasn't interested in me, as well as the fact she was so completely different than any other girl I ever knew. She was in love with a friend who was homosexual, but a brilliant pianist named Richard Wagner, and I assume she couldn't get anywhere with him other than as a friend, she consequently treated me the same way. As sick as this is, ever since, I never allowed anyone to fall in love with me unless I 'tested' them by acting as if. .. 'they should be happy enough to be in the same room with me without asking anything in return', if they truly loved me. Not a great way to accept any kind of affection or love, but that is how it went down.

Another girl that I 'dated' was Judy Saul, a wonderful pianist and a very adoring girl. .. unfortunately I didn't feel as 'friendly' to her as she wanted to be to me. But whenever we were together and there was a piano around, I would always ask her to play Chopin's Military Polonaise. I don't know why, but I loved the fact that she was gifted enough to play what sounded like a difficult piece on the piano. I suppose this was my first infatuation with talent. But because of the way I felt for Anita, I couldn't let anyone else into my heart. At least not then.

e

I remember in Atlantic City we lived at 4301 Winchester Avenue just above Ralph's grocery store. I began working for Ralph as delivery boy and general clean and stock clerk for $10 a week... my very first job. Anyway a cat began coming around the house so we began feeding her (she was a cat after all, but I never did look to see a pussy pecker). We called her Reds because of her color. She really loved me and began following me whenever I left the house. We had to lock her in one of the rooms when I went to school. Well I soon found out that when I walked to the beach which was 3 blocks from our apartment, Reds would follow me. Then when I went into the water, Reds would also follow me until she was swimming. So much for the rumor cats hate water. Many times people on the beach would accuse me of torturing the cat by putting her in the water, after which I would carry her to the shore, and they would be astonished when she again followed me into the ocean. I loved Reds and she loved me. It was easy for both of us... no sex...

e

It is about now that I experienced my first sexual encounter. It is a little 'seedy', even for me to admit, but since then I believe I've even topped this one, if you excuse the slang...

Across the street from South Broward High was a small market and produce store. Some of our group would go over and get something for lunch there. While walking around, I noticed that one of the workers, an attractive, black man (in those days they weren't called 'African-Americans') watching me, and every time he caught me looking at him he would smile, showing his not so perfect teeth. It took quite a few visits before he ever got the nerve and spoke to me. He told me his name was Will and that he would love to talk to me sometimes after his work was over. After several attempts, we make a tentative 'date' to meet around 5pm one late afternoon. I was very nervous having never really done anything like that, and I didn't really know what it was all about. When we met he asked if I wanted to take a little ride in his car, which I agreed to. We rode about 20 minutes or so to a desolate piece of land on the other side of the inlet, which had a great view of the shore hotels, etc. He then told me he liked me a lot and never felt like that before. I was of course flattered and he must have seen how inexperienced I was as I really didn't know how to behave. He started touching me, then began to kiss my neck, ultimately moving to my lips. Of course I began getting erect, and he took advantage of that with his hands and mouth. Will then gently took me out of the car and dropped my pants completely. Obviously no one was around, so I allowed him to have his way. After a while, he finally exposed himself to me and pulled my shoulders to do the same to him, as he had been pleasing me. His member was quite large, and honestly, I have a gag reflex, which didn't stop his enjoyment at all. When we finally finished he said he was beginning to fall in love with me. This was very different for me, and I suppose it was all the 'taboo' rites I was involved in at the moment ... a black man, albeit very handsome, with a little bush of hair growing out of his chin, and he was a man that I was enjoying. That late afternoon was just the beginning of a physical relationship that lasted about 3 months, and with each meeting, I was asked to do more than I even thought I could. It seemed after a while all he wanted to do was sodomize me, which was quite painful considering his manliness. But I was learning something I never knew anything about, so I allowed myself to be used. He of course made sure I had my pleasure, but he would never allow me to enter him in that way. So now I had my first male encounter and I really can't say I'm sorry for it. I suppose that because of the pain to this day I honestly do not enjoy being had in that same way... but I certainly enjoy being in the other position. After about three months he told me his family was moving out of the state so our relationship had to end. I really felt he was almost beginning to cry, which made me feel sensitive to his situation, since he obviously had stronger feelings for me that I for him. But I did learn, and he always tried to be as gentle as he could. But I still remember the pain. I cannot for the life of me understand true S & M love making. The pain never reminded me of the sex. As a matter of fact, for me it took away from the sexual arousal. What I enjoyed was the gratification I was getting out of his enjoyment ... but it was not SEXY for me... So much for my first truly gay experience!

e

It was after attending Atlantic City High School for two and a half years that we finally moved to Hollywood, Florida... me, my mother, my sister, Freda, and Freda's daughter, Sandra. One of my school chums lived very close to our home in Miami Gardens. His name was James Mom, a very good looking intelligent looking boy my own age, and we shared the same school bus every morning. Jim had a very charismatic nature about him, and my mind would wander, thinking what it might be like to be intimate with him. The closest I ever came was one night in my car in our own neighborhood, with both of us masterbating, and not each other. It was quite dark and I couldn't even catch a glimpse of him, which I really wanted to do. It wasn't until many years later, after I moved to California in 1967, that I discovered he had not only turned gay but he was interested in me the same way I was curious about him... but we were both still young and both still very shy. When he admitted that to me, I learned a big lesson. Never lose an opportunity to let someone know your feelings... we waste so much time, and even under the possibility of rejection, we can never get that time back. If there is even a glimmer of hope, take it! You have nothing to lose except valuable time that you can never retrieve.

Soon after moving to Florida, I had to go to the Greyhound Bus Station to get a ticket for my mother. While there, this man came up to me and began talking about a rendezvous we should have at his place, and he went on to tell me how it would happen, moment by moment. First I would come to his home. Then have a drink of something cold. Then we would go into the bedroom and 'get to know each other'. As he spoke I remember getting very nervous but excited at the same time. This was all talk of course, but titillating at that. Well I never did meet up with him, but I was so excited at the prospect, that I couldn't help but call Anita, the love of my life in Atlantic City and tell her what had transpired. I suppose I was internally hoping that if I told her about my possible gay adventure, she would look at me the same way she used to look at Richard Wagner. Wrong!!! She just wished me luck and told me to have a good time. Notice that I never told her about Will. .. that was just too immoral... because it really happened. And to add a little footnote about Anita's love for Richard, he committed suicide shortly after graduation, which I was not around for since I moved to Florida to finish high school.

In Florida it was very rare indeed that I would enjoy any male-to-male encounters, so I honestly felt I was bi-sexual... bi-sexual and an agnostic. After all, I was surrounded by mostly straight and non-Jewish friends. What I began saying to myself and then slowly to very close friends, "My body is a temple... even if no one goes to this church".

I've always joked with my friends that my mother really made me gay. Of course that wasn't true, but while I was in high school she and Freda would every once in a while take me to the Onyx Room on Alton Road in Miami Beach to see Charles Pierce and his act with his then partner Rio Dante. Charles became a world famous comedian impressionist while I have no idea what happened to Rio Dante since seeing him perform at the Onyx Room ... but he had a fantastic name.

I did find out that he passed away years before Charles did. Another place I would once in a blue moon attend was The Red Carpet to see another much older comedian named Ray Bourbon. That is the place I first saw Ruth Wallis and her bawdy, sexy, naughty songs. Both The Onyx Room and The Red Carpet were both gay bars that were mostly frequented by men. Neither club rooms have lasted through the years but at the time they were the top of the gay world bars in Miami Beach. And it was my mother and Freda who first introduced me to them. I remember one night going there with friends, and during a customer contest of costume lip sinking, I entered with my body wrapped in toilet paper, and I 'sang' a song that was slightly popular in those days called "I'm a Mummy". I doubt you could even find that song today. I won the contest and took home a bottle of cheap champagne!

It was that night when I met this very good looking man who said he was a lawyer in Boston. He asked me back to his hotel room, and since I didn't at that time have many invitations of that sort, I happily accepted. Once we got back to his room we began making out and I felt glorious. It was almost an instant infatuation with this guy whose name was Allen Green. He took me to bed and believe it or not we exchanged positions making love to one another. I still hated being on the bottom but I did find out that I loved being on top, although I would get too excited and relieve myself too early, or at least that is what I thought. I saw Allen probably another 2 times during his visits to Florida, but then I never heard from him again. I guess I wasn't so hot in bed. That left me with quite an inferiority complex that I am probably still at this age working to eliminate from my life. It was quite a while after this that I would experience another male-to-male encounter.

There was an Italian guy who had just come out of the closet, joined our group in high school, and took a little liking to me. We shared a little sexual activity, mostly oral or manual if you get my drift. I remember one of his 'things' was to give me head while I was driving my car. It was so exciting for both the sexual feeling and the feeling of possibly being caught, but we never were. Rick Zachara was a good guy who loved all his friends. He had a very deep voice and a very large nose, so he always sounded as if he should blow his nose to clear his voice. We remained friends for a long time. Even after leaving Florida whenever I returned for a visit I would try to look him up. Of course by that time he was happily living with someone, and we never did enjoy sex with one another again, but before then he was very wild. Years later, I heard he caught 'the disease' and passed. He was much more active than I was, and that 'craziness' finally caught up with him. So many of the good ones leave us too soon.

e

I must tell you about our South Broward High School graduation that took place at the open shell auditorium in the center of Hollywood, Florida. We had our rehearsal and there were 3 sections of chairs with 2 aisles between. We came down the right aisle in pairs, and the girl I walked down with and I were to be seated in the first 2 seats to our right after everyone else in the row was in front of their chairs. The people behind us I believe were supposed to go all the way down to the front of the chairs and sit to the left. Well, we of course rehearsed without our graduation robes. The afternoon of our graduation, we began walking down the aisle. I noticed that the graduates were standing right in front of the chairs we were to sit in. I whispered to the girl that we should go to the next row behind them since someone must have made a huge mistake to put people in front of our chairs. After all, we would have been stuck standing in the aisle while everyone else was seated. So my partner and I took the next row on the right, and went to the end of the aisle, and lo and behold, everyone else followed us, disrupting the entire plan. It was utter chaos. Once we were in front of the new seats all the way to the right, I realized that the only reason people were in front of our original chairs was that the robes took up more space. So my girl and I snuck into our own row and told everyone to scoot down 2 seats. Needless to say, the diplomas were in a certain order, so they had to stop the entire ceremony so the students could go to their given chairs. Fortunately no one really knew that I was the ass who created the new plan. But it was truly hilarious and embarrassing at the same time.

And I don't know why, but that year I began having such a strong premonition that I was going to die young. I mean everywhere I went, during my first year at Drexel in Philadelphia, whether walking or taking a trolley or a subway, I found myself looking around at the people near me and thinking, "These poor people have no idea that their lives might be cut short instantly any minute now." But of course nothing happened so I am still here to tell about it. That was a very strange time for me. I've always felt I would never reach my 30's, but this particular year was a very strong one in that respect.

After returning back to Florida and the U. of Miami, I was able to make some friends, mostly female. A good looking male student did approach me and was much more forward than I was, so after seeing him a couple of times we 'went together' for a period of about 4 months. It was fun sneaking into his dorm (I was staying at my mother's house in West Hollywood). At this point may I say that I like to maintain long- lasting friendships with some of my sexual partners if I enjoy intimate experiences with the ones I'm with. Barry Cherin was an interesting person... very fastidious and anal (not in the sexual sense though appropriate, but more in the way he handled his life). Although I have heard him tell friends in front of me years later that I was the umteenth person who ever French kissed him and the third who ever fucked him... very anal linguistically. Third... a position I have cherished to this very day. Barry later became a PR person for NBC and then became the lover of Ron Stephenson, who became the casting person of "Murder, She Wrote". More about Ron later. Barry unfortunately succumbed to pantriatic cancer a year and a half after he was told he was in remission, and passed away earlier that year. Certain people will always be close to my heart, forever.

One of my college friends in our little college clique was into costume design. He was a nice very straight and pretty good looking guy. We were close in the respect that I always liked him and he certainly was friendly with our entire clique. He later married a terrific girl named Linda, and we remained very good friends. But sometimes everything good comes to an end, so they did get divorced years later and he remarried to another wonderful woman, who seemed to be more serious minded than his first

wife. They remained married for a very long time, and then it was determined he had the beginnings of Parkinson's disease. I continued seeing him often rarely, since he did live in Florida and I lived in California. Finally they were visiting his grown son in Palo Alto a small town outside San Francisco, and I drove up to see them. It happened to be the very first time I used my GPS or navigation system in my very first Prius. I was amazed that all I did was put in their address, and the car led me directly to the front of his son's house. His disease had taken it's toll and he was shaking pretty heavily now. Once his wife left the room to get us something to drink, we were alone and he leaned forward and said, "You know, Stan, all these years I was always curious as to whether or not I wanted to try being with a man. I've thought about you ever since we were in college, and I'm sorry I never said so in school, but I really want to be with you. Do you think we could make it happen sometime before I die?" I was of course flabbergasted. He caught me off guard. Of course the thought entered my mind long before this, but I would no way manifest my own curiosity with him. But I did say, "Why not. I'll try making a trip to Florida and I think we can probably make it work if we can find the time together." We let it go then as his wife came back into the room and we never spoke about it again. Four months later, without my trip to Florida, he died, and never got to experience what apparently was on his mind for a long time. I felt so bad for him. I would have jumped at the chance to share a personal sexual experience with him, but he never moved on it or even let me think he was curious. We let so much time go by when we could be satisfying our curiosities in our lives. What a shame there is such a word as 'regret'. So many of us fill our lives with it, instead of accepting ourselves to act upon it and reach it's ultimate conclusions. Sometimes it is good to do things we are curious about, even if it is only to find out that it is not for us. I hope I don't go to my grave with any, or at least not many, regrets.

Getting back to college, one of the ways I was able to pay my own way through college was taking out a 'scholarship loan'. This loan was valid during my tenure as a college student. It had to be paid back in the same length of time that I was using it. Because I changed from Business to Arts and Sciences, at the U. of Miami many of the general necessary courses had to be repeated, which would have added some time to my graduation date. I did begin to take a beginner theatre course, as I stated before. During my 4th year of college, my friend Barry came to me and told me he wanted to take beginner ballet, and he wanted company. So I agreed to take beginner ballet along side of little 5 to 8 year olds because we wanted the basics. Well, Barry was not great at the dance, and dropped out after a month. Having had limited experience with dance, and choreographing some things at the Ring Theatre at the university, I continued. Believe it or not I enjoyed the classes and soon found my way to a more professional dance studio, the Jack Stanly Dance Studio in Coral Gables. I took beginner jazz and tap. Jack Stanly was a professional teacher from New York City who had recently opened his studio in Florida. After a short time, he came to me and told me I should take up dance seriously, as he thought I had a natural gift for it. I measured my options, and if I was going to be serious about my future as a dancer, I better not wait any longer to begin. I left college in the middle of my 4th year (but remember that I would have had to extend college another year to make up the courses from Business to A. and S. schools.... plus the extra time I had to pay back the loan I was on). So I left and began working for Jack Stanly full time for a big $25 a week subsistance. This was in 1961. While at the Stanly Studios, I had to attend as many of the dance classes as I could that didn't conflict with my chores there. I took Ballet with Jack Potteiger, Jazz and Tap with Jack and Ronn Daniels, and even Spanish dance with Maria Florentes, whose real name was Wendy Kay Fleichman. I became enthralled with both Ronn and Maria. My true bisexuality came out as I began seeing the both of them, without the other really knowing it. Ronn and I even moved in together to save money since I was no longer allowed to stay at home, having left college. So eventually Ronn and I became more than roommates. He was so into the 'dance' that we had this solo dance number that Jack had choreographed for each of us, and late at night when the studio was closed, we would go back and he always wanted me to do the "Plastique in Jazz" number which was performed with only a bench. And he wanted me to perform it wearing only my underwear and nothing else. Needless to say it was very hot. And he would get off by watching me dance. That memory still brings a smile to my face.

On the other side of the coin was Maria, who was a little older than I was, and who danced with the Jose Greco Company when she was only 16. She was a wonderful Spanish dance teacher, and having watched her perform on many occasions, I can honestly say she is the best female Spanish dancer I have ever seen. And since I am shallow and am very attracted to talent, I became infatuated with her. Obviously she felt the same with me. Our relationship got much more sexual than I had anticipated. Maria had an aunt who ran a small motel on Miami Beach of perhaps 20 rooms or so. Oftentimes we would go over there and she would grab a key to one of the empty rooms and we would watch TV, have sex, eat something, have more sex, and watch more TV It was a great time for me, although I was juggling my 'private' time between Maria and Ronn. A very funny situation occurred between Maria and me on a very, very cold Florida night in the motel. Maria and I always used protection of a kind, and she discovered a vaginal contraceptive foam called Emco, which acted like a condom in preventing pregnancy. Well, on this particular night we began our pre-sexual activity and I had to run down to the car to get the Emco, which I stored in my glove compartment. When I came back we both discovered that it was frozen solid. Fortunately we both laughed ourselves silly, trying to 'thaw' it out. This is one of those embarrassing moments so easily shared between two very close friends and lovers.

Eventually both my lovers found out about each other so I was truly 'walking on eggs' with each of them. And they both cared so much for each other as well as for me, so we all remained friends... even to this day.

After six months of training, Jack Stanly made me a student teacher, as well as a substitute teacher in Jazz and Tap. I have to say that this is truly where I learned to be a better dancer as well as a good teacher. I am a Pisces, so I can adjust to others' needs for their own improvement. And watching them dance, while I gave them corrections, helped me be a better performer myself. At least two or three times a year I would go on dance conventions as a demonstrator when Jack taught... organizations like the Dance Educators of America, or the Dance Masters of America, etc. And performing and teaching these conventions also helped me in my chosen profession. Ronn was a fantastic dancer, but was shorter than the average dancer, so Jack always discouraged his going to NYC for his craft. This way he had a very talented teacher who remained loyal to him long after he told me to go to New York. Ronn certainly should have been a contender had he had the nerve to leave and go to New York himself.

We taught a convention in NYC the summer of 1963, and afterwards Jack Stanly told me to stay there, and that he believed in me. He also told me I should change my name to Mason Jarre (this was the age of Rip Torn, Tuesday Weld, etc.), which I am happy to say I never did. I did however shorten 'Stanley' to 'Stan' ... I always hated 'Stanley' as a name for a boy. It is always the name of a nerd or dummy in film and TV.

I rented a room at the Woodward Hotel at 55th and Broadway by the week. A student friend of mine from the U. of Miami was Igor Kornich, a very talented director entrepreneur. He asked if his younger brother Tom could room with me and share the expenses ... great! Just what I needed! Tom was a gifted, straight, ballet dancer, who later became a soloist with American Ballet Theatre, and I believe now is still the artistic director of the Milwaukee Ballet. He stayed with me for a couple of months and when he had to leave, I found my first studio apartment at 408 W 57th Street, Apt. 7-K. My own apartment in Manhattan, going to auditions, and living the life of an aspiring dancer... what could be better?!? My first audition for a Broadway show was for one male replacement for "HowTo Succeed In Business Without Really Trying". In New York for every male dance audition there were no less than 250 people who showed up. This was my very first Broadway audition and I was psyched. They kept making cuts, and we would dance again. They would make more cuts and we would have to sing. Then make more cuts and we would dance again. I never felt comfortable singing, but apparently I was good enough for the chorus. Finally we were only a group of 9 dancers left, and I was one of them. They announced who got the replacement job but kept the rest of us onstage. Management then offered all of the remaining dancers the opportunity to join the road company of this show. I think everyone but me accepted. When they asked why I wasn't coming on the road, I explained to them that I had just recently arrived in New York, and wanted my opportunity for Broadway. I didn't realize then that a first class road company tour of a hit Broadway show was in itself a prestige job. I often think about how my life would have changed, had I accepted that offer.

Another audition that came along was for the musical version of "Blithe Spirit" by Noel Coward... to be called "High Spirits" starring Tammy Grimes and Beatrice Lilly. The audition was phenomenal! This time, after being one of the 8 dancers left onstage, I was asked to remain there while they released all the other dancers, after giving us all the show information. There I was onstage, alone, when walking down to the edge of the stage were Danny Daniels (the choreographer), Hugh Martin and Tim Gray (book, lyrics and music creators), Fred Werner (conductor and musical director), Leonard Soloway (production stage manager), but Noel Coward (the director) being absent. They were all looking up at me on the stage. They asked with whom I was studying voice. I told them Edna Wood (who coincidentally coached Carol Burnett). They said I still needed more vocal training, but they were all thrilled with my dancing. I was told that Noel Coward was coming into town within 2 weeks and they wanted him to meet me personally. Now the month was October and the rehearsals were to begin January 4th of 1964. Noel Coward was coming to meet me. I felt like Peggy Sawyer in "42nd Street"... I thought this is what dreams are made of... they're going to make me a star! How could I not think this? Walking on clouds for the next 2 weeks, I finally got a call from the production office to tell me that Mr. Coward was in town and he was very anxious to meet me. I was quite nervous getting dressed for my appointment with him... I couldn't even tell you what I wore. After arriving at the office, several of the bigwigs escorted me into another room where there

was a huge desk with Noel Coward sitting behind it. All the execs remained on my side of the desk. One of them said, "Mr. Coward, this is Stan Mazin, the dancer we told you about." Mr. Coward cordially offering his hand to mine for a handshake responds, "I'm so happy to meet you. They tell me you are a wonderful dancer."
I answered, "Thank you so much, Mr. Coward." After a momentary

empty moment which seemed like 20 minutes to me, I added, " I just want to tell you that it is a thrill for me to be in your show." Another seamingly 20 minute empty moment elapsed until I finally broke the ice with, "I'll let you get back to work. Again, I am so proud to be a part of this show. Thanks so much." And that was that! I never really heard anything back from them until the rehearsals. Apparently I was not going to be the new Peggy Sawyer. But, I was going to get a little more money each week along with another dancer, Ron Walken (alias Ronald Christopher Walken) for 'handling' Tammy Grimes when she took off and landed on her flying wire. But I was in my first Broadway show from the start!!!

Since it would be over 2 months before rehearsals began, I continued my dance classes ... Aubrey Hitchins (ballet), Bill Griffith (ballet), Bob Audy (tap), and a slew of jazz teachers including Matt Mattox. It was a Monday right after a Matt Mattox jazz class where I was approached by Claude Thompson and Jaime Rogers. They asked if I would be working in the near future and I responded by telling them I had signed to dance in an original Broadway show. When they asked which one, I told them "High Spirits". They said that was great because another dancer from that show was Beth Howland (of "Company" and "Alice" fame years later) and if she was able to join their show that I could join them as well. Mind you, this is only from watching me dance in a Matt Mattox jazz class. They told me that when I had to return for "High Spirits" rehearsals, they would replace me. So, that Friday I was flying FIRST CLASS from NYC to San Juan, Puerto Rico to open in a dance act for Sarah Vaughn at the Ponce De Leon Hotel on Condado. The hotel hadn't even opened yet. Now at this point working for Jack Stanly my weekly salary had grown to a big $65 a week. This show in P.R. was going to pay me $250 a week. How could I help but feel like a millionaire?

Working for Claude and Jaime was a dream. Claude and I became very close during this period of my life. I saw in him such a sensitivity and almost a loneliness that I was drawn

right into his psyche. Although Jaime's choreography was strong and powerful, Claude's was strong and smooth. Both styles were great fun to perform, but I felt Claude's was sexier as most of the movements were slower and more 'sensual'. The show was set up in such a way that our dance group was in the first part of the show, almost as an opener to the star, Sarah Vaughn. So we never did get to work with her in our dance numbers. One of the days I will remember all my life occurred during our rehearsal period in San Juan. During our rehearsal someone came in to tell us that President Kennedy was shot in Dallas. Of course the date was November 22, 1963. We were all dumbfounded. Our rehearsal was naturally cancelled for the balance of the day, and we spent the rest of it attached to the television. What an absolutely helpless feeling to not be at home during an American crisis. Not that there was anything we could do if we were at home, but being away made me feel like my family had been violated, and there was nothing I could do to protect them. I think we all remember certain tragedies that have occurred throughout the years, and each one of us remembers where we were when we heard the news. We did rehearse the next few days and I do remember those rehearsals seemed not to be as creative as before or after those dramatic days. The show of course went on as planned and was well received... after all, it was Sarah Vaughn.

My roommate in Puerto Rico at the time was a dancer named Roger Pucket. We got along well, and I assumed he was gay, but he wasn't the type I was interested in, although he was a very interesting and attractive person. When we arrived at the hotel, they weren't going to open the Ponce de Leon for another 2 weeks, and they housed all the dancers in beautiful rooms in the hotel. The rooms were beautifully decorated and the multicolored towels were all soft and luxurious. It wasn't long before the dancers began stealing the towels and sending them home through the mail. We didn't really think we were 'stealing', and they seemed to have literally thousands of them. One afternoon I went back to the room and noticed a good-sized end table that hadn't been there before. I asked Roger where it came from and he told me he saw it in the hall, obviously put there temporarily. I asked how he was going to get it back to the states, and he just told me he would package it and send it. So I helped him store it in the ceiling as we had large cubicle squares overhead covering the room. No one would ever suspect it was there. Needless to say even though I hadn't taken it, I was so nervous until he got it out of the room. How could the hotel not notice that a table was missing? A few days later Roger brought a huge brown packing box into the room. I helped him take the table down from the ceiling and we packed it with the brand new stolen towels from the hotel. Then we, some of the other dancers and I, helped him carry the package out of the hotel and directly to the post office. I could finally relax and not worry about spending the rest of my life in a Puerto Rican prison. Incidentally, years later, I ran into Roger who opened the Triton Gallery on 45th Street in NY. He was married to a woman, so I suppose that could have explained his sexuality... although I know many married guys who hide their natural sexual proclivity. And surprise of all surprises, he still owns the table I helped him steal from the hotel decades prior.

e

During our run in P.R. Claude and I got closer as true friends with benefits, and because I respected and loved his talent, I was happy with the situation. Christmas was approaching and the cast decided to have a Xmas party. Before then, Claude and I made friends with these 2 female lovers who were living in St. Thomas, an island off of San Juan that was only reachable through boats or small airplanes. They were not affluent but Claude took a true liking to them. Now I know Claude hated parties, so it was not a surprise to me when he said, "Instead of going to the party, why don't we fly over to the girls and surprise them?" I of course agreed. That Christmas Eve after the show, Claude rented a 4-seater plane with pilot to fly us to St. Thomas. What he did was change $50 into single new dollar bills, crumpled them up, and put them in a box wrapped with Santa Claus wrapping paper which we delivered to the girls. What a guy! Is it a surprise that I cherished his friendship throughout my life until he finally passed away several years ago from cirrhosis of the liver? And this was not the last time I worked for Jaime Rogers or Claude Thompson. When I did have to leave the show for my Broadway rehearsals, they replaced me with a great dancer named Sterling Clark, whose later claim to fame was as the orange colored toe shoe soloist in the mad ballet in Angela Lansbury's "Anyone Can Whistle". Another little interesting plot is that Beth Howland was privately having an affair with Jaime Rogers all the time we were in rehearsals.

And so, Beth and I had a very nice time while working in Puerto Rico. It was after rehearsals for "High Spirits" began that I moved into my studio apartment on 57th Street. It was a little hectic rehearsing days and settling in nights. I chose a color scheme of avocado green and royal blue... after all, it was the 60's. So I shopped for a bright blue sleeper sofa, and avocado drapes and carpet. I needed something large over the bed, perhaps a modern painting in my chosen colors. I couldn't find anything I liked in the stores so I decided to paint my own. I went to the art store and purchased a large canvas and oils and began my own piece of art. I was very happy with the results... blue & green clouds of color swirled over the entire canvas with one circle of pure white about 4 inches in diameter in the upper right third part of the picture. It looked great to me. Anyone who saw it asked what the white spot represented, and I would reply that the white spot was me. Everyone seemed to like the picture, but it took forever to dry. Three weeks after I hung the picture up, a friend of mine asked why it was still wet. I answered with, "I suppose it takes a long time for oils to dry". She asked how much linseed oil I used for the painting. I asked her what linseed oil was. It was only then that I learned that oils need to be mixed with linseed oil in order to dry. Duh!!! So the following day I went back to the art store and bought 3 cans of linseed spray oil, and hosed down my art work. I loved that picture, and Ms. Cohee from Thomas Junior High back in South Philly would have been very proud. Ultimately when I left that apartment I gave the picture to a friend but cannot for the life of me remember to whom... I would love to know if it still exists... somewhere.

e

Maria Florentes came to NYC to live and we still maintained our relationship, but her awareness of Ronn's relationship with me in Florida made things a little different and difficult. First of all, Maria wanted to be an actress and after beginning classes decided to change her name to Arless Bogner. She tried out some other names before she finally changed it to Cory Flaxman (closer to her own name). Some people change their faces when they are not happy. Cory changed her name. Because she was not satisfied that I acknowledged myself as being bi-sexual, she asked if I would see a psychiatrist. I agreed to have 3 visitations with one of her choice. She did not attend my private sessions of course. During those meetings the doctor tried in every way he could to try to convince me that making love with a woman is better than with a man. On our second session he even brought out pictures of a woman's vagina to tell me the correct path I should take during intercourse. At the end of the third session I was convinced that my choice was the best one because it was the most natural one... for me. It's alright to be bi-sexual, heterosexual, or even homosexual (the word 'gay' during these times wasn't as common). So although Cory didn't agree with the results, I accepted more than ever the probability that I now wanted to sexually be with a man rather than a woman. After a very long period of silence I am very happy that Cory is very close to my heart, and even if we don't see each other for a very long time, when we are together I still feel the bond between us. I understand what she went through and I completely accept her reaction to a very precarious situation. I am her family and I always will be.

e

I made some very close friends that have survived time while in the show in P.R. Two of them in particular are Shari Greene and Arline Woods. Shari and I were just dancers, but Arline besides being a dancer had her own song in the show. As it happened Arline lived not only in the same building that I was living in, but in an apartment right down the hall from me. I lived in 7-K and she shared an apartment with 2 other girls in 7-F. Arline was going with a dancer choreographer named JoJo Smith.  Soon after our gig, upon returning to NYC, Arline found out she was pregnant. She didn't want JoJo to know, so she arranged an abortion through other friends of hers. At that time there were no abortion clinics as there are today. As a matter of fact there were no legal clinics so one had to take their chances. I remember when Arline left to see this doctor in this basement to have her procedure done. She never arrived home for 3 nights. We found out that she was on death's door the entire time. When she was able to come home, she was in a terrible state. It took a lot of time to gain her strength back, but eventually, very eventually, it did return albeit leaving her a little less energetic for the wear. Arline was a great friend, and proved it to me many times over. Another friend who happened to live right next door to my apartment was this very openly gay man named Stanley Pomerance. Stanley hated his name (as I did mine) so he changed it to 'Stacey'. It took quite a while for all of us to make that adjustment, but Stacey he became. In my apartment I also bought this big black upholstered chair that opened out into a less than single bed. One time Stacey stayed overnight because his apartment was being fumigated, and he slept in the chair. In the morning he said, "You know that sleeping in that chair was

like sleeping in a big black tongue". Well, we doubled over in pain from laughter. It doesn't seem so funny now, but at the time... what is the expression???... 'you shoulda been there!' Stacey covered his loneliness with his humor. He wasn't lonely for lack of friends... more for lack of sexual partners. I often shared that feeling, not being so forward in a chosen gay lifestyle. After all I never went to gay bars or bath houses... yet. Right after we got back from Puerto Rico, Claude called me and asked if I wanted to go to a show with him to see "Boys from Syracuse" at Theatre 40. I accepted. After the show, which was a lot of fun, we went to meet some of the cast at The Horse's Tail on the corner of 56th Street and 8th Avenue. While sitting there and watching the cast come in, Claude introduced me to many of them. One in particular I couldn't take my eyes off of. His name was Dom Salinaro... a very handsome Italian man, with slight puffiness under his eyes. I thought to myself, "What a shame! A handsome guy like that and he must be drinker". I couldn't take my thoughts off Dom and for good reason, which I will mention later. He will be a very important person in my life.

While we were still rehearsing "High Spirits" I was called to do an Ed Sullivan show, with three other male dancers to back up Ethyl Merman. It was a real thrill. The other dancers were LeeRoy Reams, Bill Gusky, and Buddy Vest. I never did see that number until recently  when there was an Ed Sullivan Tribute on PBS in 2015. It was short but we all looked great. I had no idea I was as good looking as I was. It is interesting the vision we have of ourselves when we are young. Time can be an enormous enemy.

"High Spirits" opened first out of town at the Shubert Theatre in New Haven. They put us up at the Taft Hotel and my room happened to be next to Tammy Grimes' room. I'm not into gossip, but on more than one occasion Tammy had a late night visitor in the name of Ronnie Walken... need I say more? When we went to Boston I remember our opening night quite vividly. The end of the first act finale was "Faster Than Sound" with Elvira (Tammy) and the ensemble. Tammy's costume began with a very light see-through netted leotard. Over that was a silky almost scarf-like dress all gathered at the waist, with what looked like 2 scarves going from the waste over the bust and connected behind her neck, leaving the back look bare. As soon as the first act curtain came down Tammy said, "Why is it so cold in here?" She then looked down at her dress and realized that her top had fallen from aound her neck and was hanging from her waste baring her bosom, peaking through the very sheer netted leotard. Her next exclamation was, "Oh my God! I can't believe this happened here in BOSTON!" (Tammy comes from Boston). An interesting fact was that Tammy was signed to play "Bewitched", but turned it down thinking it might not be a hit, so she took this show instead. Elizabeth Montgomery got the role of Samantha instead. In 1966 Tammy starred in another situation comedy that turned out to be a flop. But she remained to be one of the most unique persons

Interesting to note that Noel Coward was not enthralled with Beatrice Lillie's performance. He was afraid in advance having worked with her in many revues that she would do her own thing and wouldn't be able to remember her lines let alone maintain a character. This is pretty much what happened, but even though she stole the show doing her own thing, her presence along with Tammy's made the show have a 375 performance run. Noel left the show during the Philadelphia tryout, explaining that he had to leave due to poor health. It was speculated that either Coward or Lillie had to go, but since she was the hit of the show, Coward departed and Gower Champion took over the direction, but Coward still maintained credit as the sole director.

Leonard Soloway was our Production Show Manager... a nice looking man with a very warm heart that I found inviting. We got together a few times and they were always very special to me. We were gentle with each other, and since I really was not too experienced, he never asked me to do anything too wild. We have remained friends throughout the years, but I often wondered what would have happened to my future if I wanted our relationship to continue growing. Several years back I went to see Leonard at his office which had moved to 9th Ave. from 1776 Broadway. On one visit to New York I went in and was greated by 2 huge Mastiffs and I was petting them and got on the floor with them so they could sniff me. Then I went into Leonard's office for a short visit. I never want to take advantage of a producer's time even though I felt a special bond with Leonard. On my way out the dogs came out and I must have made a strange but quick movement toward them and one of them instantly bit me on the lip and cheek. I was bleeding pretty profusely and I think all the people in the office went into panic mode, trying to help and saying they would call the paramedics. I insisted they not make the call, and told them I should be fine. At the time I had no idea how bad the bite was... perhaps I was still in shock. Anyway, I'm sure the producers were so afraid I would sue them, but I would never do anything like that since it was probably a movement from me that set the dogs into that panic attack. I left the office, and I swear that overnight my skin healed like I wasn't hurt at all. I went back to the office to show them and they couldn't believe it. And I certainly saw the relief in their faces when they knew I would not sue. I'm not religious, but I've always felt spiritual, and I don't believe in giving in to any illness. I've always felt we should just live our lives normally and even illness can't stay with us very long if we don't let it. Maybe that is how I healed so quickly this time, but honestly this was the shortest recovery of anything that has ever been wrong with me. I was grateful just not being scarred for life. I do hope that Leonard doesn't hold that incident against me. I think of Leonard with fond memories and hope he does the same.

e

There are so many stories on Bea Lillie. Her first number in "High Spirits" was "The Bicycle Song". While waiting in the wings, I heard her once say in the lyrics, "Give me a dyke in the sun and the rain" instead of "Give me a bike in the sun and the rain". On other occasions she would literally say gibberish and you would see the audience asking to whom they were speaking, "What was that she said?", thinking they just misread her lines instead of saying, "What the hell was that?" She had a way of making you believe she really said something you misunderstood instead of the nonsensical lyrics she made up. There was another song in the show entitled "Go Into Your Trance". Ms. Lillie would walk around the stage in a specific pattern with a balloon half filled with helium and attached to her shoulder with velcro, so it looked like Casper the ghost was following her. Her path was important because we were all dancing around her and incorporated in the great Danny Daniel's choreography were flying chairs and flying tables across the stage. One specific night upon her reentrance on the stage, she turned right instead of left, after which she had no idea where she was, and she went through the entire number chanting quietly, "I'm sorry, I don't know where to go... which way should I go... am I in your way?" and kept doing this throughout the number. We, the dancers, were terrified she might be hit with one of the flying objects. But she wasn't. But she never again forgot the choreography. Altovise Gore (later to become Mrs. Sammy Davis, Jr.) was in the show and in a part of that Trance number Ms. Lillie sings and we are all surrounding her. At one point she sang words not in the song, but they came out like... "You don't need none of them to darken your skin", she abruptly looked to her right and Altovise' face was right there. She immediately ad-libbed "Sorry!", and went on with the song. Here's another Bea Lillie-ism during the run of the show. Bea had a song she sang to her Ouiji Board called, "Talking to You". She was dressed in a pink bathrobe, hair in curlers, and bunny slippers with big ears on her feet. At the end of the number just as the applause began to die down, she would wiggle her bunny slipper ears... more applause. The next night she did a little cute walk as the applause was beginning to wane... more applause. Within a month, the shtick she was doing at the end of the number became as long as the number and the audience adored her. It was an education just watching her. She used to travel with many miniature dogs, Pomeranians I believe. She always had them in her dressing room. I remember once she told me that these elderly ladies came backstage to see her, and they told her that they thought the show was so wonderful they could hardly keep from applauding. Even she thought that was funny. One night, during the second act, both of Charles Condomine's dead wives were standing stage left by the fireplace. Madame Arcati was at a table just right of center stage. Remember that Madame Arcati was trying to have a successful seance to make the ghost wives disappear from Charles' life, and throughout the play Arcati cannot see the ghosts. Elvira's (Tammy's) line to Ruth (Louise Troy) was supposed to be, "She's too good, you know, she ought to be in the circus". One night Tammy's line came out as, "She's too good, you know, she ought to be in the chorus". Lillie instinctively turned to Tammy and just glared at her with hate in her eyes. Episodes like this occurred throughout the run and made it the most enjoyable and entertaining piece of theatre I've experienced as a dancer in any show.

e

One of my favorite of all singers of all time was of course none other than the fabulous Judy Garland. I've only come in contact with her once personally. I did see her perform her one person show in 1957 in Philadelphia while attending Drexel Institute. I decided to go see a show and my only options were this 'take-off' of Romeo and Juliet before it's Broadway run ... or Judy Garland in Concert. Well, I of course opted for Judy. She performed at the Mastbaum Theatre on Market Street around 22nd St. She was probably at her heaviest weight but it didn't matter. She was still Judy. The Mastbaum Theatre was like a HUGE barn with God know how many seats, but I'm sure more than 2000. At one moment in the show the stage manager came out from the wings and took her standing microphone and carried it off into the wings. They then turned ALL of the lights in the theatre off, including all the exit lights, leaving only a pin spotlight on her face. Then with no music and no amplification, she sang 'Somewhere Over The Rainbow' acapella ... without any musical accompaniment and in this 'city' of a theatre, with probably over 2000 people in attendance, you could literally hear a pin drop... not a cough, a rustle of paper... no sound at all but the pure unadulterated sound of Judy Garland singing her world famous song. I have never in my life experienced anything like that before or after that magical moment ... unbelievable!!!

The reason I brought up Judy here is that during our "High Spirits" run, every Monday night, the Broadway bowling league was held at the Roxy bowling alley. I wouldn't go every week, but did attend several times and on this particular occasion our show was playing "Golden Boy" and Sammy Davis, Jr. was bowling for his show. After about half an hour in walks Judy Garland because she wanted to talk with Sammy, a dear bud of hers. This was years after I saw her in Philly and she had lost so much weight. The year was 1964 and she was this little older lady with a rounded back who walked very gingerly, and didn't carry any of the characteristics of the "Judy" that always appeared onstage. Anyway, Sammy insisted that she join the "High Spirits" team. He probably knew in advance how well she bowled. I am here to tell you that it was such a joy to be in her company even though every single ball she bowled landed in the gutter no more than 10 feet from the time she let go of the ball. We didn't care at all... we were seeing the raw, real Judy Garland and nothing else mattered. This is certainly another of the memories I wouldn't change for a million dollars.

Around the middle of the run of "High Spirits", I found out about another Broadway show audition. The show was "Ben Franklin in Paris". I went to the audition and danced. Again they made cuts and I had to sing. Again they made cuts and I danced again. When the final group was chosen, I raised my hand and asked if there was anything special to do in the show. They needed an understudy to Kaiser Franklin an actor who had one of the principal roles. They gave me the sides and told me to go offstage and study them, then come back to read for them. I did this and they seemed pleased. When they said they would like for me to join the show as a dancer and accept the understudy, I was thrilled. But still trying to act as my own agent, I asked what the salary increase would be, and told them I was getting $10 more in "High Spirits" for handling Tammy on her wire, and I couldn't accept anything less than what I was getting now. What an ass I was!!! Immediately I saw them looking at each other as if saying," What kind of amateur are we dealing with here?". They told me I could leave and they would contact me. This is a lesson for anyone who aspires to raise his or her position at any audition. Never underestimate your own value. Apparently I did and they caught it. Dumb, Dumb, Dumb!!!

e

About 1 month before the end of the High Spirits run, there was an audition listed for a show called "Bajour". The book was by Ernest Kinoy, with music and lyrics by Walter Marks. And the choreography was by Peter Gennaro, who supposedly choreographed 'The Dance at the Gym', and the 'America' numbers in West Side Story as well as 'There's Gotta Be Something Better Than This', from Sweet Charity. I went to the audition and since there were about 300 dancers, I didn't push myself to the front, thinking 'my talent will show me off'. When they eliminated people from groups of 20, I was eliminated almost immediately. So I thought this show is not right for me. And I went back to the show 'on Broadway' that I was already dancing in. No ill feelings ... just slight momentary disappointment. Three weeks later I heard they were still having trouble getting good male dancers and they were holding more auditions. I thought, "Why not?" But this time I wore a bright red t-shirt, and when we danced, I put myself right up front where they would have to be blind not to see me. What a step forward for shy little me. Not only did I pass every elimination, but the same thing that happened as at the "High Spirits" audition. They all came down to the edge of the stage, and the stage manager said, "We held auditions 3 weeks ago... how come you weren't here?" "I'm sorry... I was out of town." Never ever make the people you are auditioning for feel they are inadequate in doing their jobs. Just lie, if you can get away with it. I wanted to audition for this show because Chita Rivera and Hershel Bernardi were starring in it, along with Nancy Dussault and Mae Questel. I knew "High Spirits" was going to close fairly soon, so I didn't make the same mistake that I did in "Ben Franklin in Paris". I got the job and was thrilled to get union scale. BTW another chorus dancer in the show was Michael Bennett, who happened to dress right next to me once the show opened. Working for Peter Gennaro was another absolute dream. As serious as Danny Daniels was during rehearsals of High Spirits, Peter laughed our way through rehearsals... making them so enjoyable. Peter was a short excellent dancer who spoke with a slight lisp... just charming. His work showed up very well on shorter dancers, and since I was only 5' 10" it looked pretty good on me. He had to have great assistants because each time he demonstrated any of the steps, he changed them slightly without trying to. But we caught on and loved dancing for him.

e

Our first out of town tryout was in Philadelphia. I believe the hotel we checked into was The Sylvania on Locust Street. When I got to the front desk to check in, the man behind the desk looked at me and told me that I looked very much like a baseball player he used to play with when he was younger. I asked the fellow what the man's name was and he responded, "Joe, but we called him Yussy". I started to get goose bumps. I almost started to cry when I responded, "Yussy is my father. I'm his son." It didn't really dawn on me that he probably saw the Mazin name on my reservation, but whether he did or not, he made me so proud of being my father's son. My only regret is that my father never lived to see me dance professionally.

They needed an understudy for the role opposite Chita. It was now played by an actor who looked slightly younger than Chita. It wasn't a large role... one song with her with the ensemble in the back, one dance with her as a 'gypsy' pas de deux, and one short scene with her. Totally the role of ' Steve' only had 7 lines in all. .. but everything was with Chita! As soon as we got to Philly, my hometown, they had auditions with the male dancers for the understudy.

Lawrence Kasha, the director, came up to me and asked me to please come to his room at the hotel to read. I assumed I would be reading with the stage manager, and the producers would also be in attendance. Wrong! When I arrived he was alone in the room, and offered me a drink. To this day I really don't enjoy the taste of alcohol unless it is in a blended drink where it tastes like a shake or such. I still hardly ever drink beer or wine. So I turned down the drink and asked if anyone else was auditioning that night. He said no, and he asked me to read the lines, which I did. He said I was very good and asked how much it would mean to me to get the understudy. I am not making any of this up, but this was my first experience with the 'casting couch'. He asked me to hang around with him that night and basically if I wanted the role, it would behoove me to stay. I swear I was shocked. I said, "as much as I might like to, I had to get back to my room because we had an early call in the morning". He didn't try to force himself on me, but I assumed because I didn't play with his ball, that I wouldn't be getting the role. A few days later, the stage manager, Dwain Camp, came to me and told me I got the understudy. So, apparently I was good enough without selling myself and becoming a prostitute. Mind you, I'm not above doing things like that if I find the person attractive to me, and I don't mean his looks. If I feel I am drawn to someone and I like that person, why not? We give sex away for our feelings ... why not for our feelings and possibly a little job... you are the same person... or did I just explain that I am a whore???

As the show progressed, it became a little evident that Chita's relationship with the actor playing 'Steve' was being carried offstage as well. He, being a good looking straight dancer, was also featured in the film of "West Side Story". I stayed with the show until almost the end. Michael Bennett was

leaving the show to choreograph a new version of "West Side Story" in a first class traveling show as a Lenny-Debin package for 3 months or so. I was too young when the original "WSS" was on Broadway in 1957, after not seeing the pre-Broadway run in Philly prior to it's Broadway opening. Since Michael sat next to me in the dressing room, I asked him to please let me know when they were auditioning for his show. He promised he would. So I continued dancing in "Bajour" and never had the opportunity to go on as understudy. Chita's understudy was Caroline Morris, another terrific dancer, singer, actress, and I loved rehearsing with her and the stage manager (Dwain Camp) each week. As a matter of fact Caroline and I danced in a TV Special called "Broadway Understudies and Standbys" we did in 1965. As the show progressed and right before the Wednesday matinee, Michael just showed up to say hello in the dressing room. I asked why he never called to have me audition. I wanted so much to get a chance at Bernardo. Arline Woods, my friend who lived down the hall from me, had done Anita, the role opposite Bernardo several times in the past few years. What Michael didn't know was she was coaching me with the accent. So Michael Bennett said that he was so sorry but with so many things on his mind he forgot. I now understand that so very well having been in his position years later. He asked if I could go up to Ansonia Studios after the matinee and audition. Could I ever!!! Following the matinee I rushed home to my apartment, took black carbon paper and mushed it in my hair to darken the color, put on black chino pants with a navy blue turtleneck, and covered it with a lighter blue button-down shirt with the sleeves rolled up, and put on my black Spanish boots with the 2 inch Cuban heel. I was ready! I got to the Ansonia Studios at 73rd and Broadway and found the audition room. Michael was sitting with Don Driver, the director and they were talking. Michael said to begin doing the scene with the stage manager, then immediately turned back to Don and continued his conversation. I paused waiting for them to look my way. When nothing was happening, he again said, "Go ahead!" I said, "Are you ready?" He said, "Sure." Then he again turned to Don for their conversation. I paused one more moment, then began speaking a little louder at first to get their attention. As quickly as I began with my 'coached' accent, Michael did a double-take then continued watching me, as if he had never seen me before. I now understood that when you see anyone almost everyday acting the way they act in life, it is difficult to picture them as another character. Once I gave him my interpretation of Bernardo, he liked what he saw. Obviously Don Driver liked it as well, because I got the job and arranged to sign a contract in a few days. Needless to say my dear friend Arline Woods, my coach, was thrilled because she was already signed to play Anita. Incidentally Ronnie Walken (alias Christopher Walken) was signed to play Riff This would be my second show with him. And the star was none other than Anna Maria Alberghetti, who used to tour in WWS as Maria every summer.

So, I returned for the evening performance of "Bajour" and my feet hardly touched the ground for quite a while. After signing the contract for Bernardo, I knew I was going to leave "Bajour", and I never did get to go on with Chita. I grabbed 'Steve' in the wings one night and asked if I could talk to him privately. He agreed and I simply asked him, " What will it take to make you get sick one night so I can at least do your role once?" He responded with, "Just give me one eighth of my salary that I will be docked and I'll take the night off" Great!!! We agreed on a date and that night he called in 'sick'. I was told right away that I would have to go on. Butterflies and all, I loved it. We performed the show, and I have to say that when we got to the song, 'Soon', Chita and I are on opposite sides of the stage, with the entire chorus behind us. Chita is a great singer and I know she could have wiped my ass off the stage in the song... but what she did was control her voice and I absolutely felt her 'carry me right through the song' with her. I never felt that with any other performer and I will never forget that feeling. The scene went well and the dance went great! Chita couldn't believe how I got through it without any butterflies. She should have only known that the butterflies almost made me explode, but I knew in advance that I was going on, so I psyched myself into doing the best I could. And so I paid the actor what he asked for.

Now one week later 'Steve' gave his notice. He had to have known he was leaving the show, but he never let me know that. When he left, I did indeed take over the role, but knew I only had one week to perform with Chita as I was beginning rehearsals for "West Side" the following Sunday. And so Norman Twain the show's producer took me outside the front of the Lunt Fontanne Theatre for no less than 2 hours, trying to convince me to stay with the show, and this was even before the actor left the show. I told the producer I was already obligated and he kept trying to convince me to stay by telling me I could get as many comps as I needed. The show was already running and reviewed so I never felt more people would be coming to it. I told him I wouldn't even try to get out of my contract unless I had something good to stay for. He again tried over and over to ply me with comps, because he didn't want to spend the money 'Steve's' part was paying, so we went round and round and back again. Finally he told me he would pay me the same as the other actor ... and this took 2 hours of arguing. I finally said, "Okay, now I will call them and see what they say". Well, when I did call, they would not let me get out of the contract, so I had a perfect out with Mr. Producer. They immediately announced auditions for the role the following day, which was really short notice.

Before I go any further, I must let you know how it was for me to be doing the role with Chita during my last week. The song was always a heartache for me because vocally, I was nowhere near the quality of Chita's. But night after night she carried me right through the number. When it came to the dance, I carried my own weight and it was unbelievable dancing with Chita each performance. By the end of the number we did many turns in a row then suddenly stopped on a dime, facing each other, and feeling each other' s breath. Chita breathed through her nostrils and always reminded me of the strongest bull after a long run. I was alive and on fire with her. Every night after the dance I was left with such an incredible feeling of accomplishment. The scene with her carried slightly different feelings. Within it, we have a few fiery words, I grab her by the nape of her neck and 'throw' her across the stage, then she starts to charge at me and suddenly slows up and we end in a dramatic kiss... a great scene, and I'm doing all this with Chita Rivera. So the first night the kiss is simple, looking effective, but feeling like cardboard on cardboard. At that point in our second performance I feel she is slightly opening her mouth... I oblige and the kiss seems more emotional. During the third performance, I felt a little 'tongue' activity... I oblige and the kiss is even more dramatic, if you can imagine that. On the fourth performance the kiss was sensational ... a true wild French kiss that made our bodies writhe together like forlorn lovers. That night Chita's assistant, I believe her name was Joan, or at least that is what I seem to recall, came to me and told me that Chita was afraid that the kiss had gotten so real that the people in the first few rows might begin to feel a little uncomfortable. I tried explaining that I was just following Chita's lead, but she couldn't accept that, so I agreed to tone the kiss down. The following performance... back to cardboard!!!

e

Late afternoon the day before the audition I stopped by The Open Kitchen, a very small bar restaurant. I happened to see Dom Salinaro, with whom I was enamored since seeing and meeting him after his "The Boys From Syracuse" when I returned from Puerto Rico. Now Dom was teaching Jazz at Dance Players on 6th Avenue but I never took his class. I would once in a while run into him and when I did, I got butterflies to the point of not being able to handle a conversation. But now he is at The Open Kitchen and I went up to him. "Dom, I'm Stan... I met you through Claude Thompson. Are you working right now?" "Yes. I'm in. What Makes Sammy Run with Steve Lawrence." "Are you doing anything special in the show?" "No, I'm in the chorus. Why do you ask?" Then I proceeded to tell him that I was presently doing the role opposite Chita in "Bajour", but I had to leave that weekend and they were having an audition the following morning. I honestly thought Dom would look better than the other actor or myself because he was 10 years older and his look would certainly more than match hers. I then went on to offer to help him that night after his show if he came to my apartment. I would go over the dialogue and teach him what I thought they might give in the dance. Well, I was a wreck thinking about his coming to my apartment. When I got home after my show that night, I went into Stacey's apartment to tell him about Dom coming over. He was sweet as always and said that if it got difficult we could both just come to his apartment and all just talk. I had spoken to Stacey about Dom as he was like my confidante. Being nervous I told him that we might stop by if Dom stayed long enough. I had no intention of 'pouncing' because I was afraid of possibly ruining a relationship that just might evolve. And I have never been a 'pouncer' ... I'm much too shy and inexperienced.

(Stop laughing... it's true!)

Dom arrived and I tried to be as cool as my first night with Chita onstage. We talked, and I showed him the script, which was easy for him to learn... remember, only 7 lines of dialogue. Then afterwards I went over the part of the dance that he might have to do. I couldn't teach him the entire dance as it would have taken too long. Working with him was a little tedious. Dom even began sweating while we worked ... I was sweating on the inside. After we rested a bit, we talked about shows, about drinking, and about dogs. Dom had a beautiful black poodle named 'Belle'. How can anyone not fall in love with an animal lover?!? Since we met after our evening shows, the hour was getting late. I told him about my friend, Stacey, and asked if he wanted to meet him. I knew Stacey was crazy to meet Dom, so after Dom agreed, we went next door and had a nice time for another hour, until Dom had to go home and get some rest.

Well, Dom called me the following day and told me it went very well and he did indeed nail the job. I was so happy because honestly Dom looked like he could be Chita's lover. .. both the other actor and I seemed too young to me. Anyway, my last night in "Bajour" was Saturday night, and our show was much longer in time than Dom's show. Besides, I had to pack up all my things as I wasn't coming back to the theatre. All of a sudden the stage manager knocks on my open door and tells me I have a guest. In walks Dom with a huge magnum of Asti-Spumante. I remember telling him that that was one of the few alcoholic beverages I tried and liked. I thanked him so very much for it and told him to please take it back with him, and I promised that we'd open it when I returned from the tour. He agreed, we hugged (the most we had ever done) and he left. I went home with my things and the knowledge that just maybe there's hope for me.

The following morning I called him to again thank him for the bottle and again congratulate him on his new job... that I helped him get. I also wrote him a letter the following day, which overlapped his telephone call to me. And that is how our relationship grew... through daily phone calls and letters overlapping and such. Our run in West Side Story carried us to Kansas City, Chicago, Warwick Rhode Island,

Latham New York, Mineola New York, Indianapolis, and other places, and in each place we never ran less than 1 full week or more than 2 or 3 weeks at a time. The entire tour with rehearsals ran almost 4 months, so I didn't return until near the end of September with a few exceptions.

During the rehearsals and the run, I really wanted to do something special for Dom. So during our rehearsal period, when we weren't being used, Marcia Gregg, a very close friend of mine, and Connie Burnett taught me how to knit, and my very first project with scandia wool was to knit a sweater for Dom. I was already great at following directions and the girls were great support. And so I knitted a great looking shawl collared sweater, and gave it to him the first time I saw him at one of our times off in Manhattan... a huge hit, which solidified our relationship even more.

e

During the run of "WSS" it was thrilling for me to play a great role like Bernardo. Working with Arline as Anita was fantastic. Working with Ron Walken was an education to say the least. You never knew exactly what he was going to be doing during the show. He danced very much like he acted... never allowing anyone to know his exact moves, so everything he did seemed and was more spontaneous. This made his dancing look so interesting to watch, much like watching him act in later years. Several times during the prologue he had me in a new position that I was never in before. In one of the first performances in one of the outdoor music tents in the round, he held me from behind with both arms behind my back and was swinging me around. Just then one of my own Sharks, JoJo Smith, a running locomotive in a human body, came charging down the aisle and even though I saw him, I had no control and Ronnie, accidentally I'm sure, swung me right into JoJo's head, and clunk... my forehead just to the right of my right eyebrow was slashed. Immediately bleeding I continued the show as well as I could. At intermission, Ronnie came to my room and profusely apologized. I knew he was sorry, but it didn't hide the fact that after the show I was rushed to the hospital and given 8 stitches in my right eyebrow. These happenings occurred many times during the run, and he was always very sorry, and I'm sure he truly was. Our 'Anybodys' was played by Leland Palmer, a brilliant dancer and actress, who later played Gwen Verdon in Bob Fosse's "All That Jazz". Leland was once thrown from Ronnie's back right onto the floor on her own back and was out of the show for almost a week. I could say now that during our run of "High Spirits", the same type of thing happened although there were no stage fights in "High Spirits", but it did become apparent that wherever Ron was onstage, there was a kind of 'empty space' around him as the dancers soon learned not to be too close to him when he began swinging his arms around. I have often joked about that, saying that perhaps that is how he became such a star. Anyone seeing the show might say, "Who is that dancer dancing by himself?". And so this continued throughout the run of WSS, and during the 'Quintet' I couldn't help but feel so anxious never knowing how I was going to be hurt during that 'rumble' at the end of Act I. To this day when I hear any version of the 'Quintet' my stomach turns and I begin to feel the same feelings I had when we did it. About 3 weeks before the end of our run, Ron got sick one night and even though he was in the show, it was decided that the dancer who played 'Action' would do the 'rumble' with me. Now our 'Action' was played by John Torme, a brilliant, seemingly 'method' actor and he was so strong in his role that I couldn't help but feel that even though I didn't know what to expect with Riff, Action would absolutely kill me! As soon as we began the 'rumble' John made me feel so secure. Every action he took was controlled and safe, although looking fierce and uncontrollable. Hallelujah!!! This is how I should have felt the entire time. John Torme is still acting and even though I haven't seen him since then, I have always appreciated his professionalism. I remember the last week we did the show. Ronnie came to me and said, "Man, when I punch you to start the 'rumble', you're dropping to the floor before my fist gets near your face." I said, "Fine! Ronnie, just don't hit me... I mean really... don't hit me!" That night and the following 2 nights he really did not hit me... I stayed slightly longer before I dropped to the floor and all was fine. Then the 4th performance after we spoke about it, sure enough, his fist went right into the left side of my upper lip, seemingly moving faster than usual. I immediately put my left hand to my lip and saw the blood. That was that! No more Mr. Nice Guy! When I got up, there was a short section when I went toward him and he would back up, then he came toward me and I backed up. I thought, "Okay, I have to get him!". So when he came toward me, we both had our 'switchblades' out by this point in the fight, I stopped short and jabbed him in his right forearm. By the way, these blades retracted but the fight was so fast with all the jabs we couldn't take a chance that they might not retract in time so as we 'stabbed' each other we flattened our fist into the others stomach so the blade was flat against the stomach and couldn't go into the stomach... we were always close by that time so people couldn't really see where the blade was. Then when I had him 'pinned' against the wire fence, taunting him by tossing my blade from one hand to the other, the blood was running into my mouth and I began spewing the blood out of my mouth spraying him with it... truly dramatic and exciting. During this more than improvisational fight, I couldn't help but think that I've got to get him for all the pain he caused to everyone during the run. I was going to stop short again right before the last 'jab' and punch with, blade in hand, harder than usual and knock him out. But as the moment approached I chickened out thinking I could kill him by punching him in the solar plexus, so the last stab was even more gentle than the others. As a result of his first fist punch to my lip, I had to have plastic surgery of 6 stitches to my upper lip. This was truly the most interesting and the most fearsome 'rumble' we ever fought. But truly in every performance when I was finally 'stabbed' and killed, I would be thinking, "Thank you, God, for letting me live through another one." And I still know that Ronnie Walken was truly innocent in what he did. I honestly don't believe he ever meant to hurt anyone, but he certainly kept everyone in the show more than alert during our run. I often wonder if my injuries were a little more exaggerated in my mind because I might be jealous of his career. I try being honest with myself and my feelings and no, I'm not jealous... but envy... yes, I am envious of Chris's career. I find I am often envious of true talent, and Ronnie has it!

Incidentally, after not seeing Ron for 40 or so years, I read he was going to be doing a new Broadway play called "A Behanding in Spokane", and it would be running while our group was in New York that April. I wrote him a note to tell him I would love to take him for a drink, or at least see him after the show. I never got a response, but I did arrange our group to see the show. He was of course brilliant in a role that so suited him. After the show I made my way to the stage door, and of course they had those barriers to keep the fans away from the stage door. I knocked and a man opened the door and asked, "Who are you here to see?" I responded, "Chris Walken". "What's your name?" "Stan Mazin." "Wait out here." And he closed the door. Within seconds he opened the door again and immediately said, "Come on in." Then after I went in he said to one of the other men there, "Take him upstairs." I followed the man up 3 flights of stairs and he said Chris' room was down the hall. I walked down and in the doorway stood Ronnie Walken, in full costume with his arms opened wide to welcome me. Now by the time I got upstairs it had to be at least 10 minutes after the final curtain, so I was flattered that he didn't begin to change clothes before seeing me. I brought my friend Don Tango, who was my Chino in West Side with me. Ron brought us into his dressing room and could not have been more cordial. He asked what I was doing and kept talking to me, almost ignoring Don. Another couple

entered the doorway so I started to get up to leave and he pushed me down in the chair and whispered, "Don't go yet... I'll just be a few minutes." He got up and greeted the couple, spoke to them for a few minutes, they left and he came back to us, continuing our conversation. I could not have been more flattered! He absolutely made me feel so important. And I will never forget that. Chris Walken is truly a gentleman, as well as a star.

e

An interesting bit of trivia is that Anna Maria Alberghetti enjoyed her wine. and once in a while on the road I would be driving her back to where they put her up during the run. One night (and only one), she was more tipsy than I had ever seen and she wanted to kiss me, or at least that is certainly what it seemed like. I told her we would be home soon, and I was not in the market... but I didn't tell her that. Instead I just kept putting her hands back toward her own body. She really didn't realize what she was doing. I know she was very high on wine and I never blamed her for that. To me it was extremely flattering, but the evening was never repeated again. I often wonder if I wanted to wander, the more I wondered about actively doing more wandering. What'd I just say?

e

At one of the near places we were playing close to NY, Dom was supposed to come and see the show, and possibly spend the night. He never showed up. I was not only disappointed but very angry that he didn't even call me. It just so happens that after that week's run we had a couple of days off so I went back home. I purposely did not call him as I was still filled with anger. That night late, I got a call from Sal Angelica, who was my own understudy in West Side. He called from Jimmy Ray's, a gay bar on 8th Avenue, and told me that Dom was there and wanted to talk to me. I said ok. Dom got on the phone and I was very cold to him. He wanted to come over and see me, so I said, "It's a free country... do what you want" and I hung up. When he did arrive, he began to explain why he didn't come and why he couldn't tell me. He had been visiting his family in Waterbury, Connecticut and he had his dog, Belle, with him. They had gone for a walk and without his knowledge Belle had run across the street. Instinctively Dom called for her to return and she immediately responded unaware that a car was coming very quickly down the road. Belle was hit and immediately killed. Do I have to tell you how small I felt feeling sorry for myself when he told me about Belle? I'm surprised that we didn't consummate our relationship then, but he was so distraught in telling me the story, that neither one of us could think of that. And so he left and we made tentative plans for him to come and spend the night sometime when we were playing in Latham, NY. The time finally arose and when he showed up, he brought a new almost all black poodle puppy that his brother Vito gave to him. He called her 'Pansy' and she was nothing short of adorable. We left Pansy in the hotel room when he came to see the show, and when we returned Pansy left us both a present on the bed. Everyone's a critic! When we did go to bed, both Dom and I just laid there. I think he must have been as shy as I was, and it was kind of charming with neither of us making advances. I sometimes wish we had, which I will go into later. In the morning, Dom went back to Manhattan and we felt even closer having NOT had any physical contact. I'm not sure how many people would really understand that.

e

The night I returned from the tour I went to my apartment, which I had partially sublet for a short time to a good friend of mine named Michael Shaw. I showered, changed clothes, then went immediately to Dom's apartment at 81st and Amsterdam. We opened the Asti, drank too much, and allowed ourselves to explore each other's bodies with our hands and mouths and more. I couldn't believe I was in his arms, as it was still an infatuation I had never known. And his body was gorgeous!!! He had lots of chest hair which I loved, and between his muscular legs and tight bubble butt was a body to die for. I could not believe my bliss. This was so worth the wait. Of course, with such an anticipation, there comes a moment of quiet, which I felt after an orgasm that I could not believe. We did things that normally I have learned I would prefer not to do, but I was with Dom, and everything he did to me, I did to him as well. So I felt vindicated that I wasn't letting myself just be used as I had in my first sexual confrontation. After all, I was also the dominant one, and as I've learned through the years, it was a position I preferred. From that night on, I went back to my own apartment to shower and change, and spent my nights at Dom's.

When Dom took over my role in "Bajour" (my 'understudy' role originally) the show unfortunately lasted just 3 more weeks and closed. For Dom's sake, he was able to go back to "What Makes Sammy Run". So until that show closed, he was set.

The Broadway show that I auditioned for upon my return from "West Side Story" was called "Holly Golightly" and it was the musical version of Truman Capote's film "Breakfast at Tiffany's". It was to star Mary Tyler Moore and Richard Chamberlain with music and lyrics by Bob Merrill and book by Abe Burrows. Production design was by Oliver Smith, direction by Abe Burrows with choreography by Michael Kidd. This seemed like a sure hit. (Interesting to note that for the film, Truman Capote's choice to play Holly Golightly was Marilyn Monroe, but Audrey Hepburn got it.)

Michael Kidd, the choreographer, had a reputation of firing at least one dancer within the first three days (which he was allowed to do according to Equity). We had several lovely looking female dancers, and one particular beauty named Trudy Carson. Michael had a strange sense of humor. There was a number in the show called "Lament for Ten Men" or we called it 'Dirty Old Men'. Michael went up to Trudy and told her that he was so sorry but he had to get rid of one of the female dancers and it was going to be her unless she agreed to put on old men's makeup and do the 'Dirty Old Men' with the rest of the male dancers. He had her in tears until he finally told her he was joking. He really meant her no harm and had no idea she would become so emotional. But after he apologized her seat in the show was guaranteed, because he felt so bad for her, besides the fact that she was truly beautiful and talented.

Within the first week after the rehearsals began, one of the male dancers had been fired and there was an opening. I told Dom to audition since he was free at the time, and with a little coaching he was hired. We had a friend in the show named Teak Lewis who crocheted. And during rehearsals since we had lots of 'free' time, I even taught Dom how to knit, since he was so taken with the sweater I made for him. So there we were in rehearsals with Michael Kidd, the choreographer of "Seven Brides for Seven Brothers" among other great musical films and shows. Michael would love to tell stories to the dancers and play 'kick the can' with them during our free time. Teak, Dom, and I would be sitting in the corner, Teak crocheting, and Dom and I knitting while Michael and his groupies would be joking and playing. I thought Michael hated us, but later that proved not to be true.

Mary opened the show in Philly wearing a fantastic sleeveless gown to the floor and long sleeve gloves, looking at the window at Tiffany's. I believe there was a full page picture of her in her opening costume in one of the Saturday Evening Posts. Truly she was a star. Some of the reviews compared her to Audrey Hepburn's look in the film. Within days, Mary opened the show wearing a plain trench coat carrying a cup of coffee looking at the same Tiffany window. It seemed David Merrick, the producer, never really knew what to do with the show. I personally liked many of the songs, but the show never really grabbed hold of the audience. So when we got to Boston for our out of town tryout there, Abe Burrows was fired. Truman Capote said (if you can imagine him saying this with his squeaky voice), "The only one who I will let rewrite this show is my good friend, Edward Albee!". And so the show based on "Breakfast At Tiffany's" became "Whose Afraid of Holly Golightly" ... incidentally that's my joke... not the true name. The director, Abe Burrows, was replaced by Joseph Anthony, a friend of Albee's. At the end of the run in Boston, with many future revisions to be made, most of the dancers, including myself, were let go, and older types were hired for the "Dirty Old Men" number. By the time the show began previews in New York the entire show was revamped. As I heard it, this is how the events occurred. There was an after-the-abortion scene that took place when Holly was in the Hospital. Now one of the lines that Fred (Richard Chamberlain) said to Holly was, "Holly, don't be upset. We can start over again" ... or words to that effect. Now I'm told some hecklers in the audience would shout back, "Yea, why don't you start the whole play over again?" Now this is Laura Petrie and Dr. Kildare the audience is dealing with. I don't think they were prepared to accept these characters as those of Edward Albee's version of "Breakfast at Tiffany's". Ultimately rumor has it that Mary Tyler Moore called David Merrick into her dressing room and told him in a very distraught manner that she couldn't do this any longer. So Merrick closed the show days before it's Broadway opening. Every Broadway flop has it's story, and if this one isn't true, I believe it's close to the truth.

And so up to this point in my life I have three Broadway shows and one touring show under my belt. I have a hopefully longtime partner to look forward to. During this last <u>show Dom and</u> I moved to 710 West End Avenue to a lovely 2 bedroom, 2 bath apartment, with a 'sit-in' kitchen, and a little entry room. We were only paying $210 per month and it was like a palace to us. How great it was not to have to run back to my own apartment to change clothes every day. I just wish I had that apartment now. I would think it would probably go for $4500 to $6500 a month or more, New York City standards. I remember while

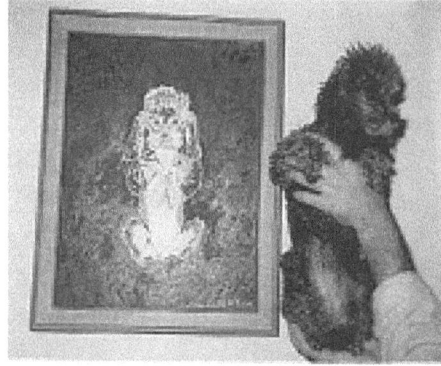

living there I painted a picture of our dear Pansy in oils, this time remembering the Linseed oil. I thought I did a good job considering... I was proud of it at any rate.

It was about this time that I auditioned for and got to dance in Paris, France at the Olympia Theatre for Lester Wilson, a fantastic choreographer, director. We were the dance act that performed the first act on the very first performing visit of Liza Minnelli to Paris. They loved her! They compared her to a female version of Sammy Davis, Jr. whom they absolutely adored. I remember so well how we used to change clothes as quickly as we could and run into the balcony to watch Liza perform with her own two dancers, Bob Fitch, a wonderful eccentric dancer, and Neil J. Shwartz, shorter and slightly heavy, but a great dancer and acrobat. This was the time Liza was just dating Peter Allen, but rumor had it that they were 'coking' together. In the act she sang a Charles Aznavour & Fred Ebb song I will never forget. It was called, "You've Let Yourself Go". Liza began the song sitting in a chair, and most of the song was about how this man who as he ages has let himself go by not taking care of himself, being the clown at parties, etc, although perhaps it isn't all his fault. During the song she gets up and circles the chair once always referring to the man sitting in the chair ... then at the end she sits down in the chair where she started and sings, "Come close to me and let yourself go". I felt chills each time she sang it. I've seen her do the number since, but to me, it never had the same impact. Look up the lyrics, as they are heart rendering. But until you do, a bit of the lyrics to the song are...

The beginning (or the setup) ...

"So we're alone again tonight, I read a book, you watch the fight"
Moving on...

"When at a party, now and then, you tell the same old jokes again"
And then...

"I couldn't hate you if I tried, and I still want you by my side"
Ending with...

''A seed we planted, still can't grow, maybe that's all we need to know Come close to me and Let yourself go... "

You really have to hear the entire set of lyrics. Perhaps then you will feel something as well.

e

It was during this show in Paris, my first time there, that we the cast were introduced to a restaurant called Le Rose Bleu. Almost every night after either rehearsals or performing we would all go there for our supper snack or meal, and the owners would keep the place open for us. After a while, the co-owner took a liking to me. I must have been cute in those days although I never was aware of it. Consequently when anyone paid a little attention to me, I was of course flattered. And since this was my first time overseas, I was curious to engage in a one-time relationship with a 'Frenchman' ... and so I did. A little time after that I showed signs of VD, Gonorrhea, and not knowing where to go, I went to the American Express office. They gave me the address of this French doctor. When I went into the office, I felt like I was going back in time... there was no modern equipment, and everything was dark and made of wood. When he finally examined me he put me in this very high wooden chair. I had to lower my pants and underwear, after which he poured a purple liquid over my genitals... I believe he gave me a shot also. I had to go back one more time and he did the same procedure on me. Now Dom was coming to Paris to spend the last couple of days there, and after the show with Liza was over, we spent the next 3 weeks traveling around Europe on Arthur Frommer's "Europe On $5 Dollars A Day", including lodging... yes, it was that long ago. I felt very bad having to tell Dom that I had cheated on him, but I only did it that one time in Paris, and I really wanted to experience something different, so if that makes me a bad person, I can accept that. Needless to say once I told Dom about it, he was destroyed... I was such an idiot! It practically spoiled the rest of our vacation. It's amazing how one bad decision can almost ruin your life.

e

Because of what I had done, the rest of our trip was very difficult. But a few things stood out. Our first time in Amsterdam we stayed in a true 'canal' house, and had to drag our luggage up to the third floor with almost ladder type stairs. It nearly killed the both of us. The owner was this Rubenesque looking woman who spoke no English, and I spoke no Dutch so we both had to converse with each other in our high school Spanish. We made it work but it wasn't easy. Anne Frank's house is a must for anyone going to Amsterdam ... and the rondvaarts were amazing, touring around the city by canal. We went to Geneva to see the geysers and Zurich to see the watches. I remember in Zurich we went to a fondue restaurant we found in the book and we've never been to one before. We of course ordered fondue and when it came it was laden with alcohol. .. or at least such a strong cheese taste that I just couldn't eat it. I'm not an alcohol aficionado since I hate the taste of pure alcohol. So I couldn't eat anything but the bread that night since our finances were already spent. And so, moving on we bought Murano glass in Venice and ate strange pretzels in Salzburg. We saw Michelangelo's "David" at the Accademia in Florence, as well as the Spanish Steps and Colosseum in Rome. Michelangelo's "David" is truly amazing.. .if you stare at it, you would swear he is breathing. In Rome we ate at a very cheap Italian bar restaurant. Now Dom speaks a little Italian. When the bartender/waiter behind the bar saw us enter, I knew he didn't want to serve us. But we sat down at the bar and Dom ordered spaghetti aglio e olio (spaghetti with oil and garlic). The waiter kept saying, "Che?", or "Che cosa?". Dom in his frustration said as he played charades with his hands, 'spaghetti ... with oil. .. and garlic'. This went on for some time until the waiter finally returned with a bowl of plain cooked pasta, a bottle of oil, and a plate of raw garlic. Dom was so upset he poured the oil, and garlic as well as his wine over the pasta and the waiter indicated that Dom was crazy, then he walked away. Now remember that we were on a financial budget, so just as I tried to do in Zurich, Dom tried eating the pasta... not a great experience. However all this throughout Europe was only $5 a day including lodging, so we ate very cheaply... and slept very cheaply... and I couldn't help but feel cheap after what I had done to Dom. He didn't deserve it and I would love to have blamed it on my youth, but it was my own mind that was to blame... and it took a very long time for him to trust me again. I swore then that if I ever 'dallied' again, I wouldn't tell him because I wouldn't want him hurt again. I did love him, but sexually we were not as compatible as we both wanted to be for each other. Love isn't everything, and in itself isn't strong enough to solve all problems... but without any love in our lives, it's a shallow existence.

e

Late in 1966 there was an opening in an already running Broadway show called "Walking Happy" starring an English star named Norman Wisdom. It also starred Louise Troy, whom I worked with in "High Spirits", and George Rose. The show was based on "Hobson's Choice" by Harold Brighouse, produced by Feuer and Martin, with book by Roger 0. Hirson and Ketti Frings, music by James Van Heusen, lyrics by Sammy Cahn, directed by Cy Feuer, and choreography by Danny Daniels, who also choreographed "High Spirits". So when I showed up at the audition, Danny Daniels was thrilled to be able to hire me again. I replaced an actor dancer named Steve Jacobs... one Jew for another. After I got the job again there was another opening and Dom got into the show as well. He replaced Chad Block a 'beefy' kind of guy, and although Dom wasn't as 'rough' looking, he always made a wonderfully strong appearance onstage. One of the friends we made who was in the cast from the start was our dear friend, Lucille Benson. Lucille was a wonderful character actress and later starred as Mother Burnside in the Lucille Ball's film of "Mame". Other friends we made or already had in the show are Ellen Graff, Tom Boyd, and Richard Korthaze (who later played the entire jury in the original Broadway musical of the original version of "Chicago").

It was "Walking Happy" that brought us to California for the first time, when we closed in New York. Actually we only played in San

Francisco and Los Angeles. We had a 6-week run in San Francisco and the show was very favorably received. On the train coming from Chicago to San Francisco (we changed trains there), a funny incident occurred to one of the male dancers. We stopped momentarily in Needles, California in the middle of the night. One of the dancers, Gene Cooper, needed cigarettes and wearing nothing but a robe, he carried $1 to buy the cigarettes from the station. Just after he bought the cigarettes another train on the track closest to the station came by and blocked his re- entrance onto our own train. Before the train that blocked his path to our train cleared the station, our train moved on leaving Gene at the station, abandoned with no ID, money or other clothes. The sheriff picked him up and brought him to the police station before they could remedy his situation. You can just imagine the look on his face as he saw our train pulling out and he couldn't get to it. I was thankful it wasn't me. At any rate, they did somehow get Gene in his bathrobe back to S.F. the same morning but long after we had arrived. Very funny situation... and Gene Cooper was about the nicest, shyest guy in our cast. I don't think he is around now.

e

We played In Los Angeles at the Dorothy Chandler Pavillion, the largest venue at the Music Center. Usually traveling plays do not play there, but at the Ahmanson if they play the Music Center at all. Our run was uneventful but lots of fun... first time in California and first time in Los Angeles. During the time we were in LA, and this was 1966, there was an audition for The Carol Burnett Show. Ernie Flatt was holding the audition and many of the male dancers from the tour went. I loved the audition and felt positive about it, so left feeling very good and proud of myself. Needless to say when I never heard anything from them I couldn't help but feel, "California people are full of crap, holding auditions for no reason." So I forgot about that and enjoyed the rest of the run in "Walking Happy". Near the end of our tour, which closed in Los Angeles, the male dancers were talking about auditioning for the Mitzi Gaynor night club act. They needed 2 male singers who danced. So they all went to the audition and I did not. I never had confidence in myself when it came to singing... so it was easy to 'let it go' and not even be concerned about it. The dancers returned disappointed that not one of them was kept. A few days later Dom and I are at our apartment at the Fireside Manor on Franklin, when the phone rang. I answered and the voice on the other line asked for Stan Mazin. I said, "Speaking". He introduced himself as Jack Bean, Mitzi Gaynor's husband and asked why I never auditioned for them, since most of the other male dancers in "Walking Happy" had auditioned already. Now remember I didn't have any confidence in myself as a singer. So when I feel like there is no way I could be involved, I don't have to stand on ceremony, and I could talk plainly. I said, "Listen, Jack, you are looking for singers who can dance... I'm more of a dancer who can sing in a group". Then Jack Bean gave me a bit of advice that I have since passed on many, many times. He said, "Let me give you a bit of advice! Why don't you let US turn YOU down, instead of YOU turning YOU down!" Wow!!! He was so right with this one. He asked if I could come to their home the following morning at 9am to sing for them. I said that I would. Before hanging up the phone, I asked how he knew of me, and he told me their choreographer was Ernie Flatt and he referred me. Who would have 'thunk' it??? So Ernie liked me after all. The following morning I showed up at 610 Arden Drive in Beverly Hills, nervous as a witch in Salem. Jack opened the door for me and we stood in the entrance to this beautiful home facing a huge winding staircase for just a few minutes. Then, like in a movie, Mitzi Gaynor comes down the stairs, looking like a true star, with full makeup on, and eyelashes that reached the bottom of the stairs 2 minutes before she did. She looked amazing. We went into the parlor, or whatever room it was that had their piano, and they had a pianist already there to accompany me. I was a wreck! I'm not even sure what I sang, but it could have been "Im Gonna Live Until I Die", which I have used before. After singing, Jack asked if I would be available to 'stop by' the rehearsal at a dance studio that same afternoon. I agreed and made my exit, still excited that I just met Mitzi Gaynor. I did indeed show up that same afternoon, and did indeed get one of the 2 vacant openings in her act. At this time her act consisted of her and 4 male dancers whom she called "The Four Fellas" ... what could be gayer than that!!! And so right after "Walking Happy" closed, before returning to NYC, I was flown up to Lake Tahoe to perform as one of "The Four Fellas" with Mitzi Gaynor at Harrah's ... Lake Tahoe, one of the most beautiful locations

I had ever been to. Now my memory gets a little fuzzy here, after all, I am old, but my roommate there was LeeRoy Reams, a fantastic triple threat... singer, dancer, and actor.

We became pretty close during our 2 week run and have remained friends ever since.

e

The second time I danced for Mitzi was in Las Vegas, after Dom and I moved to California. I remember that Dom came to Las Vegas to see our opening at the Riviera on the strip. After the show Mitzi brought all of us to this Italian Restaurant, and she was wearing a fabulous off white Bill Blass dress. Well during the night everyone was having a great time and then Dom accidently knocked his red wine all over Mitzi and her original Bill Blass Dress. I can't tell you how bad he felt, and me too of course, but Mitzi was such a lady, that even though she could have been boiling inside, she was cool and collected outside. She told him not to sorry about it, but the deed was done and there was nothing else to do about it.

e

Alton Ruff, Randy Doney's partner was quite ill one night during our Vegas stint. I mean he felt like crap and was sick to his stomach, but as soon as Mitzi came into the dancers' dressing room which she did every night before the show, Alton's disposition changed and he forced a real phony smile on his face and when she asked how we were doing, he said that he was fine. When she left I asked him why he couldn't be honest with her and he explained that she was the star and shouldn't be burdened with the health of one of her dancers. She should only be thinking about her performance. It kind of made sense to me, but I feel if we are a true family, everyone should be honest with each other and everyone could help pick up each other's spirits for a better show. There are definitely two sides of every story.

e

Whenever Mitzi came into our dressing room she would walk up to me and ask, "Stanley, what do I shmell?" She was always referring to garlic as she did in rehearsals in LA also. You see Dom was a great Italian cook and Italian cooks are useless without the taste of garlic in their dishes... so even though my tongue was green from all the Clorets I was chewing, sometimes the garlic came through. Mitzi had a nickname for Domenic... 'Lola Lasagna', and would always ask how Lola was. I loved that special intercourse we had together. Dom wasn't so crazy about it, of course. But I love Mitzi, and even though she may not be the dancer she was when she was younger, like Debbie Reynolds, she certainly knows how to handle her audiences through her humor and funny endless dialogue. She always has them in the palm of her hand. From her I learned more lessons about the connection between a star and her audience... and Mitzi is masterful.

e

With the anticipation of working on the act in Vegas I remember thinking, 'I want to take $300 and either lose it gambling or spend it taking flying lessons in a small plane. Well I had no idea how much or how little flying lessons were, but that is what I decided to do. And the $300 was enough to cover 8 private lessons in a Cessna at the North Las Vegas Airport. A Cessna is a 'high-wing' airplane that is much lighter than the low wings of a piper or other low winged planes. They claim it will fly like a kite if something were to happen to the engine. During my first lesson my instructor flew us to a height of around 7000 feet and put us in a death spiral. I was about to soil my pants when he said, "Whenever this happens to you in a Cessna, just pull back the throttle, take your feet off the pedals, and the plane should come out of it all by itself" Well, that is exactly what happened. The plane stopped spinning and as soon as it stopped, he pushed the throttle in and we began flying the plane just as before. What a thrill that was. The beginning of my 8th lesson, the instructor was sitting next to me on the plane and told me he wanted me to do a short field take off, a short field landing and a couple of other things I now forgot. As I reached for the throttle he grabbed my hand and said, "Good luck". I screamed, "Where are you going". He said, "I trust you. If you need me I'll be in the tower", and proceeded to leave the plane. I taxied down the runway, very alone, and put on my flaps for a short-field take off, and throttled the engine and started down the runway. As soon as the plane took off it seemed like we were not climbing for some time. I realized then that the flaps were still down and I lifted them and zoom... we were climbing at last. I cannot tell you the feeling of power and self destiny I feel when I lift off from the ground and I realize I can literally go in any direction I choose, within the legal rules of flight.

e

After the Las Vegas job with Mitzi was over, I continued to fly at Hollywood Burbank Airport at FlightEast, a general aviation airplane rental office. I had two major near death incidents while flying. On one of them I was flying to Apple Valley Airport a very tiny airport with no tower. Just as I was trying to land, flying against the wind as I should, there was a gust of air coming from my rear which lifted the back end of the plane so much that if I continued I would have flown into the runway. I immediately pushed the throttle forward and raised the plane into the air and flew the plane away... saving myself from a possible disaster. I was alone and didn't try landing at that airfield again.

Roz Danloe, now Roz Posner, lived down the hall from me when I lived on West 57th Street in New York. Roz was also in theatre having done "Ballroom" the musical of "Queen of the Stardust Ballroom". We have remained friends since New York. When she was living out here in California I took her for a flight, as I had to keep practicing my flying, and we landed at Fox Field, a small airstrip in the Lancaster Palmdale area. Roz knew that I knew many people and often when I was with her people would come over and say "Hello". Well Fox Field had a very small coffee shop and after landing, we went in and sat by the window and had some coffee. During our conversation she said, "How come you don't know people here?" At that point we saw a couple of people get out of a small plane, and as they were walking toward the coffee shop she said, "Look at that guy. He thinks he's Tevye." The one who looked like Tevye was dressed similarly to that character and had a scarf not unlike the one Tevye wore in the show. I looked out and immediately got up from my chair and ran out to greet Hershel Bernardi as he came into the coffee shop. Apparently a friend was flying him from Vegas to Van Nuys and they stopped at Fox. When Roz saw that I knew him and he was Hershel Bernardi, she almost plotzed. I knew him from "Bajour", my second Broadway show. After the introductions and Hershel went to another table with his friend, Roz immediately whispered, "Wouldn't you know it. You even knew someone here, and I just said you didn't. I will never say that again." When something extraordinary like that occurs, even the meekest of us is bound to get a swollen head.

e

On another occasion I had two friends with me, John King, who danced on the Carol Burnett Show many times, and in the rear seat, my friend Joan Kaye who lived in San Francisco at the time and whose brother Allen attended high school with me. We flew up to San Francisco and even though San Francisco Airport is not crazy about general aircraft landing there, once we landed and the tower asked where we were going, I said Butler Aviation as I knew they handled general aviation planes for service, and rental planes. On the return flight I didn't file a flight plan but as I always do I called for weather and was told there should be no reason I couldn't fly back to Burbank. I am a VFR (visual flight rules) pilot not an instrument rated pilot (IFR). So I am not supposed to fly in bad weather or anywhere I cannot see the ground. So we took off from SFO. I flew over USI, which south of Monterrey lies between the mountains. As we are flying I see that there seems to be a storm coming from the west and it begins to get darker, and it starts to rain. I feel as long as I can see the road below me I'm ok. As it gets darker I'm beginning to think that perhaps I should put it down on the freeway, which I choose not to do. We approach San Luis Obispo area and the road in front of me begins curving between the mountains, and because of the clouds above I am flying closer to the freeway. I make a decision to fly over the mountains toward the east and gun the engine and begin climbing. It is cold and we are immediately in the clouds. At this point I cannot take my eyes off the instrument panel as there is no way for a pilot to 'feel' which way is 'up' under these conditions. Suddenly the entire plane shutters and I realize we have hit the ice level where the water landing on the plane turns to ice. I also know that under these conditions the additional water that turns to ice creates an extra weight on the plane that could make it too heavy to fly. Now I know that there are vortexes that give me my position horizontally above the ground, but the only instrument that gives me the altitude is the pitot tube, which looks like an uncircumcised penis aiming forward usually under the wing of a plane. And I think that it may be possible that ice develops within the pitot tube giving me false readings of altitude. I have a subscription to Private Pilot magazine and in each issue there is a section about how planes go down and pilots are killed. I am now seeing my own obit in that magazine as I fight the weather. It is now freezing in the airplane and beads of perspiration are coming down my face. My friends have no idea that we might be in trouble. My feeling is that if we were to fly into the side of a mountain, it would be instantaneous so there is no reason to panic them. John on the other hand, has a great sense of humor and begins to whistle the theme from "The High and the Mighty". I say, not taking an eye off the instrument panel, "That's not funny, John". I know the height of the mountains we are crossing are 4500 feet. I wait and sweat until the altimeter reads that we are at 5500 feet, giving myself a 1000 foot advantage in case the pitot tube is clogged. After reading the vortex readings and knowing that horizontally we are east of the mountain range, I lower the plane slowly. We are still in the clouds when we reach the ice level and the ice turns to water again. We are at 1500 feet, still no ground sight... 1200 feet still no ground site. Finally at 800 feet we come out of the clouds and I see terra firma and just as I decide to put the plane down anywhere, I see US5 and turn right, toward Burbank. It is still raining and I approach Meadows Airport in Bakersfield and we land. I literally kiss the ground, rent a car, drive back to Burbank, and thank whoever she is above us for sparing our lives. Two days later I rent another car to go back to Bakersfield and fly the plane back to FlightEast.

And this still did not prevent me from purchasing a used 1969 Cherokee Arrow. A Cherokee Arrow is one in which the wheels go up, but the pilot goes down... just a little bit of pilot humor. I purchased the plane for $26,500 and did a 'lease back', which means that FlightEast could rent the plane out for me and help me pay for itself. After having the plane for about three years, I was flying up to Concord to visit Leslie and my Godchild, Zachary. Just as I approach San Jose area, this huge clanging sound begins and it is coming from the cowling (hood) of the plane. Now inasmuch as I fly, I don't know shit about the technical issues dealing with an airplane. All I know is that a small airplane has to have 'torque' in order to be stable enough to fly, and the propeller gives the plane 'torque'. With this sound coming from the front of the plane, I have no idea what it could be. I'm thinking maybe the propeller has come loose so I better not put the plane in a deep dive to land. If I lose the propeller, I lose the torque, I lose my life. So I put it in a shallow descent and continue to Concord Airport. I call the tower to tell them what is happening and they have fire trucks along both sides of the runway. It is not until we land and I pull the throttle back that I see black smoke coming from the cowling. Now when they look at the plane they see that a hose has come uncoupled in the engine, and that was the racket that was being made as it clanked around inside the cowling. With an airplane, you cannot 'temporarily' fix the plane until you take it to your mechanic. When something like this happens you must have a full examination and evaluation of the plane and that can cost 6 to 8 grand, which I do not have. So I had a balance on the plane of $10500, and I was forced to sell it to a mechanic from Hawthorne Airport for $9500. Besides the money already invested in the plane, I lost another $1000 but all that time, I had my own airplane. Unfortunately I haven't flown since. If I were to win the lottery, that may change. After all, there is nothing quite like the freedom of flight!

e

A while after settling into our home on Wilkinson Avenue in Studio City in '69, I got a phone call from another girlfriend, Harriet Freize from Atlantic City. She asked, "Stanley, two friends of mine are coming to Los Angeles... would you do me a favor and take them around? You'll love them they are wonderful people." "Of course", I responded. "If they are your friends I would be glad to show them around, as long as I'm available when they are." We spoke for a little while longer, then right before hanging up she said, "By the way, they're priests." Then hung up immediately. I was a little shocked because both Harriet and I were brought up Jewish, even though I don't follow any religion now. So the time came when her friends, the priests, were in town and they called. We made an arrangement for them to come to the house, which they did. I was nervous because I have never had any conversation with men of that cloth, so I wasn't sure what we would talk about. The doorbell rang and I answered it. There were 2 guys in jeans, and I invited them in. We spoke and they made me feel comfortable right away. First of all, one of them seemed to me to be slightly less manly than the other. But we carried on and I told them I would take them in my car. I took them to Olvera Street which is the oldest street in Los Angeles, Beverly Hills & Rodeo Drives, Santa Monica and perhaps a few places more on the way. When we got back we sat in the living room and I asked them, "Would you mind if I asked you a personal question? I've never had a conversation with a priest before." They said, "Of course." I proceeded, "Do you go to confession?" Again they said, "Of course". I continued, "Do you confess everything?" They looked at each other and laughed and one of them, Father John answered, "Of course not." Well that absolutely dropped the wall between my priestly expectation and the two men in front of me. I could then completely relax and they explained that they were 'partners' or lovers, and they were in the same church. When I asked about the religious side of their priesthood Father John explained, "Being a priest is our chosen vocation, and we are good at our jobs. But it's only a part of who we are. Not all priests think like we do but it works well for us." And so I entertained priests for the first time in my life, and it was wonderful, particularly once I found out the inside scoop about them. They left and I called Harriet to give my report. In the years that followed, whenever I took a group for a theatre tour of New York, and I had a full day free, I would drive to Philly, and Atlantic City and if they were available usually together I would try seeing Harriet with Father John. I found out that his partner was sent to another parrish and so they were no longer 'together' but still good friends. And I even had a little one night fling with Father John, so you could say I defrocked a Father. Now I don't have to call him Father John... just John... and I still consider him a good friend even though I may not see them for years at a time. And that probably has been my most religious experience since.

I did have another sort of mystical experience while I was leading some people to Yugoslavia, almost right before the war. The location was Medjugorje where these young children had visions of the Virgin Mary. And while we were there we had a meeting with one of the girls who claims she saw the Virgin. She spoke no English but we had a translator and it proved to be very interesting. We were then given about an hour break, so I took a walk and found myself behind the town where there were these huge boulders. So I began climbing across them and it was rather easy for me even though when I looked at them they seemed almost impossible to maneuver. After about 20 minutes I saw in a not too distant location what appeared to be a very light blue dress or gown which seemed to be just hovering farther away above the rocks. It looked like it could possibly have been on a hanger that was dangling from God knows what, because I didn't see any hanger really. I just stood and watched it for a few minutes not knowing what was holding it up. Then I returned back to meet the group, running over the boulders with no problem at all. Returning back to the group I told the guide what I saw. She said, "Stan, it is possible that you had a vision also." I said, "I doubt it. The dress was not white but a bluish hue" and she responded, "The Virgin Mary's dress was not white but was more light blue." I was astounded and I got chills because I had no idea about the color. I never felt religious and this didn't make me feel more spiritual, but it did indeed put a big question mark in my mind. Is it possible to be more spiritual than we are aware? Ultimately I let it go and haven't really thought about that experience in a very long time.

e

Traveling back in time, while Dom and I were both performing in "Walking Happy", Don Arden came to see the show. No one in the show knew exactly when he saw it, but before the end of our run in the show both Dom and I got a call from the Don Arden Production office asking us if we were interested in signing a contract for one of his Las Vegas extravaganzas for the following year. Dom and I talked about it and on our last day off we went to Las Vegas and signed the contracts. So now we knew we would return to at least Las Vegas the following year. So we finished the tour on a 'high' having signed contracts to be Las Vegas dancers... and I also had an extra 'high' going right into Mitzi's act for a couple of weeks.

e

I know I am jumping around in time but, on my return to Dom and New York, from doing Mitzi's act, we, Dom and I, talked about the possibility of moving to California a little earlier since nothing seemed to be happening immediately. But we waited to see if something might turn up.

It was a Monday early afternoon when I answered the phone. The woman on the other end of the line said she was the stage manager of a new Broadway show called, "Mata Hari". I knew nothing of the show. She then told me I came highly recommended as a terrific dancer, and she was offering me a job in the show... no audition... nothing, just a definite dance job in a new Broadway show. I cupped the phone and told Dom, who was reading on the sofa. I explained as quickly as I could that this woman was offering me a job in a new show and should I take it... or are we going to California? He thought for a minute, then said, "Tell her we're going to California.". And I got back on the phone and said "I appreciate the offer so much, but I wouldn't be in town as I was going to California shortly". And that was the moment we decided (Dom decided) that we would go earlier than expected. It wasn't until much later that I found out that Jack Cole was supposed to direct and choreograph "Mata Hari". Jack Cole is one of the director choreographers I would have loved working for, but I didn't know he was connected to the show at the time. I can't cry about any missed opportunity as I feel strongly that when one door closes, another opens. Events happened rather quickly after that. BTW as soon as I returned to NY, I found a 'husband' for our poodle, Pansy. So we did have a wedding ceremony complete with honeymoon pictures and all. So it wasn't too long after that phone call that Dom purchased a Nash Rambler, dark red in color, and the three of us, Dom, Pansy and I were driving to California.

e

Lee Hale, who was the musical director of the Dean Martin Show on TV, was a good friend of Dom's in New York. He told Dom that the house right next to him in Los Angeles might be available to lease very shortly. As it happened, when Dom told Lee we were coming out early, Lee prompted the owner of the house to make the house available sooner which was great news. I never met Lee until we arrived in Los Angeles, when I was introduced to him and his partner Ken Allen, an interior decorator. They lived in West Hollywood and our new address was 8752 Dorrington Avenue. The time was November of 1967 and the drive out to California through the heart of America was very cold but uneventful. Needless to say the weather as we approached the coast was a welcome relief. What I found quite interesting was that Dom was such a quiet reserved person who would never live in a wild openly gay neighborhood if he had the choice, but the neighborhood we would now live in was like the gay Times Square on a Saturday night... bumper to bumper traffic of cruising up and down Robertson Boulevard, and it often spilled onto the side streets... and our house was a mere 2 houses down from Robertson. Since I have always been sort of a quiet voyeur, I was thrilled. After all, I was never an overtly gay person, and my serious experiences in earnest happened later in my life, so I enjoyed 'seeing the life around me'. Dom and I had been together for slightly more than 2 years, since September of 1965. At this time Dom began directing and choreographing shows in little theatres around town, so I often had free evenings while he rehearsed. That seemed to me to be a little dangerous as I couldn't help but feel I never had the experiences I would have liked sexually, whereas Dom had many more than I did and that was long before I met him. I loved Domenic, and that is not even in question... but what was in question was whether or not I could truly be happy in a truly monogamous relationship. I felt I hadn't lived enough to give up the possibilities of what I never really experienced. I'm reading this and it makes me feel that I'm coming across like a bad person, but I'm trying to be as honest as I possibly can be. Perhaps that is the reason why I believe in having sex before people make life-changing decisions. I know Dom and I did not take advantage of our sexual attraction toward each other before the night I came back from my "West Side Story" tour. And it truly was quite romantic, but as our relationship grew, we both learned that the sexual activity that we preferred was the same, so in giving each to the other, I suppose we felt we were giving up too much of ourselves when we became the passive partner. What I'm saying I think, is that our sexual life was not the most perfect. That is no excuse for cheating, but if the cheating was in my mind already, then I must be a cheater. It was probably only a matter of time when that thought in my mind became a reality in my body.

e

My first automobile when we came to California was a used Grand Prix, all white... a huge son-of-a-bitch that ate up gas like water being drunk in 120 degree heat in the Sahara Desert. But I loved it. It was the first car I had that had electric windows and it made me feel rich... and it was a huge car to park. I kept that car for about a year and when my job on the Carol Burnett Show was 'cemented', I began my car obsession. The next car I had was a Toyota Supra, which at that time looked like a space ship car, very futuristic. After that I tried leasing BMWs, of which I had 3. But ultimately the lease didn't really work out for me because I was driving more miles than they allowed, and had to pay the over amount per mileage and that added to a lot of money unexpectedly. After that I had my Ambassador ... then I got into the Toyota Prius. So far I've had 6 of them over the years altogether, and I think it is true when they say once you have a Prius, you may never want a different model. I mean how can you possibly disregard the fact that you are getting about 50 miles to the gallon. But now that I no longer have a 'steady income',  I'm forced to keep my car longer, as I no longer have the luxury of changing my car every 1 to 3 years. And I am slightly addicted to that new car smell... oh, what to do? I think we all must pay for our addictions in our own way.

To catchup on my credit card balances, I became an Uber driver in 2016. What a perfect job for me. I always loved driving, and being the adventuresome person I am, and loving people as I do, it is always a surprise when I pick up someone not knowing their destination. So I always have something to look forward to. Unfortunately for Uber, I found out that 2 months after driving for them, they supported a political candidate whom I do not support. Consequently I now am a very happy and content Lyft driver instead. Of course everything may change if my lottery results ever change drastically. But the Uber/Lyft experience ... another book, I think.

e

Soon after we moved to LA I got a call from Claude Thompson, who had moved out to California a while before. He was choreographing a television special called, "Petula Clark, Downtown", and he wanted me to dance in it. I of course accepted and had a fantastic experience being a part of my first full TV Special. Of course I did several Broadway show numbers on the Tony Awards, another job on the Ed Sullivan Show with Shari Lewis and Porkchop, plus the one I did with Ethyl Merman, as well as a couple of other specials. But I can't forget the great dancers that I met on Petula's special as well. .. including Pete Menefee, who later became a costume designer, Walter Painter, who became a director chorographer and even today teaches a great jazz class based on Luigi's style, and so many more brilliant dancers that I've worked with through the following decades. And Claude called me again to dance in a Lena Horne TV Special, and we had this one sexy slow bluesy type number that she danced in as well, and I was amazed that she was really wonderful. We don't think of certain 'stars' as being able to really dance, but she could. She also had a kind of 'sailor' mouth, which I found refreshing. Personally, even though I have always been a Lena fan, I cannot help but feel that she was a very bitter person, never forgiving 'Hollywood' for the way they treated her as a black performer in the movies she made. I would have thought that she should have been fortunate to get the roles she got in the films she made, but I cannot put my code of values or theatrical ethics onto another person. Lena was certainly unique and one of the most beautiful women I've ever seen. And since I can never walk in her shoes, I will never know what caused her to become what appeared to be such an angry celebrity.

e

This reminds me of another person I used to adore... Harry Belafonte. Several years ago I was mailed a notice from the Television Academy of which I am a member. On the invitation was an invite to "An Evening with Harry Belafonte" ... or something very similar. Dom was also a fan so we RSVP'd and were so looking forward to the evening. Perhaps he would sing some Calypso songs and talk about his life, or whatever. We arrived and the place was packed. Down two of the aisles toward the stage were put 2 standing microphones ... so they were obviously going to have a Q&A after whatever event was planned. And Harry Belafonte's close friend Gregory Peck was sitting in the front row. We were excited with the expectation that he would get up and speak with his magical deep and golden voice, and talk about his good friend, Harry. Well, Mr. Belafonte was introduced and there was a standing ovation for him. We finally quieted down, and he proceeded to the microphone onstage. For the next 2 ½ hours Harry Belafonte did nothing less that put down the almost entirely white audience for supporting Israel, and not paying reparations to the Afro American community for the slave trade that we were all involved in. His speech was so political that no one could believe it. Every point he tried to make became another stab to the hearts of this invited fan club of his. When he finally finished, the people in charge, who were no doubt in shock, took him off backstage as quickly as they could, to a literal smattering of applause... no Q&A, no friends of his like Mr. Peck speaking about him... NOTHING!!! That was the last time I ever wanted to hear anything about Mr. Harry Belafonte. What makes people who are lucky enough to be singled out for their talents turn in such a way as to disappoint the people who always supported them? We all know many people who are loaded with talent who are never singled out for whatever reason... I try to appreciate everything that I have, and even being able to dream about what I want. What a gift that is... to dream...

e

Around the year 1973, I was free for a summer and even though I was working most of the year, I was able to dance in the 'Mame' number that Onna White choreographed for the Lucille Ball film of the same title. We did the number on a ranch off of 114 on the way to Lancaster and Palmdale. The time was July and most of the grass was dead, so they put Astra Turf down and we had to dance on that. Our costumes consisted of rubber boots. Think of it... July, Astra Turf, rubber boots, the heat. We could only work on the turf for 15 minutes at a time before the burning in our boots from the sun drenched turf got to us. So we couldn't remain in the sun dancing for too long. With all the athletic leaps over the hedges, and the prancing with us lifting our legs high in the air in front of us, we were sweating so much under our costumes. And during a couple of the breaks when we would go back to our benches (at that time dancers were working under Screen Extras Guild, not Screen Actors Guild, so we weren't treated like actors) Lucy would then go to her air conditioned trailer and get candy, then walk about a block and a half to give candy to all of us dancers. I never forgot that, so if anyone says anything nasty about Lucy, I always remind them about what she did during the filming of "Mame". I remember at the wrap party at her home in Beverly Hills, the dancers were invited and a very good friend of mine, Tony Barberio, who also danced in the 'Mame' number had asked a friend of his to attend the party. It was not allowed and his friend was asked to leave. Tony at this point was getting a little high on wine which was always his drink of choice. When Lucy came up to him and told him to try to behave rationally, which was unlike Tony once he was drinking, he looked at her and told her, "Go Fuck Yourself". Well she immediately had to have him thrown out of the party. He was in no condition to drive, so I left the party with him and I drove him home. So much for the epic story of Tony and Lucy.

e

Before this happened, around 1968, not long after we moved into our house in Studio City, I got a call from the Carol Burnett Show, and was told to show up at CBS, Television City the following Monday morning. I did so and was directed to Studio A on the 3rd floor. It was a huge room and the dancers were in the front of the room with Ernie Flatt and his assistant George Foster. As I looked toward the back of this gigantic rehearsal space I saw Carol Burnett and the other costars with Dave Powers, the director. We didn't have anything to do with the principals that day, but we did rehearse, and I loved being with this group of great dancers. We rehearsed until lunch, when I was asked to join some of the dancers in the commissary which I did. We continued rehearsing until 5pm, and that was my first rehearsal day. I was the new boy on the block and learned that Ernie, the choreographer of the show, used to have auditions every once in a while so he could have a group of dancers whenever he needed them. And apparently I was the first replacement since my audition several months before.

The entrance to Television City was on the ground or 1st floor. The commissary and the stages are on the 2nd floor, and the rehearsal spaces are on the 3rd. At least that is how it was set up in 1968 when I first joined the CB Show. I know that the layouts are now different having been hired at CBS since. Anyway, on my second morning of rehearsals, I get into the elevator on the ground floor, and it just so happens that I am alone in the elevator. The doors open at the 2nd floor and who walks in with her coffee in her hand? None other than Carol Burnett. The doors close, she extends her hand to me and says, "Hello, Stan. I'm Carol. How are you getting along?" Are  you kidding me? Carol Burnett took the time to find out the name of the new boy... what a woman!!! And that kindness and humility followed her every day I was on the show until it ended in 1978. I was overwhelmed.

(The only other celebrity I knew at that time who really took the time to get to know her dancers was Chita Rivera.) So all the respect I could muster toward Carol Burnett was cemented that 2nd day at  my job.

And what a job!?! I loved going to work! I loved rehearsing! The people were great... the celebs were great... and we, the dancers, were treated with respect and dignity. It wasn't long before I felt that Ernie  Flatt liked me a lot. Even <u>enough to have his partner</u> Bill Arms do a portrait of me in oil. He also liked the fact that I could tap, since not all dancers can. What I couldn't do was acrobatics, but we had great dancers like Carl Jablonski, Kathie King, and Sandi Johnson for that. Don

Crichton was the lead dancer, but whenever Ken Berry was on the show, Carl and I got to dance with him because Don was so tall, and Ken wasn't. So Carl and I loved to hear that Ken was on the show at any time it was announced. I also got to read lines on the show, which I enjoyed so much, and Dave Powers, the director seemed to like what I did. He gave me a lot of smaller roles. One time Ernie went to the director and told him if he wanted to hire actors, not to use his dancers and take them out of his rehearsals. A little bummer for me because what I really wanted to do was more acting. So from  that time on all I got to do were what they call 'under 5's'... any smaller role that had no more than 5 lines of dialogue. But on occasion I was asked to do more... like do the voice of Hitler during an entire sketch.

 But if you saw the reruns you would be bound to see me 'pop up' every once in a while. Another reason that we loved doing a few lines was that it meant a little 'bump' in our paycheck that week. But we did get to sing most of the shows, so we would pre-record the songs on Thursday nights along with the singers. Speaking of Thursday nights...

e

One of the dancers on the show when I joined was a terrific person named Bea Busch (Bea Busch Wilcox). She almost instantly made me her friend. She was married to Clayton Wilcox whom I later learned to love as much as Bea. Anyway Bea and I had this tradition of going on Thursday nights to a 'sex' or 'adult' film after every recording session. I'm not exactly sure how it began, but I do know that we used to go to laugh a lot. One particular Thursday night we went to see the original "The Devil In Miss Jones" with Georgina Spelvin and Harry Reems. This film is probably the best film of its genre I have ever seen. It has sex, comedy, music, and quite a moral. If it were not for the graphic sex scenes I would recommend it to almost everyone I know. SPOILER ALERT!!! If you would rather wait to see this film yourself, skip the following paragraphs.

First of all I have to mention at this point that the name 'George Spelvin' was used in general by actors who for one reason or another did not want their name listed in a film or stage show. Georgina Spelvin was a dancer in her younger years, and her real name was Shelley Bob Graham, born March 1st, 1936. She appeared in several films among them are Police Academy, Police Academy 3, Girls for Rent, and Back in Training. It was Harry Reems who recommended her to adult film director Gerard Damiano.

The film begins when Georgina enters her bathroom and looks in the mirror. You can see by the tired, used, and hopeless look on her face that she has nothing positive to live for. She goes to the window and looks out to see a dark, gloomy, and rainy street which only helps her in her depressive state. She then goes back to her bathroom cabinet, mythodically takes a shaving blade out of the cabinet, places it on the edge of her bathtub, begins running the water, then slowly disrobes. She steps into the bath and for a few minutes seeming to be determined in 'washing her depression' away. She then very slowly picks up the blade and we see her slit her wrists, and watch as the blood colors the bathwater. This film by the way is in black and white. Then the very next scene is overexposed and very light and slightly out of focus... I'm sure all this is on purpose. She goes into this Florida type den and she thinks she is applying for a job. One might think this is her dream after passing out in the tub, but we find it is not. The man behind the desk tells her that she is not there to get a job. She is there to find out whether she will go to heaven or hell. She asks "Why?", because she tells him she has lived a pure and good life. He tells her that she committed the ultimate sin, by taking her own life. She tells him that had she known she was going to hell, she would have done something else to deserve that fate, like committing herself to LUST. He gives her the chance to do this but she first must be taught, so she has to go through a series of rooms to 'learn'. The first room she goes into is the one with Harry Reems. The first thing he does is dishonor her womanhood by using a butt plug. I won't go into all the rooms she goes into, but the one I particularly loved was one in which she led another beautiful woman down to a cellar and proceeded to lie down on a plastic covered bed and have more sexual activities with her. The music in this scene is particularly haunting and mesmerizing. She then has a scene with herself and a bowl of fruit... imagine the possibilities! As she proceeds through this maze of immorality, her makeup gets more and more severe, and her nails get darker and darker in color. There is a very humorous scene with her, in huge golden earrings, and another woman seducing this one man. The last room she enters seems to be another kind of cellar with what looks like cement bleachers in an T shape. There is an older man sitting on the short side of the T and she sits on the other side. The man seems to be a little 'off', since he is only talking about insects. She, by this time has become a true nymphomaniac and keeps prompting him to touch her and put his member in her. This goes on and on for what seems like 20 minutes, but I'm sure it may only be 5 minutes. Then, the camera very slowly and intentionally backs up and just as you may think the scene is over, the credits begin to roll on the right side of the screen and you realize that this is how she will spend her eternity, in that room, never to be able to be satisfied again. WOW!!! Bea and I were both so moved that we couldn't speak. Both of us were taken by Georgina's acting since both of us wanted to act. Everyone in the theatre left but we were awestruck and even though this was an adult film, I will never forget how it moved us. We came to laugh, which we did, but the end meant so much more to each of us. What a lesson about morality! Is it any wonder why I recommend this film to so many of my friends?

Bea introduced me to Justin Smith whose acting class she was taking, and I immediately joined. I was always anxious before going to Justin's class, never knowing what I would be asked to do, but once I was there I was fine. I suppose this may show a hint of my insecurity. Acting class is always strange. I remember when living in NY I attended Alice Spivak's class at the Herbert Berghof Studio in Greenwich Village. We did lots of physical exercises and she always seemed to love what I did. Being a dancer I have always been more comfortable with the 'physical' aspect of acting to help me develop a role. One of the exercises I really enjoyed was just walking. She would ask us to just walk across the stage, and she would tell us what we would imagine we were wearing, and it was evident that the clothes changed or should have changed everyone's walk. One of the exercises that Justin Smith would do was to have us put a real person who was living and part of our lives in a chair across the room, but not facing us. The chair of course would be empty as this was an imaginary person from our real lives. And the objective was to tell that person anything we had on our minds, that we would never tell them in our regular lives. Well so much hidden emotion would be tripped by this request. I myself was taken by surprise when I put my younger sister in that chair, and I began telling her how I feel. My sister, Marsha, was a prostitute when she was very young to support her heroin habit, so her life was not much more than a mess. I always felt she was the best one of us. Anyway, by the time I really got into telling her how I felt, I had a complete breakdown ... screaming at her, with tears streaming down my cheeks, and finally falling down onto my

knees with my face and hands in the chair and pounding the chair. Everyone was so moved and he said I had such a 'breakthrough'. I'm not sure I knew it then, and as I think of it now, I'm still not sure I know what that meant. All I do remember is that I did face the hate I had for her former life, but through it all, she still was my sister, and still I think, most naive and deserving of love.

e

I must be honest about 'Acting'. I feel in my gut that the art of 'acting' is almost like the 'art' as it were of 'worship' in regards to religion. There are some people who really need it, and there are some whose 'spirituality' or in this case 'talent' is more natural. I specifically remember another sense memory when Justin wanted us to remember a specific emotional moment in our lives, and to describe it without getting emotional... just explaining the moment through our senses like color, location, smells, etc. Well the moment I chose was the one where I went back to Philadelphia to visit my grandfather at the place where I thought he was living. That wasn't the moment, but I found out that that place relocated him to another assisted living location. When I got to the new place, they kept me waiting in the lobby for quite some time and then a man and a woman came to me to explain that my grandfather died a year before and they had no telephone numbers of anyone to notify. Well, I felt so awful, of course. But I honestly don't remember details like color. Even in my tap class if one of my students asked me what the name of the girl in the red jacket was, and we just finished class, I couldn't remember. So trying to remember color from something that happened decades before was fruitless. But it was an exercise and I did it, creating an entire array of color from my imagination rather than my memory. And the class went along with it as well as Justin. I don't want to say he wasn't good, it's just different from the way I remember things, and if I truly did it his way, I could never have gotten through any part of that emotional recall. But I do believe that that exercise taught me to use my imagination more than I had before. Perhaps that's the lesson I was supposed to get out of it. At least that's how it worked for me.

e

Justin used to have parties at his home every once in a while and I never attended. Paul Michael Glaser, Michelle Phillips, and his other students attended regularly. So he asked me to promise to go to one of them which I finally did. I never felt I was on the same level as those people acting-wise, but I was in the same acting class. Bea and her husband Clayton would often attend and they would make me feel comfortable anywhere when they were with me. I was still shy, I suppose. So once I did attend one of his parties the first thing that happened was that I was pulled into the kitchen to sample some of their cocaine. I did try it and as it 'melted' down my throat I was reminded of the many times I would have a cold, and my mother or grandmother would make me sniff Vick's Vapor Rub up my nose. The taste wasn't the same as the Vapor Rub, but the sensation of having something run down the back of my throat was the same. Besides, I didn't really feel any sensation from the cocaine anyway. I don't think I attended any more of his parties. I do believe I am too square for them.

e

Bea and her husband Clayton were two of the original thirteen members of The Lonny Chapman Group Repertory Theatre, a small Equity Waiver theatre, of which there are many in and around the Los Angeles area. At this time the theatre was renting a converted garage on Van Ness in Hollywood. Bea invited me to a play they were putting on called "Go Hang The Moon" by Lonny Chapman. Clayton was in it as was John Petlock who has become probably my closest or one of my closest friends ever. He also appeared in Garson Kanin's "Born Yesterday" in that same season. John, who was a terrific actor, and I shared a little 'tete-a-tete' affair for a short time, but we still remained the best of friends. Through the involvement of my new GRT friends, I was convinced to join the theatre. With my limited choreographic skills (The Ring Theatre at the U. of Miami) but vast professional experience, I was asked to choreograph their next play, "The Woyzeck Follies" by Georg Buchner and adapted and directed by David Mann, and starring Richard Hatch, not the one from Survivor but the one who starred in a TV detective series from San Francisco years ago. It was a strange experience but it sort of 'cemented' my place with GRT. This is a home for me where I can create... write, choreograph, act, and direct, whenever the need arises. I've been a steadfast member of Lonny Chapman's Group Repertory Theatre for over 50 years now. What can I say? I'm very loyal!

e

The 90's brought The Group Repertory Theatre the musical, "Chicago" that Lonny himself directed and he asked me to choreograph. It's a great show and our version was the original version, which I prefer much more than the slick newer version that opened on Broadway and is still playing at this time. We had two great leads including Eileen Blake as Roxie and Valerie Miller (a Fosse dancer) as Velma. At that time by the way, Valerie had a body that would straighten gay guys... and what a fantastic dancer. So it was a feather in my hat to have her dance my numbers. The actor who played Billy Flynn did a number called "Razzle Dazzle". Our set was similar to the Broadway set in the respect that our smaller than Broadway orchestra was on a center platform. Since we also had a good sized cast I wanted 'Billy' to do the number on the mainstage with everyone else, and at one point begin a long line that he would lead from upstage left to downstage right while he juggled, which is something he could do. He asked me if he could do the whole number in front of the orchestra on the upstage upper platform. I tried to explain that with all the activity that all those people would be doing down below, no one would be paying any attention to him. I suppose it was his insecurity that made him talk to Lonny about it. Well Lonny sided with him and let him have his way over mine. Then there was the "Me And My Baby" number that 'Roxie' was to do with 2 boys. It was my idea to add a little silly spice by letting the boys wear Dr. Dentons with the back flap hangin down and have their bare asses showing. If Ron Field choreographed it, that's exactly how he would have done it. The boy dancers thought it was a great idea as everyone else in the company did. But Lonny put the Kibosh on it. I was so disappointed that I wrote Lonny a letter explaining how I felt and reminding him that the reason he hired me was supposed to be because he trusted me and my work as a choreographer. He came back with another letter telling me I took his 'kibosh' on my work too personally. I wrote back again to say he should have hired a 'yes' choreographer and not one who tries new things to bring something new to the shows he choreographs. He wrote back again and through my dismay I accepted his decision and finished working on the show. It was a fantastic hit for us, but I think it still would have been even better had my requests been adhered to. Sometimes even I have to swallow my pride and listen to someone else, even if I know I am right. Another lesson learned!

e

My position at The GRT is pretty clear, I think probably because of my longevity with the group. Consequently I've gotten to work with many other writers who belong to our group as well. One very prolific writer is Phil Olson. He is from Minnesota and he has written a series of 5 or 6 musical plays whose titles begins with "Don't Hug Me!" Others are "Don't Hug Me County Fair", "Don't Hug Me Christmas Carol", "Don't Hug Me, We're Married", "Don't Hug Me, I'm Pregnant", etc. The plays always include these same five crazy characters who are just delicious in the play, and wildly funny to watch. Phil asked me to choreograph the first one, and ever since whenever he writes a new one, I get to do the dance numbers for the cast. I've had a ball, and Phil likes my work, and I'm crazy about his talent. So if you ever get a chance to see anything with "Don't Hug Me" in the title, you'll probably enjoy it, but if you see it anywhere but GRT, chances are I didn't choreograph it. The latest play Phil had me direct was a straight comedy of his called "Birthday Club". It was done in The Group Rep's Upstairs Theatre and it was a good success. We had great actors (5 women) who each did a terrific job for us. We are proud!

e

Several years ago a new member Henry Holden joined our ranks. He had had polio as a child and walked with sticks (crutches) but it never stopped him from doing things normal people did. What am I saying? Henry was normal in every sense of the word. And his 'handicap', if you want to call it that, only encouraged him to do more than a 'normal' person would ever do in their lives. He bungee jumped, sky dived, water and snow skied, even flew an airplane. He was involved not only at our theatre, The Group Rep, or GRT for short, but was also involved in an improvisation group, a writers' group, a comedy group, a cowboy group and a gun group. Nothing he did would stop him. I remember when I first saw him at our theatre, I was about to audition for "Barefoot In The Park". Barefoot takes place in a 5th floor walkup plus a front stoop, making the climb to the apartment quite exhausting, which added to much of the comedy in this Neil Simon Play. I approached Henry and explained, "I am about to direct this play and there is a very short scene with no dialogue for the role of a delivery man and in my own special sense of humor, I was wondering if you would consider doing that, unless you thought it would be in bad taste." "Would it come across as funny?" he asked. I assured him I thought it would be hysterical. He immediately accepted and that was the beginning of our friendship. We did the play... he did his role... the audience responded, and we were both ecstatic. Since then I have directed him in other projects, as well as directed some of his writing works. I am quite humbled by his lust for life and his talent.

e

On another trip to New York I was invited to an Agatha Christie play because a good friend of mine, Lawrence Merritt, was playing the inspector. Sandra Cusimano another dear friend and actor at GRT accompanied me to the theatre and it wasn't until we saw the show that we realized the acting group was a handicapped group, even though in some roles one couldn't tell. And I'm happy to say that my friend Larry did a phenomenal job. Sandra and I got so excited to tell Henry about this group that when we returned to Los Angeles, we immediately went to see him. After explaining about the special acting troup Henry responded, "Unbelievable!!! What do you think I am?" Then he almost screamed, "I'm not joining a handicapped group!" My bad... of course Henry was anything but handicapped. We all pale in comparison to his endeavors. Henry died a short while ago from a brain aneurism. I doubt I will meet another person who led such a full and beautiful life, Henry finally left us due to a brain aneurism. He left us with a feeling that there is nothing we cannot accomplish, once we set our goals even higher than we believe possible. Henry, I thank you for all you continue to give to me.

e

Do you remember my telling you that my mother did not want me to take theatre courses in college? Well, when I danced in my first Broadway show, "High Spirits", she came to see it, and even though I was not featured, she cried afterwards explaining that she was so sorry for everything that happened about college. What a shame for anyone to do anything in their lives that they may be sorry for later. In life, every decision is an important decision.

e

Early on while still on the Carol Burnett Show, during one of our hiatus periods, I was fortunate to be asked to dance in a TV special to be filmed in Berlin, Germany. The choreographer was Anita Mann, and the show was called, "Hello, Here ist Berlin", which was strange because no one in the show was German... only all Americans and one French male singer. It was great fun being there for the first time. We shot the show in the brand new I.C.C. building which was their brand new music center. This was so long ago that now they are talking about replacing it, if they haven't done so already. Anyway one night after rehearsals we all went out to a couple of bars. I'm not too much of a drinker so I kind of remained sober. At the one gay bar I noticed this very good looking slightly older gentleman looking at me. He was dressed in a denim suit and quite impressive looking. After much prompting by my dance friends, I went over to say hello. He spoke in a broken accent, which I found quite charming. Apparently he was the conductor of the orchestra which would be playing at the I.C.C. after our tv show wrapped. And so he invited me to his apartment. I went. He began smoking hashish which I indulged in, not being used to that kind of thing at all. We began to make out and I was floating on air, kissing, cuddling, touching... and slightly more, when he excused himself for a second and returned with a huge plastic jar of Lube. I immediately knew what he wanted me to do with the lube. I had never put my fist up anyone's butt before, and I have not the smallest of fists. Well I can tell you that no matter how 'high' I may have been from the hashish, I sobered up like a non-drinking judge. I became so alert and clinical as to what he wanted me to do. The act was not at all sexual to me, but apparently it was for him. I want to slightly describe what it was like so no one has to go through this unless it's on your bucket list, in which case keep away from me. First you have to lube your entire hand and fist which is not the most comfortable feeling. Then very slowly begin your insertion. Once inside, it feels like a very moist and very fragile membrane surrounding your fist. I was so worried that I might accidentally hurt or do damage to the insides of this person. He was of course totally emersed in the sexual manifestation of our act, the complete opposite of my involvement. Once it was over, I suppose I should have felt complimented when he couldn't believe I had never done anything like this before. "You were wonderful! You should be doing this more often." Thanks but no thanks... of course I didn't say anything like that. Whatever very personal things people require to get them off, that's fine with me, as long as no one is hurt, and it doesn't make anyone sick to their stomach, as it almost made me. By the way, call me square but I have never understood the attachment that many people make of pain and sex. I don't get it... S & M... leather. .. bondage... what ever happened to good old fashioned oral and pounding??? I'm sure I'm missing something, but my life is full without making believe that I enjoy some of these strange cravings.

Another incident happened during the "Hello, Here ist Berlin" show. For a roommate, the company roomed me with Graham Fletcher, whom I did not know, but soon found out was a soloist with the Royal Ballet. Graham was a very cute, great dancer and I found out that he vied for the same solo parts in the ballet company as Wayne Sleep because both were rather short for ballet soloists. Well after rehearsals Graham and I would just sit on our beds and talk, for hours sometimes. He was very straight and never really knew any American dancers at that time. The more we spoke the more comfortable I got to sit on his bed, and just put my hand on his leg. I'm a very 'touchy' person and even though I would love to have jumped on him, I didn't, but we did get to the point where I could touch him almost anywhere, because at that point he knew I wouldn't go further and was no threat. While we were rehearsing one afternoon, when he went to get his bag, it was gone. Someone who walked into our rehearsal took his bag with all his documents and all his money. He had at that point I believe about $600 in his wallet from the previous weeks earnings... and it was gone. He was the only foreigner other than the French male singer I mentioned before. All the American dancers felt so bad about the incident, that without Graham's knowledge we all collected enough

 money to give him the sum of $500. He was so taken aback that when we gave it to him he just about cried with gratitude. He truly was awestruck. He said that British dancers would never ever be that generous. He couldn't thank us enough. Today Graham is married to his wife Jane, who was an excellent soloist with the Festival Ballet, and they have a grown son, Dillan who is a champion sailboat competitor. Dillon sails and wins competitions throughout the world. Graham, his family and I

have been great friends ever since that TV show in Berlin, even though I see them barely once a year.

e

Doing the Burnett show was so thrilling for me. Sometimes I would be in a grocery store and while waiting in line someone would say, "Don't I know you from somewhere? I know I've met you." They would ask if I knew such and such a person, because they thought they knew me personally, and only when I asked if they watched the CB Show did I get, "That's right! That's where I've seen you before!". What a hoot, being recognized from television ... me... one of the kids from South Philadelphia.

One morning that I will never forget is when the phone rang interrupting my sleep. I answered quickly, as I am a very restless consequently light sleeper. The voice on the phone said, "Where are you?" I responded, "In bed. Who is this?" The voice answered, "Do you know what time it is?" I looked at the clock and it was 10:30am. 10:30??? I'm supposed to be at work at 10. Well I don't know how I did that but I was at work within 20 minutes, and I live at least 15 minutes from Television City. Of course I hadn't showered and barely put toothpaste directly onto my teeth when I left the house in a speed that I had never known before. I am a reliable person. I've always considered myself responsible. But let me tell you, once you are late, even though it was only a matter of minutes late, you never ever can make up that time lost and it makes quite a mark on the clean record you have in your own mind. No one ever said anything once I got to work, but there is hardly a day that goes by that I don't think of that guilty time while I was sleeping when the phone rang.

e

At CBS I became acquainted with a page working on "The Young and the Restless", Gary Warmee. I found him very amusing. It was through his love of animals that we connected. Later, Dom and I began to rely on

Gary to house sit and care for our animals while we traveled. I didn't realize at the time how much he would come to mean to us.

e

Watching the principals on the CB Show was an education. Watching Vicki Lawrence learning so much from the 'family', (Carol, Harvey, Tim, and Lyle) was like taking an acting lesson... especially watching her character as Mama in the 'Family Sketch' develop. And Harvey was such a truly fine actor that it was evident he could have

done Shakespearean as well as Burnett material. Harvey was a terrific person and quite friendly to the dancers as well. It would only be when he was negotiating any new contract that he would walk down the hall and not talk to anyone. We all knew what was going on. And Tim on the other hand was very shy... or so it seemed to me. But how brilliant he was. Every sketch he was in, he would take a part of it and do his own 'Tim Conway' bit. No one ever knew what he was planning. He would for instance go to the construction crew and tell them to make an oversized doorknob that was strong enough to support his weight. Then when he played a butler with white gloves, he would attempt to turn the knob and of course it would slip with his gloves. He then proceeded to put one leg onto the huge knob, climb on it with his back to the door, then very slowly revolve himself until he was upside down while still on the knob of the door. Fans of the Burnett Show will no doubt remember this bit. He was always doing shtick like that that was absolutely hysterical. Who could ever forget his Siamese elephant story in one of the family sketches? Brilliant!!! Many people thought that Harvey cracking up at Tim was a rehearsed bit. Well I am here to tell you that Harvey never knew what Tim was planning. No one did! It got to the point that all Tim had to do was catch Harvey's eye and Harvey would absolutely break up in anticipation for what Tim was planning... and he honestly never knew. A perfect example of this is seen in the 'dentist sketch', one of the most hysterical sketches in TV history in my opinion. It never gets too old to watch these 2 geniuses over and over again.

And then there is Carol. She can do anything, and do it so perfectly that one is in awe of her talent. And since the Burnett Show she has proved herself as a serious and more than competent actress as well. I couldn't have enjoyed working with any other TV group more than with this family, and they made all of us dancers feel a part of it. It was certainly a prestige job and I stayed with it until the last show that we did in 1978, when the dancers did a number called "Firebird", with music by Stravinsky. My main partner in this number was Bobbie Bates, whom I happily danced with many times during the run of the show. In one particular lift, Ernie had me standing with my back to her, and Bobbi would run toward me and do a grand jete (big leap) right by my right side, and I was not supposed to look at her, but catch her mid air. Ernie would say, "Just do it. You'll know she's there by the wind." It always made me nervous because I certainly didn't want to hurt Bobbie, and I never wanted to disappoint Ernie. We did it and I don't know how. But Bobbie and I were always wiping our brow once that lift was over. And through the years Ernie Flatt always did things like that to the dancers. Once we were doing a western number and one of the girls was supposed to jump from the roof of the saloon and the male dancers were to catch her. Well we were waiting and figuring out who would put their hands where, and lo and behold we hear, "Here I come!", and Ernie flings himself from the roof of the saloon and we in desperation caught him with no idea who was catching what part of his body. We were not about to drop the choreographer. And after catching him and putting him back on his feet he said, "That's it! Just like that!" And we were all white-faced at that moment. And Ernie was indeed a stubborn Irishman. On another occasion he gave us a combination that no one could do. Oh we got the footwork, but Ernie would often add arm gestures that completely went against the footwork or the music, and for some reason not even Lorene Yarnell (later married Robert Shields, the fantastic mime) nor Don Crichton (the lead dancer on the show) could get it right, so Ernie would in frustration say, loud enough for all the dancers to hear, to his assistant George Foster, "George, remind me to have another audition soon!" But we knew he loved us. And every rehearsal would begin on Monday morning, and if Ernie was 'cooking' with choreography we knew he got his ideas while sitting on the throne in his home before he left for work. He even told us that's where he thought about the routines and what he would do with them. It became a little family joke we all shared, including Ernie.

When Betty White was on the show, we had a combination and Ernie asked me to do a double pirouette while 'cork-screwing' down to the floor. I've always had a very bad left knee, and that is the knee I was to 'hinge' or put my weight on while lowering myself I kept falling out of it, and explained to Ernie that one of the other dancers should do it as I didn't have the strength in my left knee. He said, "Don't worry! You'll do it!" Stubborn. Well, when the time came for my little pirouette, I indeed fell out of it, although recovering very quickly, that non-dancers might not even notice... but I know Ernie and the dancers knew. Ernie never mentioned it. He liked me. I know he liked me because much later, I had a party and one of my close friends confided in me that Ernie told her that if he were to have to keep one of the male dancers, he would choose me. You have no idea how great that made me feel. Although for all I know he could have said that about each of his dancers at one time or another because I know he loved us all.

e

I used to have a party every year at my house and I would invite the cast, crew, and even the production people. That first year, when I approached Lyle Waggoner he told me that he and his wife, Sharon, might be busy with her visiting family, and I just thought it was an excuse. So in the middle of the party, the phone rings and it is Lyle and he says, "Stan, I am so sorry but we cannot get away from Sharon's family tonight. Please ask us again." Well, every year after that when I had my party, Sharon and Lyle ALWAYS showed... every single year. Harvey and Tim showed up once or twice, and Vicki showed up sometimes. Some of the camera men and secretaries showed up, but Carol never did. I got a personal call from her secretary explaining that if Carol came to my party, she would be obligated to go to everyone else's party, and I understood completely. I thought it was great that Carol told her secretary to contact me directly. I respected her so much. BTW, 2 years after the show closed, I was at the old Westwood Theatre seeing a performance of "Little Shop of Horrors". Now the Westwood Playhouse was laid out in such a way that the aisles in the theatre would turn toward the center aisle and then through a little tunnel into the lobby. Well at intermission I am walking up my aisle and just as I turn to go toward the center aisle I hear... , "Stan, Stan." I look up and it's Carol leaving the people she was with and when she gets to me she grabs my arm and asks, "What are you up to? And what's happening with you?" Now I'm not generally in touch with her and I don't even have an address other than a fan club address for her. .. and I haven't seen her for 2 years. Well, that's a typical story for Carol Burnett, as warm a person as anyone I know. I am so lucky to have worked with her on her show!

e

During my yearly parties, I always had some sor t of entertainment. One year I had Tahitian dancers including a fire dance number with real lit torches, one year there was a male and female belly dancing couple, one year Birl (one of the regular dancers on the show) sang with his wife Anushka, and there were magicians, etc. I always tried to  have a 10 to 15 minute show that was a little different from the year before. And I was not the only one who threw a Carol Burnett Party... Bonnie Evans, Randy Doney, and Bobbie Bates I believe threw some also. I think Bonnie's was special because she requested a 'costume' type party where the men dressed as women and vice versa. That's the year that Dom, my partner since '65, and I dressed as nuns... this was during a time that I was sewing my polyester pants for rehearsals for the Burnett Show, so I made the habits, and borrowed the accessories from a friend who worked for Universal and got the nun paraphernalia from the film, "A Mule for Sister Sarah". It was a real hoot. Being a little sacrilegious, I didn't wear any underwear, so every so often I

would moon someone for a laugh... very quickly... I doubt anyone would want to see my moon for any extended period of time now.

One predominant dancer who never threw the dancers a party was Don Crichton, the lead dancer on the show. I did find out just a few years ago that Don was paid as a principal and not a dancer, but that wouldn't have made any difference to us. He was always a good dancer and great to work with and no matter to whom he spoke, he made them feel as he made me feel like a close friend. But still... no parties. He would ask me, "How could I have a party? What would I serve? Hot dogs?" I would respond, "Why not hot dogs? We're dancers... we will eat anything!". The only time I did see the inside of his home was when he left on a trip and a good friend of Dom's and mine, Don Rehg was house sitting for him. Don R. invited us into Don's beautiful home. Don Rehg was one of the dancers in my second Broadway show, "Bajour". And what a lovely home Don Crichton had. It would have been a great location for a Carol Burnett/Ernie Flatt dancers' party.

e

During my 'tenure' as a working dancer I have learned that all too often the job you are working at is not only for the job you are working at. Of course that means often jobs lead to other jobs. While on Burnett several of the male dancers were asked to dance in a huge charity event run by a large group of ladies called the 'Share' ladies. This group is made up primarily of either very famous women mostly in show business, or the wives of very famous men in the business. We never got paid to do the shows as it was of course for charities that Share would choose... for instance two of their charities were the 'Children's Wing at Cedars-Sinai Hospital' in Beverly Hills, and 'A Place Called Home' in downtown Los Angeles, a building or house to help keep troubled children off the streets. So I danced with many partners over the next few 'Share' shows, and they were always performed in the spring, usually at the Santa Monica Civic Auditorium. And I met so many of those ladies. There were Joanie Horowitz who later became president of Share, Neile Adams who was married to Steve McQueen for almost 16 years, Maxine Smith who is Gary Smith's wife, Dolores Narr who is a fabulous dancer in her own right, Tadd Tadlock who is another great dancer/choreographer, a gorgeous red-haired Nicki, and fantastic Gloria Franks, among others, and of course Miriam Nelson who used to choreograph the shows. Needless to say all these women helped sponsor and get sponsors so each year hopefully the charity would collect more money than the year before. And I also met Mrs. Milton Berle, Rosemary Stack and a slew of other luminaries connected in one way or another to show business. Many of these ladies I still consider close friends like Neile and Miriam.

One of the parties that Share had, not the show mind you, but a party for the performers in the show, was given at Rosemarie Stack's home... Mrs. Robert Stack. I remember she had a tent put up in her backyard and it was all catered, truly a high class party, as all of these parties were. I went into the house to use the bathroom and had to go through a 'trophy' room. Robert Stack had wall to wall pictures of him with all the dead animals that he had shot. I repeat wall to wall with no space in between. It was like watching the photos of accidents. As much as it horrified me, I kept looking at the pictures when I realized how sick to my stomach I was getting. I wasn't sick from the food, but from gazing at this room of death. To this day I do not understand why there is such a thing as hunting for sport. The excuse is that these animals would overrun the areas in which they live, but I doubt that has ever happened. Murder is murder when it isn't for survival or self-defense. I am probably in the minority but I never again want to experience that helpless as well as ill feeling I got in that room of blood. I'm probably being too small minded about that part of the human 'sport', but just think about it... killing for sport... it makes no sense at all. If men want to involve themselves in this type of activity, they should join other groups of 'hunters' and 'prey' and really feel the power of the hunt by hunting each other. Enough said!

e

During a particularly bad time between Dom and me, when we were having little spats or weren't even talking at all, which happened

throughout our years together, I had been invited to a party and I met a couple of new friends. One in particular who was paying more attention to me than the rest was a very cute little Greek guy named Demitri Piteris. He was truly exquisite as an example of Greek art in the most handsome of ways. He knew how good looking he was but even that became charming to me. I began seeing him fairly often and I believe the feelings of both of us began to grow. I was always honest with him about the existence of Dom, my partner, and even though he said he didn't want to get involved with a person who was already connected to someone else, our feelings nevertheless continued to grow. And as that happened the relationship I had with Dom continued to deteriorate, to the point that Dom seemed to be taking me for granted in every way, talking 'down' to me whenever he spoke, and when I tried bringing it up he wouldn't talk about it... he would just leave the room. I've always given advice to other friends about writing a letter when conversation was impossible. So in this case I decided to follow my own advice which I rarely do, and I wrote Dom a six page letter. I know that no matter how angry someone is, and they cannot talk, they certainly will more than likely read a letter as long as the person is not near them. In my letter I wrote how I felt about his talking down his nose to me, and how bad I felt that he seemed to be taking me for granted, and if I did the same I was truly sorry. I did say that I felt a little needy and because I wasn't getting the attention from him at home, I looked elsewhere and found it outside our home, and had unfortunately began falling in love with someone else. I didn't want it to happen but it did. And I wanted to know if he wanted to try to save our relationship or just let it go. It was up to him. He came to me with tears in his eyes and told me how sorry he was for the way he was behaving with me, and he did indeed want to save us. So I did in fact let Demitri, my Greek savior and god, go. I always think of him with fondness, and even though I hardly ever

see him, when I do, my heart <u>still flutters</u> like a little girl's. Dom and I did do much better for the next bit of time at least. I think at that point we knew we had a special thing going, and even though it may not have been traditional, I did know and so did he that we still loved each other. And that is the way it basically has been with more 'ups' than 'downs'.

e

Dancing on any show for over ten years, you learn a lot about the celebrities who are invited on the show from time to time. You learn as I did from our show, how great certain people are... like Jim Nabors

who always starred in each of Carol's first shows of the season, a great person who was always friendly with the dancers. I used to judge celebs by the way they acknowledge our presence... and I still do. Cass Elliott was the first one who was so great to us. Ken Berry was a dream to work with... and Chita Rivera was so real and

down to earth, she always learned the names of the dancers because she loved them, Much like Bernadette Peters ...

Shirley MacLaine was always fun because she could dance... and Gwen Verdon, when she was on we did a kind of silly 'children's' number

94

with her... Ben Vereen, the number we did with him was almost non dancing, I remember I was a tree... and Steve Lawrence, such a multi talented person, a true triple threat... and his wife Edie Gorme', who used to constantly stop Peter Matz' orchestra because she thought she heard something wrong musically, until the production team 'wised up' and pre-recorded her orchestrations so she couldn't stop the flow of the show, but boy, could she sing!... and a slew of others some very talented and a few less so. I remember when Karen Black was on the show she kept overseeing Dave Powers the director, suggesting he do this or do that during sketches that she was not involved in, but when it came to her doing her own song on a long set of stairs, she couldn't even stop on the correct stair for her closeup... but she sure must have wanted to direct.

e

Another incident occurred that I find very amusing. Tony Randall was guesting on our show. He insisted that there would be no smoking in Studio 'A, our huge rehearsal space. So the producers put signs up everywhere in the studio. Consequently smokers would go out into the hall and do their thing. Well, it was like walking through a cloud of smoke, just to enter the room. Where was Tony Randall? He would be in the hall talking to his friends, and not even caring about the smoke. I found that so hypocritical, and quite funny when you think about it.

When Gloria Swanson was on the show, Don Crichton was too tall to partner her, so I was lucky enough to do so for part of her number. Somehow there was a picture taken by the professional photographer that had me dipping Ms. Swanson in what turned out to be a glorious picture. Well apparently she used that picture a lot. She even put it into her autobiography, "Swanson On Swanson", but my name is not mentioned. What a great picture! About a year or so later (it might have been sooner than that), Carol came up to me and said she received this newspaper clipping from Gloria Swanson and asked if I wanted it. On the front of this Italian newspaper was a picture of Gloria and me and above the photo in the margin, Gloria wrote...

"Dear Carol and Joe,

They will probably use this picture in my obituary if Im lucky.

Love,
Gloria"

Of course I was thrilled to have the clipping, and it remains on my office wall above my computer. By the way, my office looks like the remnants of a bomb blast, but that's a different part of the story.

e

Leslie Uggums was a guest on the CB Show also. I have a slight background with Leslie. While I was teaching dance at the Jack Stanly Dance Studio in Coral Gables, I was going out very seriously with Maria Florentes, which I mentioned before. And Maria became a good friend of Leslie. She also introduced Leslie to another very good friend of hers named Eddie Albert. But this was not the famous Eddie Albert, so he had to change his name and the name he chose was Jeff Turner. Well not too long after that, Jeff and Leslie became romantically involved. This was of course before Leslie married Grahame Pratt in 1965. Well, when I moved to New York, Stacey Pomerance had Jeff, Leslie, Cory Fleischman (Maria Florentes real name) and I to his apartment to play charades. So I knew Leslie, who is an absolutely great singer and actress, slightly more than as a fan. And whenever I run into her, she is always as cordial as can be, asking how I am and if I ever see Cory (Maria). I love people who remember their old friends.

e

Julie Andrews was always a close friend of Carol's. They did "Julie & Carol at Carnegie Hall"", which I was not in since I hadn't even met Ernie Flatt or Carol Burnett yet, and "Julie and Carol at Lincoln Center", which I was fortunate enough to have done.

Another of Carol's guests was Nancy Dussault. Now I know Nancy because she was one of the stars in "Bajour", my second Broadway show. And years after the Burnett Show was over, I was asked by Bob Wright, who produced the CB Show, to direct and choreograph "Bells Are Ringing" with Nancy at the Norris Theatre in Palos Verdes. I of course accepted, but was not aware that I only had Nancy the first week, as she and Karen Morrow (of whom I am also a great fan) were going to be in Texas for a concert they were both giving together. By the time Nancy returned, we were already in tech so it was quite difficult putting Nancy in the show while I was also taking care of all the final preparations. Nancy withstood all that I threw at her, and ultimately she was terrific. I truly felt I could have done her more justice if I had her for all the rehearsals, but we did the best we could under the circumstances. And she and her husband Val always give me a warm greeting whenever I see them. I never felt she got the attention to her career that she deserved.

e

I never worked with Helen Reddy before Carol's show, but afterwards, in 1987, I was asked to choreograph "Anything Goes" at the Terrace Theatre in Long Beach. The director was John Lowe, the son of Ruby Keeler, a famous tapper of the 30's and 40's, who made her comeback in "No, No, Nanette" in 1971. Helen could tap although she was a 'very thick' tapper, that is to say not so graceful, but more of a hoofer. I remember there were certain numbers that I was to choreograph and certain ones John said he wanted to stage. When it came time for his staging of the opening number, he was having a conversation with I believe one of the producers. I approached him several times and he said he'll be right with us. After the third time, I took hold of the reigns and began staging the opening. I remember by the time he joined us, I had everything done, so after showing the number to him, he seemed quite pleased. Now, when I choreograph, I really don't like doing anything ahead of time. So for me it becomes kind of like an improvisation, since I like the dancers to learn the material as I come up with it. I think I learned that from Danny Daniels as well as Ernie Flatt. That's the way it always worked for me... not necessarily for everyone else. And since I never choreographed the show before, everything was new to me. Mickey Deems played our 'Moonface' a role he recreated from the original revival of the show in 1962. While I was doing the 'Heaven Hop' number, I watched him watching me. When we had our first run through he came up to me and said, "You know I never thought what you did in that number really would work. But I have to tell you you know what you're doing, because you made it work, and very well. .. good for you". Needless to say that made me feel terrific. The reviews were mixed with one paper calling my work shallow. I got a letter from Rikki Lugo, a wonderful director choreographer in her own right whom I later became friendly with, telling me she loved what I did, and went on in detail. That certainly made me feel better, and made me realize that once you see something of value, let the people involved know how you feel. Those feelings will not go unnoticed... or unfelt. "BTW, Helen Reddy was a dream to work with, and we became friendly enough for me to visit her several times at the Motion Picture Home in Woodland Hills. I hope she is ROARING in heaven!

e

Sand Dabs!!! I will never hear 'sand dabs' again without thinking of Carol Channing, when she was on The CB Show. I do believe that Carol was as daffy off the show as on. She was lovely, charming, sweet, and a little crazed. She was going through some type of diet when she was on the show, and she brought sand dabs with her every day, and the smell was absolutely awful.

When she would begin to eat her sand dabs during lunch in Studio A, at that time, the largest studio at Television City, the room would very quickly empty out. To this day I'm sure only Carol Channing knows if her sand dabs were raw or rotten.

e

Everyone involved with the Burnett show was absolutely thrilled at the prospect of Eileen Farrell and Marilyn Horne, two opera divas, appearing on our show. Well between Ernie Flatt the choreographer, Bob Mackie the costume designer, and Dave Powers the director, and Carol of course, the number that they did was I think one of the classics. They did, believe it or not, 'Big Spender' from "Sweet Charity", dressed in beautiful 'Gibson girl' turn of the century dresses, with gorgeous huge hats, and each lady carrying a long walking stick. I remembered how down to earth Marilyn Horne was to work with, never worrying if she said the four letter 'S' word while trying to remember the steps. And she was very good at doing the number. Eileen on the other hand had difficulty even walking in time to the music. If you gave her literally 3 steps beginning with the right foot, she would somehow wind up on the wrong foot. But the concept of the number was fantastic. And even though Carol claims she cannot dance, throughout the years she has proven to us dancers that she can do whatever she sets out to do. I cannot respect a person more.

e

Early on during my first few years on the CB Show, I met a travel agent, Jim Bradford, who later became a friend of Dom's and mine. He was already doing theatre trips to NYC. He told me that if Dom and I had 10 friends who wanted to join in on his trips, he would allow us to go for free. Well it wasn't difficult for the both of us to find friends of ours who wanted to join a group and travel to New York to see Broadway shows, since most of our friends were in show business. So this became a yearly 'thing'. Remember that in the early 70's trips were not as expensive as they are today, so it would be easier to 'comp' a person or two when they brought enough people to more than cover their expenses. Today I doubt you could find any trip that would allow a complimentary passage for only 10 persons. At any rate, these trips were a blessing to the both of us... to be able to travel to NYC to see shows, when it only cost us for dinners and the extra shows we attended. Eventually Jim began traveling to London, and he offered the same trip to us but we would have to get 15 people to join his group. And there we were practically travel agents and getting our theatre tours for free. An opportunity presented itself to me in the form of adult travel agent classes during the evening sessions of Cal State LA. I didn't want to become a travel agent... I just wanted to see how the travel agent dealt with the group leader, which I considered myself. The beginning of my first lesson the teacher got up in front of the class and said, "There are no travel agents living in Beverly Hills, who bought their homes from travel agency money". I thought to myself, "That's fine... I don't want to be a travel agent anyway". She then said, "But, if you like to travel. .. " and my ears perked up. She continued, "... there are familiarization trips that companies offer travel agents that allow them to travel for next to nothing with the hope that they will organize groups and trips so their company will be used". Wow!!! That means I could travel around the world and it would cost next to nothing. I spoke to the teacher, Sarah Barnett, after class and she was so impressed with the fact that I was already organizing groups to travel to NYC and London. She said, "Stanley, don't be a fool! If you were a travel agent you could be making your commission besides getting your free trips". And so during the 6 week course I learned how to hand write flight tickets, and lots more. Sarah and I became close friends and she gave me lots of advice. I was afraid that I would have to be working in an office for 40 hours a week and I had to have my free time available for show business jobs... after all that's the life I have chosen. She explained that I could work as an outside agent, so I wouldn't have to go into the office. After the course she introduced me to Sharon Weiner, the owner of Inter-Dome Travel, who was very business like, although she loved the fact that I already had my 'group' clientele. The girls in the office were wonderful to me. They were, Joanne Glick, and Sharon, the owner, and I was an outside agent as was Carol Tedeski, the only Italian amongst all of us Jews.

Actually I considered myself the only Jew... they were all Israelis, or at least they all spoke Hebrew except for Carol. I learned how to run my own airline tickets on the computer, so the girls didn't really have to help me very much, and I enjoyed my visits every time I went into the office on Ventura Blvd in Sherman Oaks. There were other inside agents who worked for a couple of years, then went on to other locations. I remember Mercedes whose friendship I cherished very much. And Caroline, my Italian 'goombah', and I became very close friends, until she recently passed. During my years with Inter-Dome

Travel, so many events occurred. Sharon divorced, then remarried and had her 3 girls, Carol disappeared then came back into my life a few years later. Originally the travel business belonged to Sharon's mother, but she had just recently passed when I joined the office. Her father Nathan would stop by every once in a while but then he had heart problems and I remember before his operation, he came into the office and told me quite confidentially that he was very afraid of this procedure. I tried to comfort him by telling him that they do these things all the time now, and he surely was worrying for nothing. The next day he went into the hospital and died on the operating table. I cannot tell you how I felt. What should I have said? Sharon was almost inconsolable for a while. Eventually Sharon sold the business to other Israeli's and for several months she worked in the office of Travel Galore, and I joined as an outside agent. Joanne Glick didn't come with us, so I believe she retired. I was very happy to get in contact with her after all these years to find out she is alive and as well as she can be. My new boss was Freda, who took over the business after she and her husband divorced. The other girls in the office were Pazit, Rachel, and Varda, all lovely women, Israeli of course. I'm not sure if it was because I was an outside agent, but as friendly as they were to me, I honestly still never felt I was one of the Israelis in the office... I loved them very much but they would always be speaking Hebrew in the office and I was the outsider who never learned the language. The little I learned from my grandparents was Yiddish and not Hebrew. And I am so sorry now that I insisted that my grandparents learned and spoke English instead of Yiddish or Russian during my childhood. It should have been so important to be in a situation where I could easily have learned another language. If only we could be a little smarter a little earlier in life.

But I was still taking my groups to New York, London, and now other places around the world. I went on lots of Fam trips early on in my travel agent 'side' career. For my very first Fam trip I chose to go to Kenya to see the animals. It was truly a thrill for me to see them in their natural environment. Since then I've been to Kenya probably 3 more times. I remember in one of the trips, I was videoing the remains of a 'kill' when the vultures were picking at the remains. I zoomed very closely into the flesh that they were eating, and then my very next shot was a zoomed in video of breakfast hash on the following morning's buffet, then slowly zoomed out. Whenever I show it to people, they cringe when I zoom into the flesh remains, and continue to cringe when I show them the following breakfast 'hash' scene and laugh very much when I zoom out showing the entire buffet line of food. To see it is more meaningful than my describing it.

Once the CB Show was over, and "Mama's Family" was on TV, my friend James Smith, who worked as assistant stage manager on the CB Show, became stage manager for Vicki's show. I did three spots on the show as an actor, once as Billy Bob, a waiter, once as a referee on a women's wrestling competition, and one other that I forgot. When Vicki began her night club act it consisted of Vicki and Mama. Don Crichton usually choreographed her numbers, but when it came time for her to do her finale, Don's partner Dean was having health issues so Don wasn't available. Vicki called me and asked if I wanted to do it. I knew somehow it wasn't going to pay, but I was so happy that she asked that I said yes. The number was "One" from "Chorus Line", and it was Mama's number. I did the number and she and Al Shultz, her husband were very pleased. Incidentally I saw her act 2 years later and she was still using the same number I staged for her. Jim Smith was now her production stage manager for her act. In 2008 Jim decided early in the year that he would join me in his lifelong dream of going to Egypt with my group in November. He had told Vicki and her husband Al (Shultz) from about March on, and kept reminding them what his plans in November were. They kept saying not to worry about it. So, about 2 weeks before we were leaving for Egypt, Vicki tells Jim that they had a gig in another week and a half. He reminded her that all year basically he kept telling them about this trip. Vicki said, "That's fine. Just call us when you return". When we returned after an absolutely phenomenal trip he called her. She basically shrugged and said, "That's nice. My son is now doing your job." I cannot forget this even though Jim has accepted it. I suppose I carry a grudge longer than most people. It's too bad people aren't the way we want them to be.

e

I've been so very lucky as a dancer in my life... especially when we all know so many truly talented people who just don't get the right breaks.

Early during the Burnett Show in 1972 I got to dance in my very first Academy Awards Show. The number was "Shaft" by Isaac Hayes and it was choreographed by Donald McKayle, one of the best choreographers of his era... or should I say 'our' era. Other choreographers I've worked for on different Academy Award Shows are Walter Painter, Ron Field, and Carl Jablonski, to name a few.

Danny Daniels, who hired me for 2 Broadways shows, also hired me and several other dancers from the Carol Burnett Show for a Perry Como Christmas Special to be shot in Madrid, New Mexico. Madrid was kind of a ghost town just outside of Santa Fe. Among the other dancers was Jude Van Wormer, a terrific dancer as well as a terrific friend. Jude and I always had this kind of 'sexual' tension between us... whether it was a joke or not I really couldn't say, but we enjoyed teasing each other. Well, while in Madrid, Jude had several dates with this one cameraman, and each time, the cameraman had to cancel because he was working overtime. One night the dancers were all at this restaurant that I believe was called El Nido in Tesuque while Jude was supposed to be on her date. She came in right after we ate and was crying because her date disappointed her again because he had to work late. When we all left, she was feeling quite low, so I said that she should come to my room. I meant it innocently, so she said, "What would we do?". I responded with, "We'll laugh... what do you think we'll do?". Well she did indeed come to my room, and we laughed a little, talked a little, and surprise of all surprises, did our naughties together ... come to think of it, we didn't laugh very much. Well, we did have such a great time that the following night she came back and we 'laughed' again. In a way it made me feel almost heterosexual. .. but I am what I am, so the evenings were never repeated. When I think back on that time, it still brings a warm smile to my face... and my heart. I still have the warmest of feelings for Jude.

e

It was in the mid 70's that I was asked to coach Cybill Shepherd in tap. She was going to be starring in a musical film called "At Long Last Love", to be directed by Peter Bogdanovich. Most of the private lessons took place at their home on Copa de Oro Road in Bel Air. Cybill was pleasant to work with and a beautiful woman. These coaching sessions went on for about 2 months. Cybill even brought me in to introduce me to Peter once or twice. I felt we were very close then. However once she began to film her TV series, "Moonlighting", she didn't really have any time to say hello to me. I stopped by the studio a couple of times when I happened to be working on the same lot but after leaving messages for her she never seemed to have the time. Perhaps she never really got my messages. I have no way of knowing. But I do respect and love celebrities who always remember the people they have worked with. I often wonder whether she would have responded had I become a celebrity in my own right after we worked together. We'll never know, will we?

e

I specifically remember going on a trip to Egypt. Of course everyone in the office couldn't understand why I even wanted to go to Egypt. But that first trip was absolutely awesome for me. I flew into Cairo and was to spend 2 nights there, then take a train to Luxor, and do a 4 night cruise from Luxor to Aswan, then fly back to Cairo for another 2 nights, then fly to Tel Aviv for 4 nights, and finally fly back to Cairo and spend my last 2 nights there before flying home. Well, I wanted to spend the first 2 nights in a true Egyptian hotel... and I did. When I checked into the Nabila Hotel, at least I think it was called the Nabila, no one seemed to speak English. I believe at that time it was listed as a 2 star hotel. 2 Stars were certainly overrating this hotel. My room was large, but only had 1 dim light bulb so it was difficult even to find what clothes I wanted to wear, because my view of the only window in the room faced a brick wall not 3 feet from my window. I was already warned not to speak to any arabs as all they would want from me would be money. I think that advice probably came from my office workers. I did have a video camera with me but in those days the camera was fairly large and my camera case was a good sized one that hung from a strap over my shoulder. After checking into the hotel, I remind you I was alone and didn't join any group until I arrived in Luxor, I wanted to take a walk to see the surrounding area, which I am prone to do in any city that is new to me. The hotel was only about a block and a half from the Nile River, and I immediately walked there. Here I am walking along the shore of the river, with very few people around. I spot these 2 young men sitting on the bridge abutment and I walk past them. I hear, "British?" and I respond as I keep walking, "No, I'm American!". Immediately both jump off the abutment and only one of them speaks in broken English. Now of the 2 young men, one was absolutely gorgeous and tall, a very Egyptian looking man, and the other looked like a nerd, but he was the only one who was speaking. He says, "We love Americans!" Between his dialogue with me, they would say something to each other in Arabic. Hesham is the name of the taller of the two and the other I believe was called Ahmed. Ahmed asks me, "Do you mind if we walk a little with you?" I respond, "I don't have any money for you, but it's your country, do what you want." He answers, "We're not interested in your money, we just like to practice talking with an American." I say, "Okay." We continue walking... all the while I'm carrying my video camera case over my left shoulder. It's a very warm night and every so often we run across a cart that has ice cream or sodas for purchase. They would ask if I wanted something to drink and when we reached the 2nd cart a couple of blocks away, I was hot and thirsty, so I said yes. We all had a soda and I wanted to pay, but Ahmed said, "You don't pay. You are in Egypt!" In the beginning of our walk I was very suspicious of them, but as we spoke I was more relaxed. By the time they bought me my first soda, I felt quite honored to be in that situation. After another while and other idle conversation, Hesham said something to Ahmed in Arabic, and Ahmed asked if I wanted to see the section they lived in since we were so close. He told me it was called the Kit-Kat section of Cairo. I thought... 'Kit-Kat'??? It is either a show biz neighborhood or it sounded like it might be their 'red-light district. Either way I thought, "What an adventure!" So I said, "Sure". We then walked past this open market with carts on both sides of the pedestrian street, and the aroma was not very pleasant. We continued up the road and in front of me down the street is what seemed like a coffee house, with a bunch of Arab boys sitting on the stoop of the store. Ahmed asked me, "Would you like to meet some of our friends?" "Why not?" I responded. My heart was racing... I was full of excitement, nervous, but still in control. After all, I was an athlete (dancer) and I could always run. We sat down on the stoop and there I was, this Jewish kid from South Philly, surrounded by about 8 Arab youths. For the next hour and a half we told jokes to one another. I would tell Ahmed a line from a joke, he would translate to the others, then I would proceed to tell another line of the joke, he would translate again, until I got to the punch line, he would tell them in Arabic, then they would all laugh. And the jokes were repeated in the same fashion when one of them wanted to tell me a joke. It was truly an incredible experience. We finally left their friends and continued to walk another block and Hesham, the good looking one told Ahmed to ask if I wanted to come up and meet his family. Again, I have to say that although I was still slightly suspicious, I threw caution to the wind, and thought, "What will be will be". I heard that from Doris Day. So we climbed three sets of stairs and went into his flat and I met his mother and father, and his brother. His brother was shorter than he was and his build was more muscular than Hesham, but not overly so. I was told that Hesham and his brother were wrestlers for the Egyptian Olympic team, and unlike our wrestlers who appear to look like body builders, their wrestlers have swimmer type bodies. Well, when they finally walked me back to the Nebila Hotel, it was late and I couldn't thank them enough. They were all busy the following night and they told me that if I came back from the cruise to try to look them up. At that time they didn't have cell phones as prevalently as they do today. So I absorbed my fantastic evening as best I could, and wondered if I would ever see them again.

The overnight train to Luxor was very interesting. I was given a compartment with one other man, and unfortunately the man had a body odor. I suppose he was disappointed that he didn't get his own compartment, so after half an hour he disappeared and never returned. Perhaps I was the one with body odor. Great! I now had my own compartment on a train, and loved it. My ticket included a meal which was delivered to me on a tray in my compartment. And such a meal. .. there were so many plates of different foods, and even the tray was very large to contain the assortment. I ate, walked the train a bit, then went to sleep. We arrived in Luxor early in the morning, and the train station was much like the airline terminal when I first arrived. It seemed like I was in a 1920's movie with all the hustle and bustle of a very old station, with people shouting and reaching for different bags. But throughout this adventure, I never lost my bag, and indeed people were very honest in helping me with whatever I needed. I was met at the station and taken to the boat, which at that time was a much smaller boat than the sizes they have now. I believe the boat was called the Cleopatra, and it was beautiful. All shiny and wooden with accents of what looked like gold, but I'm sure was not. It probably only had about 15 cabins on it, so compared to todays standards, it was tiny. The cabins were fantastic and very luxurious. The food onboard was fine. Each stop contained tours of the towns and temples. We stopped at Esna, Edfu, Kom Ombo, and finally Aswan. Being in Egypt for the first time was quite mind blowing. Having never been to a country with many temples, I was like a sponge, on that first trip. And the kindness of the Egyptians was unlike anything I had experienced before. In many countries you are greeted with, "Welcome to... (whatever country you're in)... " But when the Egyptians say, "Welcome to Egypt!", you feel it ... the warmth ... the generosity... the caring... the truth. When you go into a person's bazaar, they are so honored that you took the time to see their store. Even though many of the bazaars have the same souvenirs, I would always say to them, "You have beautiful things here." And they would beam with pride. More often than not, the owner would give you a good luck scarab, to take with you, whether or not you purchased something. The entire experience is one of humility, kindness, and acceptance, usually on both sides.

e

After the cruise, I flew from Aswan to Cairo, and this time had had enough of the Egyptian 'experience', and wanted to stay at a better hotel, for the next 2 nights I stayed at the then Sheraton Hotel right in the middle of the Nile. Today the hotel is called the Sofitel Cairo. I was very excited to get back to see if I could find Hesham again. So that first night back I walked up to where I thought Kit-Kat was and found the coffee shop where we were telling jokes that first night, then continued walking until I thought I was in front of his parents apartment. I yelled out very loudly for Hesham, and finally he came to the window and looked down and saw me. He ran down to me and even though he spoke practically no English, he got in touch with another friend who spoke more than he did, and we went for Sheesha, a water pipe. Before this trip I assumed all water pipes were filled with hashish... traveling teaches you so much about different peoples and their cultures as well as being an education in old lies we are told about 'foreigners'. Through his friend's translation I was invited the following afternoon to a wrestling practice match, and it was at an Egyptian military base. I was so excited. I took a taxi to this base and was met by someone else who brought me inside the base to where the wrestling was taking place. I watched many of the matches including Hesham and his brother. After the match, Hesham took me into the locker room, where the wrestlers were changing clothes, showering, etc. I was in absolute heaven... Hesham knew not what he did... still very innocent. I was sitting in a corner watching all these Egyptian beauties around me and couldn't believe it. He had on what looked like a black and white bathing suit under his wrestling attire.

For some reason I never did get a glimpse of him in the nude, but saw many of the others, to my delight. After the match he took me back to my hotel, but he wouldn't come up, as in Egypt they are not supposed to... I think I may have mentioned that before. The following morning I flew to Israel for a few nights before my return back to Cairo. In Israel I floated in the Dead Sea, visited En Gedi, a biblical site, went to Masada, toured the Old City of Jerusalem, visited Yad Vashem, went to Tel Aviv and visited Old Jaffa. Also visited one of the kibbutzim in Israel. .. I could have sworn it was called Gloria Kibbutz, but the girls from Travel Galore said there was no such kibbutz. I did take a walk along the ocean behind the Tel Aviv Hilton and found that even Israelis cruise around for a little sexual activity. It was a very full few days indeed. At the Tel Aviv Airport, we were lined up and one by one each asked a series of 4 simple questions, each of which we had to answer to no less than 4 people, each asking the same 4 questions. I think if you stumbled in your answers you would have been pulled out of line, but I never was.

Arriving back in Cairo, again I wanted to upgrade my hotel so this time I stayed at the Ramses Hilton, right behind the Nile Hilton. I just got into my room and began to unpack, when the phone rang. I picked it up and a voice asked, "Is this Mr. Stan?" I answered, "Yes." He immediately continued with, "My name is Tareq. I am a friend of Hesham. Hesham cannot meet you as he is in a wrestling competition in Alexandria." I said, "I know, he told me last week and asked if I could go, but I knew I wouldn't have enough time." Tareq continued, "So Hesham sent me to take you around Cairo." I met him downstairs within minutes and off we went. We walked, we talked, he spoke even better English than Ahmed the other friend of Hesham. We even took one of the truly Egyptian vans, that once you get it, if you are in the back, you pay the money to the person in front of you, and he passes it onto the person in front of him and so on until the driver receives the money. In the States, the driver probably wouldn't even get all the money that was passed. Tareq wouldn't let me pay for anything. We wound up in the Cairo Zoo, sitting on a metal fence across a wide walkway from a man selling cotton candy. And we talked about everything, from politics to the Israeli Palestinian conflict (a common discussion amongst young Egyptian men). After we were sitting there for almost an hour, and the time did go by very swiftly, the man made 2 cotton candy treats and brought them over to us. Tareq wanted to pay and the man refused to accept any money. This is Egypt, after all. Tareq finally gave in and accepted our gifts. A little while later we began talking about getting something to eat. I said I wanted to take him to a restaurant as he was so kind to me the entire day. He said, ''Absolutely not!'' I said, "It's difficult to argue with you when you find it hard to even accept a gift from one of your own people. Do you understand how good it makes you feel to be able to give me your time and you won't take anything from me?" He answered, "Yes, of course." I responded with, "Well that's how I want to feel. Let me have a little selfish feeling to be able to do something for you, by at least taking you to dinner." He insisted, "No, absolutely not!" I then said, "Okay, let's go to a restaurant and we will sit down and I will watch you eat." Tareq thought and finally said, "Okay, I will let you take me to eat." He then found the cheapest restaurant he could find because he didn't want me to spend any money. We ate and went back to the hotel. He said Hesham gave him something to give to me. Also, his (Tareq's) girlfriend had died 1 year ago and he was still heartbroken. He penned a poem for her, and he wanted me to help him put it into a better form of English than what he had written. I told him to come up to the room and he gave the receptionist at the hotel his papers, so he came up for a while. Once in the room he went into his bag and told me, "Hesham gave me this to give to you". It was his black and white bathing suit. I wanted to give something to Hesham as well, and the only thing I had was a pair of gray shorts with a "Hollywood" logo on it, so I told Tareq to give it to Hesham. We then worked on his poem and it truly was beautiful but in English I had to clean up some of the grammar for him. After doing this he read the poem and began to cry. It was such a close relationship we had at that moment. He gathered his things and left . . . of course I brought him down to the lobby. I found these Egyptians, Hesham, Ahmed, and Tareq to be quite innocent but still full of Egyptian hospitality, which is full of love and acceptance.

e

It was many years since that first time in Egypt, until I returned. This time I was bringing Americans to Egypt to tour, and of course I would come with them. I remember on 2 separate trips I missed the boat once in Esna, and once in Edfu, and I am the travel agent. The first time I missed the boat was in the afternoon, I was buying a galabia (a man's robe that many of the older Egyptian men wear, like a mumu). The salesmen and I were waiting for one of his men to return with another galabia from down the street. I said that I didn't want to miss the boat, and he said not to worry as they would toot the horn before leaving. So we are standing outside his store and we see his man coming down the street with the galabia, when we see my boat leave the dock and THEN toot the horn. Well, we ran across the street to the dock and were screaming at the boat to come back, which eventually it did, after having to make a complete circle in the middle of the Nile. They were not pleased but at that time they didn't have a system to tell them everyone was not onboard. The next time I missed the boat was in Edfu on a different trip of course. After taking my evening walk through Edfu, I wound up talking to the security soldiers guarding the dock. We were smoking my cigarettes (I was a smoker at that time), and it was extremely late. Having talked to the head security office, this very large, black skinned Egyptian, he told me that the boat was scheduled to depart at 7am. Well this was getting to be around 430am, and again I was with 2 soldiers only one of which spoke very broken English. So again, seeking these special experiences, we were again telling jokes until my cigarettes ran out. I said, I'll be right back as I had more cigs in my cabin. In those days and today, often the boats are stacked side by side, so to get to your boat you might have to go through 3 or 4 boats if the dock was very busy. So I go very quickly through the first boat, through the second boat, through the third boat when they asked where I was going. I said to the Moon Goddess, and they, the people in the third boat said that boat left already. What an empty feeling!!! I ran back to my friends and told them to find the head security officer, which they did, and explained that I missed my boat. He was absolutely furious because he was told the boat wouldn't leave until 7am and it left at 415am. So he gets on the phone, and begins to shout over the phone, of course all this is in Arabic. Every once in a while he would 'cup' the phone with his hand and in a very polite voice to say, "Not to worry... the boat she come back", and then immediately begin shouting into the phone in Arabic again. This happened several times until he finally cupped the phone and asked, "What was the name of your boat?". He finally found the boat as it was approaching the Esna lock, and he told them to stay there and send a small boat to pick me up, which they did. After about 20 more minutes or so, a little rubber dingy with 3 men in it approached the dock and I had to jump into it as there were no stairs for the dingy. As we approached the Moon Goddess, it got larger and larger in life the closer we came, thoughts of Barbra Streisand singing "Don't Rain On My Parade" came into my mind. When we were next to the boat, I had to lift my arms so the men in the lobby level could lift me up to the lobby. The lobby was filled with the workers from the boat and the captain came to me and implored, " We are so sorry we left you in Edfu, and so happy to have you back with us." My response was, "And it's so good to be back on the Cleopatra again." He screamed, "Cleopatra??? This is the Moon Goddess!!!" I said it was a joke and he almost fainted. The following morning I'm taking my morning walk and coming back to the boat, and I pass two of the workers whom I haven't seen before, and one of them says to me, "You miss boat!" I found that particularly amusing... now the workers on the boat remember me.

e

My name is Stan Mazin. Ancestry is Russian on both sides. We pronounce it with a long 'a' as in 'maze'. Now in Arabic the name Mazin is pronounced with a short 'a' as in 'Oz', or 'Ahhh's'. Pronounced

that way it is an Arabic name also. So when I travel to Egypt I tell everyone that they can call me Abu Mazin, who is really Mahmoud Abbas, the president of the Palestinians, but it is easy to remember for them. So oftentimes I will be walking in my galabia down a street in Luxor or Aswan and I will hear, "Abu Mazin... Abu Mazin ... " And they are talking to me. Now when I go to Egypt, I travel with one pair of pants for the planes, and about 15 to 17 galabias in various colors and styles. The Egyptians see my 'gringo' face wearing a garment that many of their elders wear, and doors fling open to me. Conversations begin automatically. While taking people on a side trip to Dendera and Abydos, 2 temples about 2 hours drive north of Luxor, I was walking with some friends in my galabia, when a boy of approximately 10 or 11 year of age came up to me from behind, and tugged at my galabia asking, ''Are you Abu Mazin?" He remembered me from the year prior. Of course I love the Egyptians. Many times I would be walking down the street with an Egyptian friend and a woman would be sitting against a wall on the ground, not begging, just sitting there. And my friend would take out a piestra bill, ten ($.03), twenty five ($08), or fifty ($.16) and just hand it to the woman ... who wasn't begging, but obviously needed it. These are a 'giving' people.

e

A very dear friend of mine is Mohamed Salah, the travel agent in Cairo who arranges all my Egyptian trips from now on. We are indeed like brothers which he keeps reminding me, and I love his wife and his two children so very much that they make me feel like I am truly family. On one of the trips after a very long absence from Egypt, I asked Mohamed if he would mind driving me around Kit-Kat to see if anything looked familiar and if we might possibly find Hesham. He agreed and we began driving through the area. Nothing really looked

112

familiar. And I couldn't remember Hesham's last name, so all I knew what that the family had two sons who were wrestlers. We stopped by a man who was getting into his car and asked if he knew of a family who had two wrestling sons years before. He explained he didn't know but right around the corner a friend of his had a business for quite a while and he might be familiar with the family. So off we drove around the corner and met with his friend. We asked the same question and he thought and said that there was a business back where our car came from who might know the family, as their sons who were very young were studying wrestling. So we drove back around the corner, parked the car, walked up to this athletic shoe store, and I looked at the man behind the counter, and it was a mature fully grown almost gray haired Hesham. He looked at me and said, "Stan Mazin!"... I couldn't believe my eyes. I had given him a business card of mine with my picture on it years before, and he had it displayed under the glass on his counter. I wanted to cry. He had his own boys now, three of them and they were all studying wrestling. We talked and his English was better now. Every trip I take to Egypt now, I make sure I see my good friend, Hesham. I will admit that when I first met him, the feeling toward this good looking Egyptian was not so pure... but now it is the purest. How can I not love these people and this country so much when I have these kinds of experiences that remain so personal to me in my life. And there are so many more stories that I have stored away in my mind.

e

One of the many interesting people I have met who have traveled with me is a woman named Jean Charney. This is an elderly woman who is truly beautiful, but who will never tell you her real age. Age is such an interesting quality in that when we are younger, we want to be older, then we are happy we are the age we are, and finally when we are older we try to pass for younger than we are. Jean almost reminded me of Marion Lorne or Billie Burke. She wasn't as funny immediately, but the questions she would ask after our tour guide just explained in detail what she wanted to know, would be quite humorous. But she is such a kind woman. Once in Pompeii, on a particularly hot day our group was leaving and she stopped to pet one of the stray dogs. There was only one direction to go toward the exit, and we waited an hour and a half for her. Finally Bix Barnaba, another dear friend of mine, and I went back to try to find her. She went out of her way to try getting some water for the dog, which was no easy task in Pompeii. On another Egypt trip, while driving toward the pyramids, the guide was giving her spiel about the area, when Jean asked, "Why does she have to tell us so much?" These were the questions she would ask which made her a very special woman in my mind.

Another good friend who traveled with me was Anne Jeffreys, who was married to Robert Sterling. Together they were the most beautiful couple in Hollywood. Anne and Robert starred in the television version of 'Topper' in the 50's which also starred Leo G. Carroll. Annie J. as she likes to be referred to was always dressed to the 'nines', and always fabulous looking. I didn't really know what kind of sense of humor she had until our first trip to Ireland. When I go to a new town or village, I love to go to their stores, clothing and food markets. Well since Robert wasn't traveling, Anne paid for a gay male friend of hers to come along, and the three of us became good traveling friends on that trip. We went to a good 'supermarket' in this particular village, and in the frozen food department found this box of Mr. Brains Pork Faggots. We were hysterical. It was a good 14 or 20 minutes before we could calm down, and no one else knew why we were laughing so much. That Christmas, I went to a party at another fantastic woman's house named Miriam Nelson... more about Miriam later. I saw Annie J. there and she said, "Stan, I have a present for you. Remember to take it with you when you leave." I thanked her, we spoke throughout the evening, and I left with her present to me. When I got home I opened the beautifully wrapped gift and under the wrapping was this beautiful blue Tiffany box. I opened the box to expose this Tiffany's silver picture frame and in the frame was the lid cover from Mr. Brain's Pork Faggots. What a phenomenal woman Anne Jeffreys was... and what a sense of humor.

e

In 1971 Diana Rigg and Keith Michell starred in "Abelard and Heloise" by Ronald Millar and Robin Phillips at the Ahmanson Theatre before it's Broadway opening. Dom, my partner was the production stage manager for the show. One night he told me he invited someone to dinner on Sunday after the show and I should make dinner. I asked who it was and he said, "It's a surprise". I told him I had to know so I would know what to prepare. After a little argument, he said, "Okay, if you insist. Diana Rigg!" Diana Rigg!!! I was going to make dinner for  Emma Peel! I was ecstatic! I loved "The Avengers" on TV and adored Diana Rigg. Dom told me that her dresser Bill told him about the time Diana was telling him a story and was in the wings wearing a robe ready for her nude scene. In the middle of her story, she said, "wait a minute", she disrobed, went onstage, did the scene which was very heavy, walked back into the wings, put her robe on and continued the story without a break. That's the kind of actor I would like to be, someone so sure of her talent she never had to do a 'method' preparation for the scene. So now I had to think what to make. I chose Chinese food because I love it and I had a great Chinese recipe book. I was so excited that Diana Rigg and Bill were coming to our home. I couldn't wait to cook, so I started when the matinee started. I know that Chinese food is cooked very fast, but I was making about 5 dishes and wanted to make sure it would all be done. Well, by the time they got home from the matinee, it was pretty late and my food was overcooked... all of it. I had to serve it and she was a true lady about it but honestly it was a disaster.

e

Ever since Dom worked with her, every time we would go to London with our group, if she were performing in a play, we would go backstage and sit in her dressing room with her. After we saw "Medea"

115

at the Wyndham Theatre, we went to her dressing room. She had a couch against a wall and 2 arm chairs diagonally facing her couch one facing each of the front corners of the couch. She was sitting on the sofa and Dom and I were in the arm chairs. She leaned forward and said, "They are talking about bringing this show to New York. What should I ask for?" She was asking two Broadway chorus boys what she should get to star in "Medea" on Broadway. Dom said he didn't know. I didn't want to seem like a 'chorus boy', so I thought a second and reminded her she hadn't been on Broadway since "Abelard and Heloise" which was years before, and even though she starred in 'The Avengers', that was quite a while ago. I continued, "But you are a star and I would think you would probably get at least ten thousand dollars a week." Without waiting a second she added, "And a car!?!" I said, "Of course. They couldn't expect you to take the subway." I couldn't believe that conversation. Incidentally in case you weren't aware, she won a Tony for her performance of "Medea" on Broadway. I never did find out what she was paid. I love Emma Peel!!!

e

One of my favorite travelers was Jane Kean. Jane played the role of 'Trixie' in the color TV version of "The Honeymooners" as Art Carney's wife. She used to travel with her husband Joe Hecht, an older comedian. Both were talented and everyone loved them. After Joe passed away, Jane continued to travel with me, and she was truly a delight. She was this very elegant woman who always was very elegantly dressed, but had a very low down sense of humor, so it was always a pleasure for me to call her a 'dame'. And she went everywhere with me... all over the world just about. And she had the most spectacular Christmas parties in her home which included notable guests like Margaret O'Brien, Betty Rose (David Rose' widow), Charlotte Rae, Jane Withers, Marni Nixon (who used to dub the singing for every Hollywood star), Millicent Martin, Connie Sawyer, and so many others. One night she slipped in her own apartment and hit her head on the coffee table. She was taken to the

hospital and after fixing her up they released her. A few days later she fell again and this time other tests were taken and she apparently had a blood clot in her brain from the first fall. She never came out of the hospital and we all miss her so very much. No matter what troubles she had in her life, we were not aware of them, and she kept 'doing her thing' to the end. Another lesson to be learned. No one knows what is in our minds but ourselves. John Donne said it... "No man is an island." I disagree. "Every man is an island." And I think that is a good thing.

Now let's talk about Miriam Nelson. She remained with us for  98 years, looking as lovely as she ever was. She was the first wife of dancer director Gene Nelson and remained married to him for many years. She was choreographer for many movies, shows, and many years for the Share ladies, a charity group of stars and show biz wives. Even at that age, though perhaps needing a chair to hold onto, those magic feet still went a mile a minute. And a nicer woman I've never known... never ever a bad word to say about anyone in the business, which is very rare. Miriam has traveled with me extensively and remained to be one of my best friends till the end, which still makes me so very proud. Miriam left us recently taking a piece of my heart with her. Miriam asked once what my first experience with dance was. My mind of course took me right back to my childhood ...

e

My first memory is that of riding in a baby carriage when the ladies in South Philadelphia would stop my mother to admire her baby son. I remember our row house on Sheridan Street just north of Shunk. I remember Pearl, the girl 2 doors down from our house, with whom I attended Kindergarten and elementary school at Taggart. My mother enrolled me at Lou Crescenta's School of Dance on Moyamensing and 16th Street. It was a combination class of ballet and tap and a very little acrobatic. It seemed I excelled in tap. It was difficult for my father to pay for my dance classes... and when he came home from work on the day I had my class, he would more often than not say, "Okay. Show me what you learned today." As much as I may have wanted to, I was so shy that I couldn't just dance when he asked me. Invariably he would wind up hollering at my mother. "What the hell am I paying for dance classes when he won't even dance for me!" "I will, Daddy... I promise, I will". But I only felt that, I never said it.

e

Sometimes when we are young we do things that are embarrassing to talk about when we are adults. I remember once when we lived on Sheridan Street I almost burned our row house down. I forget how young I was but I was more young than stupid. In our kitchen I saw a knife sticking out from a shelf not noticing what was holding it down. I wondered whether or not the knife would melt if heated. So we had matches and I took a chair and slid it under the shelf I climbed up on the chair and struck the match and held it under the knife. Just as I thought the knife was going to melt, the complete corner of the shelf above the knife ignited and the kitchen corner was ablaze. You see, there was an entire box of blue tip matches sitting on the knife, keeping it from dropping. I ran outside and was shy about admitting it, but told my parents who were sitting outside on our stoop (this was South Philly after all) that I might have done something bad. They ran inside and somehow poured pots of water over the fire. I was sure I would get the strap, as I did sometimes, but very rarely. My mother and father were very kind to me. When I thought I would be hollered at and punished, they sat me down and explained why I must never do that sort of thing again. I couldn't believe that I was free of guilt so easily, but I remembered doing that for the rest of my life, so I suppose the guilt has lived inside me for a very long time.

I remember going fishing, if you can believe it, in some kind of lake in South Philly with my grandfather. We were not fisherman, but every once in a rare while he would take me. I remember that I did catch a gold fish and I told him I didn't want to hurt the fish. He said in his Russian accent, "They are not hurt. This does not hurt them." When I looked at the squirming fish in the bucket of water I replied, "I think they must be hurting, otherwise why would they be trying to get out of the bucket?" My grandfather reassured me again they were in no pain,

118

which of course I didn't believe. It reminded me of another time when I got 6 Easter chicks and built a chicken coop myself I would guess I was about 9 or so. Anyway I raised them for at least 4 months and other than 1 of them dying who got caught somehow in the mesh wiring, they all grew to a good size. One day they were gone and my father told me that he and my grandfather took the chickens to a farm in Jersey where they could be free. My grandmother cooked lots of chicken over the next couple of weeks and I never put 2 and 2 together. When I think of it now, what can I say!?! I am an animal!

e

Growing up I wasn't really into sports. I always seemed to want to play with the girls. I now understand that that may have been the reason or choice in lifestyles while I was growing up. But I wonder what caused that, and I have no idea. All I remember is that when I was prompted to play stickball with the boys in our neighborhood, I was bad at it. I probably needed glasses, but at that time people rarely thought that might be a problem, but I could never hit the ball. Consequently I was always the last person to be picked. Let me correct that... I wasn't picked. I was the last person that one of the teams would be stuck with after everyone else was chosen. That was a big reason I had such low self esteem, certainly when it came to sports. Playing 'Jacks' or jumping rope with the girls was always more pleasurable. I'm sure that's just another reason why whenever my father wanted me to play 'catch' with him, I never wanted to. You see, my father was this huge baseball fan, and he was chosen to go to the summer camp for baseball players to possibly be chosen for the Phillies team. But right before he was to go, my mother became pregnant, so my father did the 'right thing' and stayed with her in Philadelphia. But he always had a hand in baseball. And when he got too old to play, he became an umpire for little league teams in Philly. He was always disappointed that I didn't hold the same love for the sport that he did. So I decided to go in a different direction.

e

I remember my very first recital at Town Hall on North Broad Street. We did a number called, "Sentimental Journey", with older dancing couples and my partner and I were the youngest and smallest of the students in the number. At the end of the finished number, my partner and I were in the middle of this large semi-circle of the other couples... very cute! I also did the recital the following year where I danced with other people to "Anchors Aweigh". Then I stopped... I don't think my parents could afford it any longer. At the time I was 5 and 6 years of age.

During the summer all the mothers would sit on pillows placed on the bottom of the window panes, so you'd see these ladies sitting in the windows, fanning themselves because in those days there was no air conditioning. If they weren't in the windows, then they would sit outside on the marble stoops in front of their houses. I remember when I had to pee, instead of bringing me upstairs to the second floor (no one had bathrooms downstairs in our area) my mother would stand me at the curb and take out my pecker and I would have to pee in the street with God knows who watching... I know Pearl was. As I think back at that moment, my mind reels... was I six or sixteen!?!

e

I didn't dance again until my 12th year. I went back to Lou Crescenta's to take tap, and in the recital that year I danced to "Sweet Sue". The excitement of the evening comes back to me in spurts... the mothers putting makeup and costumes on their children in a very crowded back stage area. I am dressed in a common suit, as we really couldn't afford to buy a fancy costume. My solo began and I'm onstage and suddenly a spotlight hits me and I can't see a thing. I get to the middle of my dance and forget the next step. I freeze for a second, look into the wings for I don't know what, then make up 'jibberish' with my feet until the next step that I remember that comes with that part of the music. This was probably the first time onstage I was truly embarrassed ... the first time offstage was my mother making me pee in the street outside my home. And it was during this time that I was enthralled with another student, Bernice DeCroce... she was so beautiful. It's interesting now when I think back at that time the embarrassing moments meant more to me then, than the ones that have occurred since I was young. I must be growing up.

e

On each of my yearly New York Theatre Tours that I run, we have many truly interesting travelers. And on each trip one of the highlights is the optional Sunday Chinese Dim Sum breakfasts. We all meet at Mott and Pell with another very dear friend of mine, Didi Shapiro, who takes us to this huge Dim Sum restaurant where we are usually the only caucasian faces present in a sea of Asians. The food is fantastic and when we all chip in, we are stuffed and the meal is generally $10 each including a generous tip. Incidentally Didi is a fine artist as well as a fantastic friend, and both she and her husband, a terrific actor named Bill Rowley, used to be members of Lonny Chapman's Group Repertory Theatre before they moved back to New York City. At any rate one of the interesting characters who came with our group on these trips was Lynn Cartwright, an actress who used to be a member of Lonny Chapman's Group Repertory Theatre also, and who was also married to a wonderful character actor and author Leo Gordon. Lynn was Gina Davis as the older woman in "A League Of Their Own", but they dubbed in Gina's voice. Lynn used to travel with me on my New York and London theatre tours but after Leo passed away, we hadn't heard from her in quite a long time. Then one year I got a call from Tara, their daughter, and Tara said Lynn wanted to come with us to New York that spring, so we made the arrangements. Now I hadn't seen Lynn in years and the first time was on the plane going to New York. I said hello as I entered the plane. Lynn was seated on the aisle of the first row and there was no business or first class. I was seated in row 7 on the opposite side with a 3 and 3 seat configuration. I buckled in, and just as we began to taxi, Lynn began shouting, "My dog! Where's my dog? What happened to my dog?" She got up and started down the aisle and I told her that her dog wasn't on the plane and she should go back to her seat, which she did. She stayed there a few minutes and we started down the runway and lifted off. As we were climbing, again she had the same outburst, and running down the aisle. I told her that if her dog was at the airport, that Tara had taken her dog home with her so she didn't have to worry about it. She sat back into her seat after the stewardess came over. After another few minutes the same thing happened. The man sitting right behind me suggested he take her seat and she could sit right behind me, since I seemed to be able to calm her down somewhat. They changed seats and she seemed calmer with me sitting right in front of her. I wondered whether that was a fluke and at least hoped it was, since I had a lot of people to deal with and I would be very busy taking care of business. The rest of the flight went fine, with very few interruptions. I had 17 people on the theatre tour and Lynn was only one of them. I gave Lynn a roommate named Beverly Goodman, a younger very bright woman who had almost no social skills... I actually thought she was a savant, because anything you wanted to know, she seemed to know. She had traveled with me before but always had her own room. Since both these women wanted to save some money this year, I put them together as roommates. We landed, retrieved our luggage and were taken to the Best Western President Hotel on West 48th Street. We all checked into the hotel without a problem. As a New York tradition, we, those who want to, meet about an hour after check-in, in the lobby and walk over to Bella Napoli on West 49th Street east of 7th Avenue. The food is great, the prices are reasonable, and it's close to the hotels we use. I've used the President before, but after this trip I was able to get into the Edison whose location I like even more. Now we are at the restaurant. Lynn tells me she'd like to use the bathroom and I lead her to it. She enters and I go back to my seat. After a while we hear very loud banging coming from the bathroom. Lynn is inside and is screaming that she can't get out. The manager of the restaurant comes back and we try to calm Lynn down until she tries to follow his instructions to open the door. This incident did take about five minutes before the door was finally opened. She came back to her seat and everything after that seemed normal. We paid our bills and went back to the hotel. Everyone went to their own rooms and I went to mine. I never have a roommate... I used to but there is no amount of money that can take away my personal privacy now. I've learned that, after rooming with many different people who needed to have a roommate. So I am almost asleep and the time is approximately 2am, when the phone rings, and Beverly is on the phone. She is crying, which I have never ever seen Beverly do, and she says that she cannot tolerate Lynn's rantings any longer. I go into their room and explain that I will try getting them their own room. Lynn seems fine with this idea. I go down to the lobby and explain the situation to them, and with great understanding they offer me a single room just down the hall from my room where we could put Ms. Cartwright. I take the key, go to their present room, and pick up Lynn's bags and bring her to her new room. By this time it is almost 3am. I tell Lynn to stay put and I will be right back as I have to go down to sign some papers for the hotel. On my return to our floor, as the elevator approaches, I can hear loud banging coming from one of the rooms. Lynn is again screaming my name through the door, and at the same time banging on the door. I tell her to calm down and slowly unlock the door from the inside so I can come in. I enter and she immediately is calm. I tell her where my room is, and that she can call on the telephone when she needs to. I leave and return to my room. Not 20 minutes later, the phone rings, and it is Lynn. She asks questions about her daughter, Tara, and her dog. I explained that we were in NYC and they were safe in California. I come back to her room and bring Lynn to my room. After much talk Lynn finally settles down and lies down for a nap. By this time I am so riled up I don't think I can sleep. About 5am I ask Lynn if she would like to go to her room and she says, "Yes!". I drop her off and go back to try to sleep for a couple of hours. The phone rings around 6:15am and it is the front desk. "One of your ladies is walking around the lobby area in her pajamas. Could you please come and take her back to her room?" And so I dressed as quickly as I could, went downstairs to get her, brought her back to her room, went back to my room to shower and shave as quickly as I could before I returned to pick her up for breakfast. I now know I cannot trust her to be on her own. With the 3 hour time difference between Los Angeles and New York, I leave Tara several messages. She finally calls me back around noon. I explain the events of the previous day and night, and tell her she must come and either stay with her mother, or come and bring her back to California. She agrees to fly out that day as soon as she can. I stay with Lynn most of the day until she says she is tired and has to rest. I bring her back to the hotel and make sure she takes 2 sleeping pills, and I don't leave until she lies down and begins to sleep. I then go to meet Bix and Patti Karr, an actress who starred in a show called "Walls" at the Huntington Hartford Theatre in Hollywood in the early 80's. Patti used to be the general stand-in for Gwen Verdon and Chita in many of their shows... so she is a fantastic dancer as well as a wonderful actor (the term 'actor' is now accepted for both male and female actors). Bix, Patti, and I eat at Mee's Noodle Shop on the corner of 53rd and 9th Avenue ... great food, very low prices, huge menu... all this great food coming from a kitchen the size of a large dining room table... after all, this is New York! My cell phone rings in the middle of our meal and of course it is the President Hotel telling me that 'one of my ladies' has been walking around the lobby dressed in a robe and talking to herself They have brought her to the basement offices and had to restrain her to keep her from getting away. She is now in one of the offices with the lady who runs that office. I explain the situation with Lynn to Bix and Patti while we proceed to the hotel. We take the elevator down to that office, and Bix and I go to the office while Patti tells us she will wait by the elevator for Lynn's daughter who is supposed to arrive any minute. Once I am there Lynn settles down and becomes rational once more. We are talking to the lady and coming down to the room is Tara followed by Patti, who is telling her she had no right to allow Lynn to travel. Tara enters the room asking, "Who is this crazy lady who is yelling at me as soon as I get off the elevator?" We all calm down and I explain to Tara that her options are to stay with Lynne in her room, or to leave for California early and take Lynn with her. She agrees to stay. Hallelujah!!! Now while I am in New York or London, I will see a show every single night. After all, that is my life and I might see a show I might possibly be able to appear in, or see a show I could possibly direct, etc. So that same night after the last breakdown of Lynn Cartwright we all go to see a show. After the show I usually, when in NYC, go to Barrymore's, an after hours theatre bar and restaurant, which I went to on this night. Before doing so, I saw Tara bringing Lynn back to the hotel. I could relax.

We often stay at Barrymore's for 1 ½ or 2 hours. It was a great place to unwind... and I needed to unwind everything. We are walking back to the hotel and I see Tara coming from the opposite direction without Lynn. I asked where she was and she replied that she was upstairs sleeping. I tried to explain that she was not safe being alone. Tara went out for cigarettes and went right up to the room. I can just imagine if Lynn had come down to the lobby, gone out of the front door, and turned in either direction, she would have been lost, without even knowing the name of the hotel she was staying in. I am giving

Tara the benefit of a doubt. Perhaps when Lynn is in her own home surrounded by her own things, and the people she knows, perhaps these events don't occur.

But on the other side, I am suspicious that Tara just might want me to be a 'witness for the prosecution' in case she wanted to have Lynn committed. That didn't happen. I'm told that Lynn passed away of 'natural causes' one year later. When I think of how great a person and an actress she was before this trip... Lynn Cartwright was a wonderful person and was also a member of our theatre... she is missed.

e

Being a Pisces, I've always considered myself as a jack-of-all-trades... master of none. That hurts me a little as I would like to think that some things I do, I do well, but everything we do in life is judged not by ourselves, but by the people around us. And so we must accept what our friends say, even though I don't think we should really believe too many of the accolades. There are too many egos in the world as is.

e

Early on in the 70's I was called to come down to interview with Larry Heimgartner to possibly choreograph their summer musicals at LA Harbor College. Larry was a real buffed up guy, very attractive, looking more like a football coach than a theatre director. The head of the drama department was Marge Chandler, the widow of actor Jeff Chandler. Since Larry was directing the summer musicals, he was the one who interviewed me. I think one of the main reasons he was impressed with me was the fact that I was presently working on the Carol Burnett Show as a dancer and actor. I really didn't have too much experience choreographing professionally. But I was hired nonetheless. The first show I did that summer was "Roar of the Greasepaint, Smell of the Crowd". Apparently Harbor College gets more money from the government depending on how many students are in their shows, so there are always at least 40 to 50 or more singers and dancers in each show. Out of a group like that, certainly there might be a smaller group of about 6 to 8 persons who have danced before, if we are lucky, and hopefully 5 to 8 people who can sing better than I can... believe me, anyone can sing better than I can. My job was certainly difficult, but

I love challenges, and I was also good at teaching dance, which came in handy with my rehearsals at Harbor. We were fortunate to have the role of 'Cocky' played by Fred Bishop, a fantastic musical talent who has the charm of an angel, and the role of 'Sir' played by Jim McClure, a big blustering sweet guy, both with exceptional voices. Cocky was the butt of all of Sir's jokes, so he was always getting into trouble in the show. And Fred did everything I asked him to do, including doing a huge slide headfirst off of a high ramp into the arms of the other people down below, right at the end of the 'Put It In The Book' number. I had a ball working with all the people. I proved to myself that I could do it. This was the very first book show I choreographed for anyone, because it was before I even joined GRT... the Lonny Chapman Group Rep Theatre. The show came out fine and during each performance, Larry Heimgartner, the director would stand in the back of the auditorium and applaud and cheer more than anyone else did in the audience... so much so that oftentimes the audience around him would look up as if 'who is making all that racket?'. But Larry loved his cast. And watching him work with them was very much like watching a coach work with a football team. That was an education by itself. About a year after this show, Marge Chandler, who I learned was not too well, gave up her drama department crown and handed it down to Larry. Debbie Heimgartner, Larry's beautiful wife, was in every show, and had lots of talent in her own right. I thought she would make it very big if she turned professional, but apparently her choice was to stay in Wilmington with Larry. They made a beautiful couple, and I did so love working with her as well. The next show I worked on the following summer was an original called "Grab The Ring". It was more of an exaggerated children's show. Other shows I did the succeeding summers were "Jesus Christ Superstar", "Cabaret", "Joseph and the Technicolor Dreamcoat", "Can-Can", to name a few. I remember Norman Church in "Superstar". Rehearsals had begun and we had to replace one of the male 'dancers', and Larry implored me to hire this techie named Norman Church. Now we had auditions every year for each of the shows, and without doubt Norman Church was absolutely the worst mover let alone dancer of every single one of the kids. I told Larry that Norman couldn't even walk right. He begged me and told me that Norman would work harder than anyone else in the show.

I acquiesced and Norman Church joined our company. I hate to be wrong, but by the time we opened "Jesus Christ Superstar", during my speech to the cast, I would tell them that if anyone loses their place and forgets what to do onstage, look for Norman Church, because he knows exactly what to do and he does it well. I learned such a lesson from that experience, and I've repeated my 'Norman Church' story to many shows since that time. I would tell the lesser talented dancers in the show, "I want you to be my Norman Church!" I'm sure Norman never had an inkling as to how his presence in that show affected me... and still does.

During my last show at Harbor, we were voting on the California ballot for or against Proposition 13. I was in favor of it, but Larry told me if it passed, I might be out of a job. I thought we needed it to protect our homes, etc. Well Prop 13 did indeed pass and I never could work for Harbor again. I'm sure they didn't have the budget, but I voted my mind, and had to accept the consequence, which ultimately I did. I still love Larry and Debbie so very much. He gave me a chance to hone my craft, and I always learn by doing... and I will ever be indebted to him for that.

Apparently someone saw one or two of my shows at Harbor College and I was approached and asked to direct and choreograph a group of mostly non-pros for a big charity organization called "The Footlighters". The only true celebrity who was a member is Barbara Billingsley, from "Leave It To Beaver" fame, and because she never wanted to sing or dance she hardly ever appeared in any of the shows. The director I replaced was Jonathan Lucas, who directed and choreographed the show for the past 4 years. Apparently no other director/ choreographer has done the Footlighter shows for more than 3 or 4 years.

When I saw tapes of former shows there were always places in the show when there were pauses for costume changes, etc. And there were more speaking lines as well. The group is not made up of actors who do well with lines. Also the choice of songs were not always known so the audiences never really felt 'connected' to the shows. As soon as I took over, I made sure that the numbers we did were familiar to the audiences we got, so many of them were standards. But I would also always add a 'twist' to the number. The men who were invited to participate in the show were husbands and friends of the Footlighters ladies. I remember one number that began with cavemen in a tribal choreographed number, very simple, that the men could have fun with. During their part of the number, they rolled out a huge caldron onto the center of the stage, and just as the caldron stopped rolling, the next musical intro began, and Marilyn Silva slowly arose from inside the caldron singing La Habanera attired in full Spanish costume with a Mantilla on top of her head. Marilyn could sing so it sounded great, but the concept was so off the wall that people kept laughing, which was my goal with the Footlighters. We also had two 'diva' singers who each always tried to outdo the other. Whenever we had a run-through, each would come to me and say that the other's song was longer than hers, and so on ... they were even counting seconds. They would also vie for which number was last in the run of the show, thinking that that position was the best one. I loved those two ladies. One was Rena Old, an English woman who flew in every year just to do the show. The other was Peggy Edwards, who was married to the man who was the architect for the Hilton Hotels, consequently she and her husband lived on the top floor of the Beverly Hilton Hotel when I began doing their shows. Both of these ladies I believe used to sing with the bands in the 40's and 50's. And the shows were performed at that time at the Beverly Hilton, as Peggy got some kind of a deal for them with the hotel. They were friends, but foes when it came to their numbers in the show. I was the first director to put both of them in the same number, which was 'Bosom Buddies' from "Mame". When I took over the shows I made sure there was a minimum of dialogue and a maximum of familiar songs that were relatable to the audience members. I began every show with a large number of the members, then usually a solo or duet, and build from there. We always had a 'Showgirl' number for the lovely ladies who didn't really dance or sing, and I always had a 'Tiller' line of about 8 dancers, that I worked with made up usually of about 3 or 4 girls who could dance, and the rest broke their backs to learn the numbers. We tried to do a little tap dancing in each show. And since we didn't have much of a set besides only a backdrop, I tried to use props that we could make ourselves. Once, the girls who could <u>sing, did 'Gotta Wash That</u> Man Right Outa My Head' from South Pacific. We built 6 portable circular showers on wheels that they could move around in different patterns, and the showers had shower heads above them with

128

silver streamers hanging from the 'showerheads', so that from far away it looked slightly like water. I was so proud of each and every woman in the show, and each and every woman in the show had a special thing going for her. Certain women always did certain types of numbers.

My dear friend Sue Casey, who used to swim in all the Esther Williams movies, besides being a good dancer, was always in the Showgirl numbers along with Carole Emmett, another long legged beautiful woman. Charlene Chase was always dancing for me, as well as a slew of others that I relied on so much. Nikki Lewis another English lady also danced for me along with Barbara Mortenson, Barbara Billingsley's daughter. By the way, it was Nikki Lewis from whom I got my first

2 Cavelier King Charles Spaniels, but that's another story for later. I shall never forget the ladies of "The Footlighters" ... Carol Masters, the first producer who hired me, and she was a great performer that I could rely on anytime...

Sandra Young always danced for me and she was a terrific dancer and she hired me several times when she produced.... Tanna Havlick, an always fun dancer for me in only 2 shows but she never believed she could do anything, and she was wrong... Kit Joyce was a dream person although she admitted to me that she thought she had no talent, but I always enjoyed working with her... Rosemary Herd was always a showgirl and once in a while she would let me put her in the tiller line... Helen Lambros danced for me and loved being onstage any time I asked... Linda DeMetrick was always in the tiller line and it was

great fun having her dance for me, who would always say she couldn't do certain steps, but she wound up doing them very well... Vera Bernard a strong woman who had a little tiff with me one year, but whom I've always respected... Victoria Miller a great dancer whom I used to assist me several times over the years... Denise Genova, a lovely singer who turned out to be a lovely artist in her own right, but unfortunately succumbed to cancer years later... Lynette Treffinger, a marvel of energy who made Josephine Baker come alive to this day... Diane Fisk another wonderful singer who had to be patient through the years before she began soloing... Mary Jo Blue who did anything I asked of her, and through her connections in show biz supplied many of our set pieces

through the years... and so many many more, each and every one of them made me so proud when the show finally came to fruition. But if someone were to ask if I had a favorite, it had to have been B. J. Humiston. B. J. was an original Copa girl so she had the looks, the body, and the ability to really dance... and I love dancers. We became very close and she and her sister Beverly even traveled extensively with me. It was such a joy to always have her to work with, as everyone loved her. It was so sad when in later years her abilities weakened and she had to succumb to an inactive participation. That happens to all of us as we get older. So I encourage everyone to use their talents early

on and never say 'no'. And speaking of people who never said 'no' to me, the men of the Footlighters shouldn't be forgotten either. There was first and foremost Jack Garrett, whose wife Barbara always worked the financial end of the shows as she was always good with money, and Jack was always in a comedy number, every once in a while

even in drag; he was truly hysterical, and he could tap... Rocky Miller, Victoria's husband could sing, and on one occasion he sang Nelson Eddy to Jack Garrett's Jeanette MacDonald (need I say more?)... Peter Bernard, a reliable guy who would also do whatever was needed to help create any idea I came up with, and in his real life he used to work with the police... Bill Joyce, Kit's husband, a good singer but always seemed to have some kind of accident during the show. One year the men were supposed to take their jackets off onstage, and his shirt came off with it leaving him the only bare-chested guy onstage. And one time it happened with his pants... but he could really sing. There was Tony DiMilo, a friend of The Footlighters who was always ready to dance for me... Dennis Genova, Denise's husband, who always arrived with a great sense of humor... Dave Buffington, whose wife Dolores was always helping with the production, was a great person to work with, shorter than most, always smiling, and hysterical in a number where the men began singing in tuxedos and later it was revealed through the lighting that they all had on bright red patent leather high heeled women's shoes... between him and Jack Garrett, I didn't know who to laugh at first... what a sight gag surprise... and Michael Bernstein, the husband of one of the 'bigwigs' of The Footlighters, among others. I did a number where the men stripped down to funny underwear, but nothing too graphic. Michael Bernstein of course was in the number called 'You Can Leave Your Hat On' from "The Full Monty" film, and when we rehearsed the number he had different funny underwear on. When we did the show, the underwear he chose had an enormous 'penis' looking appendage as part of his costume. Always trying to make the shows as palatable and classy although funny as possible, I was furious. After the show I ran back to the men's room as that was the room sometimes the men had to use as a dressing room. Michael was not changing but I thought he was in one of the bathroom stalls. I began screaming at him, saying things like, "How could you do this to us? That's not professional at all!. What was the big idea? You should be ashamed of yourself". The other men in the room who were changing were just smiling. After a few minutes, this man, not from the show, but an older man who was just one of the audience members comes out of the cubicle with a strange look on his face. I apologized profusely and Michael had walked in out of sight as I was giving my tirade. Even

I thought it was so funny. God only knows what that little man thought I was talking about. Anyway, it was too funny for me to remain angry with Michael. I enjoy laughing at myself in predicaments like this one.

Barbara Billingsley was hardly ever in my shows unless we had a fake awards section as part of the show and she was a presenter. But one year it was time for my dear Kit Joyce, who professed she had no talent, to star in a number. I came up with the concept of dressing Kit like Charlie Chaplin and doing a mime number with background music only. In the skit, Charlie Chaplin sees this lovely lady come to a bench, who sits down, reads a letter, and begins crying or at least looking very sad indeed. She crumples up the letter and takes a few steps away from the bench, then without seeing him do it, Chaplin puts a rose on the bench. The woman, Barbara Billingsley, returns to the bench, sees the rose, picks it up, and a smile comes across her face as she slowly exits. Simple but very effective in the show, and it did exactly what I wanted it to do for both Kit and Barbara.

I directed and choreographed "The Footlighters" show for the next 4 years consecutively, after which some of the women felt they needed a change from me. That was fine, as I was so proud of what I had done to make their shows go faster, better paced, and more full of audience enjoyment. So they gave me a break, of about 2 or 3 years. Then I got a call from Sandra Young, stating they wanted me back and as producer of that year's show, she wanted to hire me back. I went back and did yet another 4 years. Remember that the limit to any director/choreographer's length of service prior to my employment was 4 years total. Here I did my 4 years and they brought me back. Over a period of about 30 years I did their shows 17 or 18 times. I never worked more than 4 years at a time, so in fact, I broke all their records for the return of any director/ choreographer. That gives me a true feeling of accomplishment and honor. Many of the Footlighters have passed during the balance of my employment with them. And it seems like it was difficult for them to capture younger members who were interested in their goal, so now it seems they never do their show any longer. It truly is a shame because it was an opportunity for them to be humanitarians with the charities they supported, as well as the opportunity for most of them to perform, which in real life they would hardly realize. I think we worked well for each other... I made them look good... and they certainly made me look good. And one of the highlights of my life came from The Footlighters. I was always a paid professional to put their shows together. And I was proud to be with them for so long. Well, every year they would honor one of their own. And one of the last years we did the show, they decided to honor me along with my dear dear friend Betty Jo Humiston. It was an honor I will remember forever, having these women love and respect me so much as to make me one of their own. Some memories will never die.

One of my favorite numbers for the Footlighters was where I had Betty Jo Humiston dressed as Miss Piggy and she was in a complete head mask dancing with all the men in tuxedos to "Dancing in the Dark", and I was so very proud of that number. B.J. almost fainted as it was difficult for her to breathe in the mask, but she insisted she wear it since she knew I wanted it in the show. When my B.J.'s health diminished and she finally left this world, her daughter supposedly took care of everything. They never had a public viewing, but the family had a private one at the mortuary. B.J.'s daughter and son-in-law didn't attend as they were on vacation. But because we were so close with B.J. and the rest of the family knew it, they invited Dom and me to the mortuary where she was laid out. Nothing was done to her appearance, meaning her hair was not done, no makeup, and she was laid out on a hospital gurney only covered by a sheet. We all went up to her and I wanted to lighten the situation with the family, who were pretty resolved with the situation at this point. I said, "Look at her. She still has those 'bizams'." Without hesitation her sister Beverly responded, "Why not? She paid enough for them." We all had a great laugh over that. But I miss B.J. more than I realized I would. Not only in The Footlighters, or as a traveler, but as a close friend. I am proud to say I knew her as a lady, and as a great 'dame', and I use that term with tremendous love and affection.

e

I want to talk about our animal family. Before we left NYC, we found a husband for our Pansy, our miniature poodle, and since she was almost all black, we found a husband who was all white, but smaller than she. We had a ceremony with wedding pictures and the works. So it wasn't too long after we arrived that Pansy went into labor. She was often in my lap so when she wanted to get there, and she was getting larger, I would lift her and she would nestle right there, where she seemed most comfortable. Well just in case, we had an enclosed box for birthing in the corner of the living room, and another enclosed box next to the television. She went into each of the boxes, then came out and waited to be picked up for my lap. I didn't think anything of it, so after lifting her, she began to tremble slightly and seemed like she was contracting her stomach and she began licking her private parts. I told Dom to get a towel just in case as she was acting peculiar. He returned with a towel I put under her on my lap and she continued to lick her vagina. In just a few minutes I saw what looked like a light bulb beginning to emerge from her vagina. She didn't cry, she didn't wimper. She kept on licking and finally there was a release of this 'bulb' and she kept licking it until the membrane was gone and I could see it was a moving puppy. We lifted the puppy and Dom took it away into the shedded newspapered shoe box for temporary housing, while Pansy continued to lick again, when a few minutes later, another membrane covered bulb appeared, and she gave birth to a second and last child. I was a mother! At least it felt that way with her having given birth right on my lap. The closest thing I will ever have to birthing my own children. What is amazing when you watch animals doing things like this by instinct, is that they were never taught... it is the most natural thing in the world and I suppose it's as instinctive as any baby or animal when they look at you. They automatically look right into your eyes, as if they already know that is the pathway to your soul. Why not your nose, chin or ear? No... just the eyes... they know!!!

e

At this time we now had 3 dogs, Pansy, Rudy and the 3rd dog we almost didn't name because we were going to find a nice home for him.

We named him Butler because he was more black and white and looked like a butler. By the way, both puppies were boys. When Butler was 7 weeks old we found a proper home for him and we did sell him for very little money. But we were sure he had a good home. Rudy stayed with us for a couple of months, and my mother wanted to take Rudy when she was in California for a visit, so we let her, thinking it would be wonderful for her to have him. Well, my mother was married to Harry Kleinman then, having broken up with Freda a couple of years before. She met Harry at the Elks club and I think I mentioned that before. At any rate after a couple of months, my mother called me and told me something happened with Rudy. My mother and Harry were living in a high- rise condo on Miami Beach, not far from his bakery business. My mother was going someplace with a friend and they took Rudy with them. She started the car and after half a block heard some yelping when she realized that her friend had the leash but the other end of the leash was through the door, which means right before they took off, Rudy jumped out of the car. She jammed on the brake and found Rudy on the passenger side, all bloodied as he was dragged on his chest till he bled. That was it. He would recover but there was no way in hell I would keep him there. Once he recovered I had my mother ship the dog back in a crate and I picked him up at the airport. He has never left our home again. And because of the care that both Dom and I gave to him his actions became a little peculiar. He became very possessive of me and of his food. I could never offer him any food from my fingers, as he would snap the food and possibly bite me. I would have to put it in the palm of my hand. And if I were sitting next to anyone, and I would touch them, he would growl and snap at me, telling me he was jealous. At the same time if anyone touched me on my leg and he was there, again he would snap not at them, but at me for letting them touch me. That happened even if the other person was Dom… he would always be snapping at me. That strange behavior made me feel very important and special. I knew he loved me.

Both Pansy and Rudy had wonderful lives with us. I could never take them to work as I couldn't be sure they wouldn't start barking at some point, but we did take them many places. I remember we brought them once to Tijuana and they let us into Mexico with no problem, but on the return, they didn't want to let the dogs back into the states without health papers, which they never told us when we entered Mexico. I wasn't about to give them up, so we argued for hours before they finally allowed them back. The Mexicans must have realized by how we argued how much the dogs meant to us. They warned us that the next time we needed health cards for both of them in order for them to return with us. How close we came to losing them... wow!

There was a time when Rudy developed an eye abscess very quickly and his eyeball one morning was literally hanging out of its socket. Dom and I immediately took him to the vet. He told us that Rudy would have to have his eye removed. But Dom and I didn't want to do it that day so we told the vet we would talk about it and bring him back. He reminded us we really had no choice. We took Rudy home and that night the phone rang. It was our dear friend Lucille Benson, who came out to California with us in "Walking Happy". Lucille heard the sound of my voice and she asked in her southern accent, "What's the matta', honey? You sound like somethin's wrong." I told her about Rudy, and she responded, "Oh, poor baby. Don't you worry about him. I'll do a treatment on little Rudy." I asked, "What time do you want to see him?" In actuality I had no idea at all that our friend Lucille Benson was a healer in her church. She said, "I don't have to see little Rudy. Don't you worry, he'll be just fine!" We finished our conversation and that was that. I cannot tell you what happened or how she did it, but I swear within 2 days, his eye went back into its socket and the swelling went away. We brought him back to the vet and the vet couldn't believe what he saw. I explained about Lucille, and of course he 'poo-pooed' it saying how the body does strange things to heal itself I don't care what he said because I saw Rudy's eye just about to drop out of its socket, and I know that it was Lucille who cured him. To me she will always be the good white witch. Years later of course, after her success in film, she got to the point that casting people were asking for 'Lucille Benson' types. That is a true sign of success in this business.

Lucille every once in a couple of weeks would ask Dom and me to dinner, either at her home or she would take us out. We of course also had her to dinner at our home many times. I remember once we went to a restaurant I believe in the Diplomat Hotel on Wilshire Boulevard in Westwood. Our waiter was this very lively and talkative fellow who kept telling us that he was going to have his own TV show soon. When

Lucille asked his name he replied, "Richard ... Richard Simmons". Enough said.

e

During our stint in "Holly Golightly" Dom and I made very good friends with Mary Tyler Moore's secretary Barbara Ware, an Afro-American woman who was a dream to be with. Well, after we moved to California she invited us to Mary's house to swim and have lunch every now and then. When Barbara invited us to her church one Sunday, Dom and I decided to invite Lucille to come with us since she said she was a member of that church, not that specific church but of the order. I will never forget it. They asked Lucille to speak and she went up to the podium. Here is this white southern woman in front of hundreds of black faces. She leaned forward and said into the microphone, "There is one God". Well I must tell you the roof practically came off the church. They roared and shouted for what seemed like 10 minutes. She knew just how to reach them. Her warmth knew no color, race, or discriminatory factors, just love. This was yet another of those almost miraculous moments to cherish forever. 'Cherish' ... 'chersh' (southern pronunciation?)... 'church' ... I never thought of that word association before.

Dom and I both adored Lucille and I loved our relationship with her. Many years after this, she went back east to visit her sister, and had a heart attack and unfortunately could not heal herself But she will always be remembered for being Rudy's healer when it seemed impossible, and for being a wonderful friend to the two of us. She certainly is one of the unforgettable ones.

e

As the dogs grew with time, so did their bodies dissipate slightly over the years. Animals give us so much love, it's too bad that God's plan, or whoever she is up there, didn't include a life span equal to ours. They both had different health problems, as Rudy developed a breathing problem and Pansy developed a form of epilepsy. But we took care of them the best we possibly could. Ultimately Rudy's trachea box flattened which caused him to be coughing almost constantly. He was around 12 years old at this time. I took him to Sherman Oaks

Veterniary Office and they told me the only option if we didn't want to put him to sleep was to try an experimental operation where they would try putting 'rings' into his throat to keep his trachea opened. Of course I tried the operation, because I would rather take a chance on something rather than accept the existence of nothing... ending a life that had given me such joy. I brought him into the vet and went home. I remember I was working at the time, and I got back from rehearsal and my mother was visiting. I walked into the kitchen where she and Dom were, and on their faces I saw what I feared... Rudy was gone. I practically fainted, and couldn't stop crying. When I recovered, the following morning I called the vet. He told me that the operation was going on and all of a sudden Rudy came out of the anesthesia looked around and panicked, and had a heart attack. I did that. But was it wrong to at least give him a chance? I couldn't just end his life. In the years after this episode I've had to do just that many times over.

Pansy persevered and continued with her medication to live a very long life for a poodle. She began going blind at 16. By 18 she was blind and could hardly smell, but she still enjoyed eating and even though she couldn't see, she was comforted when we picked her up and sometimes even walking around we would see her wagging her tail. By this time we had moved to our Leghorn home and we had a pool. Because of Pansy we had a board about 8 inches high going from one side of the back patio to the other, preventing her from getting on the pool side of the board. Whenever I put her outside and I was in the kitchen, of course I spent more time watching her than doing anything I was doing in the kitchen, whether it was cooking cleaning reading, anything at all. Dom  loved to do his crossword puzzles from the LA Times. But Dom was very unidirectional, in that he wasn't too good at multi tasking. When I came home from work one day I saw the look on his face. He put Pansy in the back yard and was doing his crossword puzzle. The next thing he knew he couldn't see her on our side of the board. He looked into the pool and Pansy was at the bottom of the pool. He jumped in and got her out and was screaming so much that the neighbors even came to our house. It was too late. I just know that once he put her outside, he went to his puzzle and didn't look up. She must have gotten herself pinned into a corner of the wall and the board which was supposed to block her from the pool. She panicked as she couldn't see, and in her struggle twisted herself to the other side of the board. Walking innocently she must have walked into the pool and I can imagine how she must have felt going under... "They'll save me... they'll save me... " To this day, even with Dom gone, I think I have resented him all these years since then. I never said anything, but I think I still blame him. We should have put her peacefully to sleep long before this happened. Now... even now I cry when I think of Pansy in that pool. "They'll save me... they'll save me..."

e

Remember when I mentioned that Nikki Lewis, from the Footlighters, was the person who first introduced me to Cavalier King Charles Spaniels. She had to get out of her apartment very quickly and she had 2 Cavaliers, Magna (full name Magna Carta) and Bentley. She was desperate when she asked if I could possibly take care of her dogs for just a couple of days until she could find a home for them. Magna was a 'ruby', all red, and Bentley was a tricolored, black and white with some red, so it shouldn't be a problem finding a home for them. Well, I brought them home and Dom was furious. He wouldn't even look at the dogs, which surprised me very much, as I always thought of him as a true animal lover. .. and not the kind that just loves barbeque sauce. Well, the more I got attached to them, the more detached he seemed to get. Finally at the end of the 3rd night, Dom, in anger, shouted, " I know what you want!. You want to keep these dogs yourself" "Yes", I said... "That's what I want... I want to keep these dogs... these dogs I want to keep... yes, that's what I want!". The answer came back at my face, "Well if that's what you want... fine! Then you are going to be the one to take care of them!" What? Did I hear right? He said it was okay as long as I took care of them. He was giving me permission to take them into our home. I couldn't believe it. From that moment on, I could hardly take them away from Dom. He was always fondling them, helping in every possible way to take care of them. It wasn't that he didn't want them in the house. He didn't want to bond with them if they were going to leave our house, and once he committed me to have them, it was all right for him to love them. Dom was truly a remarkable person when it came to our animals ... or any animals for that matter.

e

With all the experience that Harbor College and The Footlighters gave to me under my belt, I was ready to do more once The Carol Burnett Show was over in 1978. By this time I had done the show almost consistently for ten and a half years, with a 2 week exception when I contracted hepatitis. To this day I don't know if I had A, B, or C hepatitis... because I don't know the difference. I know I never contracted it by needle, as I never was a 'user' of needles. I may very well have contracted it from food in Tijuana, as I often went down to Avenue De Revolucion and shop at a store called Sara to buy Homme men's underwear. It was lower priced there than in West Hollywood at Ah, Men or International Male. And it felt so good to be in a foreign country which was only 2 hours drive from LA. Dom and I would make a day of it. We oftentimes would eat the torts from the street venders, thinking nothing of it. Interesting that I caught hepatitis but he did not.

Each year at the end of the season's taping on the C.B. Show, Carol would have a party for everyone connected with the show. It was always, or almost always, catered by Chasen's on Beverly Blvd. in Beverly Hills. We always had their fantastic salads, their renowned Chili, vegetables, and great desserts. We usually had it on our stage at Television City. Following the dinner we would have what we call a 'gag reel' show, which would be taped. Carol would have to sit in a chair on the side of the stage, and just watch, as everyone who wanted to would do a parody of a sketch, a song, or just poke fun of one or more of the celebs who were on the show that season. It always covered a range of very funny, to hysterical, to devastating, but always, ALWAYS, entertainment, and Carol, being the sport she is, would sit there and laugh. You know, I have never ever heard her say a nasty or derogatory word about anyone. That's one of the reasons everyone wanted to work with her. Here's a bit of trivia you might not know. Lucille Ball adored Carol and Lucy was very anal about her comedy, that is to say it was planned and not improvised. So often when Lucy was invited to any guest spots on television, she would ask Carol to go with her, because she understood that Carol instinctively brought out the comedy in another person. Lucy learned that early on as she guested on Carol's show a couple of times. The next time Carol is on an interview program with another person, watch closely. You'll learn a lot from this woman.

The final season of shows were taped without Harvey. Apparently there may have been a tiff, or financial misunderstanding, I don't really know. So Dick Van Dyke was the guest star throughout that final season. Dick was a terrific person, very friendly, but again, his comedy wasn't the same as Harvey's. Harvey's comedy was so very character based, whereas Dick's was more physical, almost always seeming to play himself in different situations. Playing comedy differently does not diminish anyone's ability in this field. I so enjoyed watching both of them attacking a sketch... albeit differently.

A few years ago, I got a call from Chris, Harvey's son. He told me Harvey was at UCLA Hospital and it was quite serious. He thought if I wanted to I should go by and see him. Apparently there were only about 3 male dancers that he especially liked and I was one of them. I immediately went to the hospital. Harvey was in intensive care. I buzzed outside and they just let me in. I was greeted by his present wife, who asked, "Who are you?". I told her I was one of the dancers from the Carol Burnett Show and she asked who told me to come there. I said, "Chris". She asked, "Chris who?". I said, "His son, Chris." She rolled her eyes back and said, "Oh". Then she left the room. Harvey was already gone, as he seemed to be staring in the direction of the television that was on, but with no response. I took his hand and began talking to him. I really can't say whether the squeezes I got from him was a reaction to my talking, or just an automatic muscular 'tick', so I can't say he really knew I was there. But I knew it and that was good enough for me. Harvey died a few days later, and I did go to the memorial in Pacific Palisades. Chris, his son, was very grateful that I saw him in the hospital and happy I was at the memorial. He was a special talent, Harvey Korman. One of those you can never forget.

e

I had started teaching tap almost as soon as I got to LA. I used to teach these classes at the Greek Theatre stage for only $.50 a class. That is the students paid $.50... we were paid nothing. My partner Dom also began teaching jazz there. We then switched over to regular classes at the Falcon Studios on Hollywood Boulevard, in Hollywood. After a couple of years we both changed teaching studios to the Moro-Landis Studios at Vineland and Ventura in North Hollywood. I always considered myself a better jazz dancer than a tap dancer, but I hated the exercises so tap was always easier for me to teach. I was more of a 'soft-shoe' tap teacher than a rhythm tap teacher. I appreciate the sounds that those rhythm tappers make, but all too often their upper bodies look like crap. Give me the Donald O'Connors, Gene Kellys, and Fred Astaires... not the 'hip-hop' versions of tap. Dancing has to be with the entire body... not just from the knees down. I was never really a popular tap teacher, but my students were loyal and inspirational to me. And that's all I felt I needed at the time. Of course I have my regulars whom I adore, Johanna, Robert,].].. Barbara, Elaine, and some others. I still consider them friends, and all the while, I am choreographing new material in my tap classes, so they were making my mind work for me.

And even though I never considered myself a ballet dancer I've been taking or trying to take one or two classes a week for several years now. It may be depressing that I'm not dancing the way I used to when I was younger, but at least I am getting my body moving, and at an older age, I suppose that is all we can wish for. Of course I love getting to class when Kate Kahn, probably the brightest of my female friends, Audrey Trent, married to one of the most successful Hollywood dancers, Jerry, and Lysa Kline, who herself was highly successful in films, are present, because with them there it becomes a friendly coffee clutch without the coffee. So at this age we share in our aches and pains, and remedies... one of the perks in getting older is to share these things with surviving performers.

When the Carol Burnett Show ended in 1978, I wasn't sure what was going to happen to my career, if anything. But very soon after we finished our last taping, I was offered the job to choreograph a new show called "Festival", which would be directed by Wayne Bryan, whom I never met before. The show was to star Gregory Harrison and Brian 'Stokes' Mitchell, (later starring in 'Trapper John'), and

Stephanie Zimbalist from 'Remington Steele' fame. The writers of the music, lyrics, and book were Stephen Downs and Randal Martin. My assistant was a terrific dancer named Sonja Haney... no relation to the ice skater. The other Broadway notables in this show were Michael Rupert ("Falsettos" and "Mail"), Bill Hutton ("Joseph and the Amazing Technicolor Dreamcoat"), and Roxann Parker ("Moulin Rouge!"). The cast was great to work with and they all showed up very well here at the Las Palmas Theatre in Hollywood. As an interesting note, on opening night, I got a very special gift from Gregory that he had me open in front of the entire cast. It was a huge black dildo, which I still have, and which is still unused. I did happen to catch a glimpse of Greg's body while he was changing clothes once, and the similarity to his gift to me was awesome.

Every single review that came out featured one of our dancers named Robin Taylor, who was a spectacular actor, singer, and dancer, and made more out of everything I gave her to do, than I would ever imagine. Consequently she was always pointed out in the reviews and write-ups. She had a dance with Stokes, just the two of them, that was so fast and furious... that at the very end, in one split second she went from standing on her feet next to him to jumping up onto his chest with her legs wrapped around him and they both finished in a pose so the audience basically saw two pictures, one with both of them standing and the other in the final pose. I don't even know how they did it, but I asked to try it and they did. When we played the Ford Theatre in D.C., Stokes was replaced by Leon Stewart, Bill Hutton was replaced by John Windsor and Stephanie was replaced by Maureen McNamara. I'm sure they had other professional obligations. When we went to New York with the show, Frank Levy the producer told us that Universal was looking for a show to back that year. "Best Little Whorehouse" and ours were the two shows Universal was looking at. Frank told us that if they chose 'Whorehouse', we couldn't run. Well Universal backed "Whorehouse" so we couldn't afford to stay in NY. But at least we got there. Ah, the 'business' of 'show' ...

I almost choreographed a show starring Martha Raye and the Hudson Brothers. Frank Levy produced "Festival" and he also saw a show I choreographed for Harbor College, so he asked me to choreograph "Minnie's Boys". He did warn me that he hired Stockton

Briggle to direct the show and he, Stockton, wanted his boyfriend to choreograph it, but he was sure once I started working with him that he would like me enough to keep me on. So I went to work one day and met with Martha and the Hudson Brothers and began to do what I was hired to do. I never saw Stockton that day, but heard that he automatically went to Frank and told him he just could not work with me. And that was that! Frank came to me apologetically and explained that since Stockton insisted, I had to go. It's quite interesting to me that sometimes the jobs we get... are not the jobs we get.

But before I turned around I began getting other choreography jobs. One of which was for Jerry Gordon who was directing a musical about Jewish immigrants. The show was called "Ferguson, The Tailor". It was to star Roslyn Kind, Barbra Streisand's sister, and Peter Kevoian. If anyone is lucky enough to work with Roz, jump at the chance. She is a delight to be with. She absorbs like a sponge. And many musical critics have said her voice is more like a musical instrument than is her sister's. Peter also was great in his role as Ferguson, always humble and very touching in his portrayal. 'Ferguson's' music was composed by Carol Weiss, who also has her own Musical Theatre Workshop. The show was fun to do and it was very educational dealing with the immigrants coming to America after the turn of the century. We also had wonderful character actors like Dorothy Constantine and Paul Keith, who couldn't have been more humorous in this piece, with funny lines like, "It's not a bad sausage", a line I have used many times since. And the end still brought a tear to your eye. I remember that I did a waltz in the show, and had great dancers like Cheryl Baxter, Tina Paradiso, Cornelia Whitcomb, and Lloyd Gordon to name a few. Anyway, I liked what I came up with and thought it was appropriate for the show. We did the show at the Beverly Hills Playhouse, a small theatre on Robertson in Beverly Hills. Well, years later, and I'm talking about at least 20 years later, I went back to see another show at that same theatre. The woman at the box office said, "You look a little familiar to me... I wish I could remember where I know you from.". Then a little later she came up to me and asked if I ever choreographed a show years ago at that theatre. I told her I did and reminded her it was "Ferguson, the Tailor", and she immediately said, " That's where I know you from!. I still remember that beautiful waltz you did in that show... I never forgot it." When

144

someone tells you something like that, about something you did years before, there is no better reward than the way that person has made you feel at that moment. I still beam!

Shortly after "Ferguson" I was hired to choreograph an original 'hot tub therapy' musical called "Walls". It was written by Jonna Gault, produced by her husband Milton Phillips, directed by Al Rossi, and starred Patti Karr and Dick Patterson. This is the show that first introduced me to Patti Karr whom I mentioned before as covering many of the roles that Chita and Gwen played on Broadway. My assistant for this show was one of my favorite dance partners from the CB Show, Bobbie Bates. We rehearsed here in LA first, then we played the Burt Reynolds Theatre in Jupiter Florida, before we returned to play here. I remember they put us up at a fabulous 2-bedroom condo in Jupiter, overlooking the ocean. That didn't matter too much as we got up very early in the morning and by the time we returned to the condo, when we looked out at the ocean, all we could see was black. I think that is why even today I'd prefer having a view of the city or even the freeway, because it is always alive with life, whenever you look at it. The producer made arrangements to video a copy of the show, and I was to get $2500 to have my work put on video. I have no idea what Al, the director was supposed to get. It was really important to me to try to get a copy of this show because it was my first truly professional Equity contract as a choreographer. Milton Phillips came to me and asked if I would give the money back to him for a copy of the show. Of course I said yes. It's called 'kick-back' and not too legal, but the show meant more to me than the money. So at the end of the run in Jupiter Milton asked me to go to his house. I went and had the check with me. He asked if I had it and asked me for it. I asked when I would get the copy of the show. He said I would have it opening night. So I told him he'd get the check opening night. He was so upset that he threw me out of his house. I suppose the same happened with the director, but I don't know for sure. All I know is that we were told immediately that we were both being replaced. The choreography was to be taken over by my dance captain. And Milton hired a woman from NYC, Miriam Fond, to take over the direction. Well we all left Jupiter, and after another 2 weeks, one of which included one week's rehearsals for "Walls" for the preparation of the LA opening, I got a call from Janna's secretary telling me, "Well, we're ready for you and Al to come back to rehearsals. We just wanted to get the cast more prepared for you.". Apparently they were not happy with whatever it was that the other director and my dance captain came up with, so they liked what we had more than what they were doing. I came back to watch one of the rehearsals and sat in the balcony. Afterwards I went down to the stage and was introduced to Miriam Fond, the soon to be ex-director of the show. As soon as I met her, I loved her. She carried a real New York attitude and I loved it. So I asked her if I could talk to her. She had no idea she was being replaced ... that's how this producer 'works' apparently. She was so taken with my honesty about her being replaced, and appreciated my telling her so very much, that we established a very special bond that remains today, although she lives in NY and I live in CA. And since then I have learned she is very funny, talented, and loves theatre and dance. She performs and directs cabarets and shows often, and I will not visit NYC without seeing her. That's the one good thing that came from my connection with "Walls", other than the work itself and the alliances I made doing the show. An interesting note is that Faith Prince was hired in a small role when we did the show in LA. I never did get a copy of the show, so at the time, I just put the check in the bank. I would really like to have gotten a copy for my own personal possession ... and I suppose for my ego.

e

In 1980, Carlton Johnson, one of the dancers on the CB Show, got a gig to choreograph "The Blues Brothers" starring John Belushi and Dan Aykroyd. He asked if I would like to do a little 'bit' in the film. Of course I agreed. The scene took place in Bob's Country Bunker, and I wore a red cap and was tap dancing like a drunk on a little table, until I fell off. It was a simple bit which Carlton let me choreograph since he was not a tapper. We shot the scene which had what seemed like hundreds of extras in it, and it all went well. Mind you, I was toward the back of all the action so I was not featured, even though I did get principal salary for it. When we finished shooting the scene, I was walking toward my dressing room when John Belushi came up to me and said, "Man, you did a terrific job. You really did. Thanks so much for doing this for us." I was flabbergasted. The star came out of his way to thank me. I didn't even know he noticed what I did in the shot. I thought he had such a rep on being like a drug addict. Perhaps I was wrong. The following Monday I wanted to return the rehearsal tape to Carlton, so I went to Moro-Landis where they were rehearsing another number. I slightly opened the studio door and saw Carlton working with Aretha Franklin. I signaled him to let him know I had the tape, and John and Dan were talking in the far corner of the room next to the windows. The next thing I know John saw me and immediately came over and shook my hand and basically said the same thing he did after I did the shot. Not only did he appreciate what I did right after I did it, but he even remembered it over the weekend. I feel I definitely got him wrong. Whatever the rumors were about his drug practices, he certainly was not practicing them while he worked on this movie. I had a completely new respect for John Belushi, and I am very happy to be wrong again.

Incidentally, Carlton, who was a divine person, certainly acted gay, but was not only married, but was a grandfather as well. He always took care of his wife. Carlton was a joy to be around, always funny, and always exceptionally talented. Ultimately he became victim to the disease going around gays since the 80's. I could not attend his funeral as I was on an international group trip, but I am told from the other dancers who attended that the minister began speaking in a regular tone of voice. But as he got more into his speech, he basically blamed Carlton's death on his show business friends, saying we gave him the disease. The minister made all of Carlton's friends feel extremely awkward. I'm so glad I couldn't be there for that shameful a happening.

Carlton would have been boiling if he were at a service for another friend, only to be put down like that. Carlton was better than that, and we, his show biz friends will always remember his life, not his death.

In 1981 I worked for Alan Johnson who was the choreographer and one of the producers for Mel Brooks' "History of the World, Part 1". The movie is made up of several scenes from the world's history, and the one we were involved in was 'The Inquisition", a musical parody of the Spanish Inquisition done a-la Mel Brooks style. We didn't deal directly with Mel, but it was obvious he had his handle on every part of the movie, as he should, being the director. In watching Ronny Graham and Jackie Mason run the first part of this episode over and over again, mainly because Jackie couldn't lip sync too well, it was evident how much patience Mel had with the actors. And we dancers had a ball at the fun choreography. Dom and I both danced in it, and I even had a little solo line, although the voice was not mine, having been pre-recorded long before we were ever hired... "Who knows, Tuck? You might win a buck." The dancers were scheduled to work through a certain date, and the second A.D. (assistant director) kept reassuring us that we would be paid through that date. Well, we must have been very good as we finished that number about a week ahead of schedule. I was the deputy so when some of the dancers came to me to make sure we were paid through the last date on our contract, I reassured them what the A.D. kept telling me. During the last week we were supposed to be paid, there were a couple of big auditions that occurred so the dancers wanted to be reassured. When we were paid, we were not paid for that last week and I got many calls from the other dancers demanding that we should be paid what we were told. In my naivite, I didn't realize that Alan Johnson was also one of the producers, so when he called me to ask what I was complaining about, I said, "Alan, this shouldn't even concern you... ". Then when I tried to explain what had happened he said, "I don't want to hear another word about it!" And abruptly hung up on me. It was a long time since that job that Alan even talked to me and I felt awful about that. I liked Alan very much and he was a fantastic choreographer. Just look at Shirley MacLaine's act and the part she does dancing in other choreographer's style and you'll see how versatile and clever he is. The next time I worked for Alan wasn't until 1995 when I danced in another Mel Brooks film, "Dracula, Dead and Loving It". All that time because of a huge misunderstanding! Again, time and friendship lost for no reason.

e

At this time I was beginning to dance in more films. Dom and I both danced in "Aria" which was shot at the famous Madonna Inn in San Luis Obispo. Each room is decorated in a uniquely different motif The room we had was the Victorian room, all pink and a bit froufrou. If you want to have a laugh, look at their rooms at http:// www.madonnainn. com/features.php.

148

e

I received a call from Tab Hunter. He told me I was recommended to him to choreograph two numbers for his film, "Lust In The Dust". We made an agreement and in about a week I flew to Albuquerque and was picked up and driven to Santa Fe to meet with the people I was to work with. As soon as I got there I was taken to the makeup testing room and introduced to Divine, who became an immediate cult success by literally eating dog doodoo in the film "Pink Flamingos". He was not wearing any makeup nor was he wearing a wig.

Just this balding, probably middle aged, silver haired (what he had left), very charming and intelligent man. We sat and talked and every once in a while he would throw in, "Look, she's still in that chair!" What he was referring to was Lainie Kazan, as she was sitting being made up for her own makeup test. Apparently Divine was waiting for her to finish before he could start, and he must have been waiting a while before my arrival. His interruptions with the same remark were  quite amusing. In essence what he wanted from me was for me not to do dance steps for him. He wanted to 'hot-dog', which was like improvising at the same time 'selling' his number with physical movements... but no steps. His song was called 'These Lips Were Made For Kissin'' and we did have fun with it. In the number besides giving him a few arm gestures, all he wanted was for me to tell him where and when to be in a certain location for the cameras. After talking it over with Tab, I agreed. Now I'm told that Lainie's role was originally intended for Chita Rivera. But Lainie certainly did the role justice. Now with Lainie, she wanted a little more of a structured number for her song, "South Of My Border". In the number her boyfriend (Henry Silva) was just killed and is laying over the bar. We begin her number with her wailing over his body, then suddenly throwing him off the bar into a chair when she begins singing. I had this idea of seating her on top of Henry Silva's lap and using his arms as hers during part of the song... of course she is the one manipulating his arms. When I explained it to her, we both laughed a lot. It still makes me giggle when I think of the moment I thought of it. And that was my only connection with Tab Hunter, although I wouldn't have minded a different connection. He was still such a good looking man. And even though the film was directed by Paul Bartel, I watched Tab and he had a say in everything Paul did, probably to the dismay of Paul himself. But whatever he suggested, I agreed with, so I thought that Tab would also make a good director. Now Tab is gone also.

e

A little while after this I got a call from Michael Nesmith (The Monkeys). I went in to talk to him about my choreographing his "Eldorado to the Moon" for a TV video called 'Television Parts Home Companion'. We came up with the concept of his little girl at three stages of her life, so I used Michelle Elkin, a fantastic dancer who used to take my tap class, Tina Caspary, another fantastic dancer who later had her own dance company and school, and of course my personal joy, Bobbie Bates, whom I try using whenever possible. The number came out okay, but I had no control over the final editing. I thought it looked fine, but...

e

"Babes" was the first sitcom I ever choreographed. It starred Wendie Jo Sperber, Lesley Boone, and Susan Peretz, all very talented girls. The series follows babes a trio of plump siblings who had other things on their mind besides their weight: like work, relationships, popularity, and starting a family. I only choreographed one episode, but Dolly Parton was a guest star. I choreographed a simple number that the girls and Dolly were to do together. Dolly came to me and requested, "Honey, please don't give me dance steps". I said, "Dolly, they are very simple". And she replied again, "Please don't give me any dance steps". It became evident that she knew her limitations. It's always interesting to me that some great singers, do not make the musical connections with their bodies. I not only respect that self-acknowledgement, but I praise it. Allowing Dolly to do her own thing, only enhanced the number. If

I made her learn the steps, she would have been self-conscious. It was a thrill and a learning experience to work with her. I still adore Dolly Parton.

e

Twiggy is another star I choreographed a number for, this time a tap number. She did a short lived sitcom in '91 called "Princesses". I did the number in one of the episodes where she danced down a spiral staircase. What a doll she was to work with.

e

A few years later Fran Drescher starred in a successful sitcom called, "The Nanny". I choreographed three of them. I remember one particular episode when I staged a ballroom dance between Fran and Charles Shaughnessy. For the tech run-through, Fran had to do an interview at the same time, so I got to dance her part opposite Charles because her stand-in never learned it. Need I say that I loved that? On one occasion I was supposed to stage a number with Fran in a football locker room. I kept being told that they would give me time to work with Fran. I waited and waited, and was told the same thing... "You'll have time to work with her". Finally they announced that they would camera block the number. I told them, she doesn't know it because I never got her. So they took a 10 minute break and I finally got Fran to learn a simplified number since I had such limited time. Renee Taylor was in one of the audience seats watching us. After I blocked the number for Fran, she called me over. "Listen, kid, have you seen 'Bermuda Avenue Triangle' yet?" I said, "No but I want to see it". Renee and her husband Joseph Bologna wrote and were appearing in this play with Bea Arthur. Renee replied to me, "Well Joe wants to put in a dancing bow number at the end of the show. Can you see the matinee tomorrow?" "Sure, I'd love to". So the following day I went to the Canon Theatre where it was playing. I saw the matinee and worked with the cast right afterwards. They only gave me one half an hour, since the cast was doing another show that evening. Everyone worked on their feet, except for Bea. She just stood on the side and watched. So I stayed for the next show and during the bows everything went awry. Once the audience left the theatre, the cast remained onstage, everyone except Bea. She stormed onto the stage saying, "I didn't know it was going in tonight! No one told me it was going in tonight!" Well, I suppose because of that they never did the musical bows again. I thought Bea was angry at me but she wasn't.

e

Years later, my good friend Billy Goldenberg invited me to come to the Booth Theatre in NYC because he was onstage playing for Bea's Show, "Just Between Friends". I loved the show and Bea's naturalness in front of a live audience. After the show Billy brought me into Bea's dressing room to meet her. Now years before this, I told Billy about the episode with "Bermuda Avenue Triangle", but assumed he forgot that I told him the story. Well when Bea said, "I am so happy to meet you, Stan", Billy said, "Oh Bea, you met Stan before". I was dying. He continued to tell her about the episode with Renee and Joe. I wanted to disappear. Then Bea said, "What you don't know, Stan, is that I was not getting along with them at that time. We had a disagreement". Thank God! I was so afraid she was going to hate me for what had happened.

e

A short time later I got to see Elaine Stritch in her ''At Liberty'', another socko performance by this true Broadway legend. But the main difference I noticed was that when Elaine spoke, if someone in the audience began to react or applaud at the mention of a city or something that was close to them, Elaine kept on going like a locomotive. In Bea's act, she mentioned a city and she interrupted her script by talking directly to the person making the slight outburst... EG., "It's a great place, isn't it?", if she mentioned his city. So I felt Bea's was the more personable act where she made the audience part of the act, whereas the audience was just an audience in Elaine's act. At least that's what I felt... and I was surprised about Bea's informality.

And she did make me feel great meeting her after her performance. I really thank my friend Billy Goldenberg for that.

Incidentally Billy had a sister, Lucy, who was smarter than a whip, but had difficulty walking from a childhood disease. Bea would go to see her in Long Island where Lucy was housed often, and sometimes even by herself, if Billy was working. That is a very good person. Lucy liked me very much from the time we met when Billy was playing rehearsal piano for "High Spirits". I was visiting Billy once and we went out to see his sister in Long Island. She was always happy to see me, and so was I to see her. Once we arrived without her expecting us, and she took us to see her bedroom. There on the wall was a poster of "Bajour", my second Broadway show, and on it she had written, "Starring Stan Mazin". She knew I was only in the chorus, but she followed my career as well. Billy was a terrific brother to her, and could not have done more than he did. We all miss her so much now that she is gone... Billy also I am so sorry to say.

e

I've also done some daring stunts on my own while traveling to various parts of the world in my travel career. I remember on my first trip to New Zealand and Australia I traveled with other travel agents on a familiarization trip, and we flew first class to Auckland. While we were there I was talking with some of the agents and mentioned that I was very afraid of heights. One of them told me I should face my fear by doing something outrageous like bungee jumping or skydiving. I immediately told them that if I were to do anything like that I would only trust a company called A.J. Hackett, as they were doing that for such a long time, and I had seen some footage on TV about their company. I knew they were based in Queenstown, New Zealand in the South Island. As we traveled around, I suppose the 'news' of my bungee jumping had spread throughout our tour, so by the time we got to Queenstown, the group was just waiting for me to bungee jump. They kept telling me that I had to do it for each of them. I really did not anticipate even attempting to do anything like that. I remember the day before, when we all went on a boat trip through Milford Sound. It was drizzling the entire day, and the captain passed me by and I stopped him, "Captain, is it always raining like this here?" He looked out the windows, turned to me and said, "In Milford Sound, this is a clear day." We laughed and he continued along his way. The following morning we were heading toward the airport, and the group told the guide not to forget to stop so I could bungee jump from the nearby bridge. I told her to please not change any plans as we had a plane to catch. She told me that they had built in the time for me for the jump.

My stomach then began to churn. We stopped at the closest bridge, the Kawarau Bridge, which was closed to traffic and only used for A.J. Hackett's Bungee Jump business. After much coaching I paid my fee, which I must add is non- refundable if you should change your mind. This young man brought me out to the middle of this unused bridge and sat me down on the ground, while he wrapped towels around by ankles. The wind was blowing very hard. And this was a very young man. He told me as he proceeded that they can drop me any length over or into the water, and he asked if I wanted my head to go into the water. Remember the wind was blowing like mad. I said, "My head? Don't do that! I just did my hair!" He didn't get my joke, just slowed up for a second then continued tying my ankles. Then he helped stand me up and with my legs almost shackled together I very slowly inched my way to the edge of the bridge where I had to manipulate my body through this cross beam to get me to the outside edge of the bridge. There were 2 planks going out above the river below. He put me on one of them and attached the bungee cord to my legs. Now they weigh you in before you even get out to the bridge. And I noticed that the bungee cord I was given was heavier than the ones used right before me. I also have to say that I watched a program before I left for the

trip about botched bungee accidents. I saw a kid do bungee at a carnival and he bounced right up and hit his head on the platform he leaped from. I saw another guy jump out of a helicopter and you saw he bounced once, then on the second bounce you saw the knot in his ankles untie and he dropped to his death over a canyon. I was not looking forward to this at all. But I was on the spot as all of the other travel agents were looking up to me at this moment in time, and there is something within me about responsibility to others that propels me onward. So I edged my way toward the end of the plank, all the while holding onto the back bar without letting go. Now there were outlines of your two feet just showing ¾ of your feet with your toes over the edge of the plank. I was bending so low gripping the bar behind me in such a way that he said to let go and re-grip so I could be more secure on my feet. I did so and it really scared me to let go of that bar for even a fraction of a second to re-grip. They said, "Do not look down!", but you have to see that your feet are in the outline on the plank, so you must look down. You see your toes over the board and see the vast space below before you see the water underneath. As soon as I re-gripped the bar, he started to count backwards from 5. I was certain it would be slow like... 5... 4... 3... 2... 1, so the jumper could muster the courage to jump. Now I really wanted to not jump but with all the agents watching me, I had to do it. So he finally began counting so quickly... 5,4,3,2, that on the count of ' 1' I screamed and bent my knees, pushed off and did the highest and best swan dive I ever did in my life. All the while I was sailing down toward the river, I had all those thoughts in my mind about the bungee accidents, and I began wondering if I was still connected to the bridge with the bungee... it seemed a very long time and then finally, I felt the tug of the cord and I knew I was connected to the earth. I began to swing over the water, and my head did not get wet, so it was true that they can decide whether or not you want to get your head wet. When I stopped swinging, they finally lowered me to a boat that came by to pick me up and take me to the shore. I had to climb huge boulders to get to the walkway, which would slowly get me back to the top of the bridge. All the while I was walking I kept thinking, "God, I hope I didn't soil my pants". Well that was a successful jump and it made every one of the travel agents very happy. And I think I was the happiest not to disappoint them.

As for my fear of heights issue, I don't believe this took care of it, because a few months later I took a few people on a Grand Canyon tour and while there we saw an lmax movie of the discovery of the Grand Canyon. In the film, native Americans were walking along the edge of the canyon and each time one of them went toward it, I held my breath and grabbed the sides of my chair... a true sign of acrophobia ... and this was a movie.

On another flight I was talking to the stewardess about my bungee jump and she told me if I really wanted to get over my fear, I should skydive from a plane.

155

Ok! I thought to myself that will never happen. Well, on another cruise I took friends and clients on a 2 week New Zealand to Australia cruise on a Royal Caribbean Cruise Line. While we were in Auckland, a few of us did a little side trip to Rotorua where they were sky diving. You guessed it! I signed up to do a sky dive and the same conditions applied... once you pay... no refund! So I was given a parachute and harness over it, and another guest and I went in this little Cessna, similar to the ones in which I had my flying lessons when I did Mitzi's act in Vegas. We each had a professional skydiver that would be attached to us. I had this short cute young man who, in the plane attached himself to my back straps. I told him if I had a baby I would name it after him. He laughed. We were the first to leave the plane. He reached over and opened the door and there was one little pedal used to enter the plane. He said to step on the pedal, and when he tapped my shoulder, just lean forward. Again the wind was very strong with the plane door opened. He said that we would not be doing a somersault so just relax and he'll do everything. Well, he must have underestimated my weight because once he tapped me on the shoulder and I leaned out of the plane, all the while thinking, "What the fuck am I doing?", we both rolled out of the plane and did one complete somersault before flattening out parallel to the ground with him on top of me. What a great feeling that was, falling toward the earth with no motor sounds, just the wind whizzing by my ears. When we got closer to the ground he opened the chute and directed us toward the landing sight. And surprisingly we landed on our feet without having to fall. It was an interesting experience and the only part that was scary was falling out of the plane. Bungee jumping I felt was much more of a challenge. But yet... I'm still afraid of heights.

e

Mark Wilson, a pretty famous magician called me into his office to talk to me about the prospect of directing his show in Seoul, Korea. He was not going to appear in the show but we would hire someone to do the magic and also hire dancers and use some of the Korean dancers already working in the line at the Sheraton Walker Hill Hotel there. Altogether we could only hire 8 dancers and the lead magician had to come from those hired. We had auditions, and Vernon Willett was hired to be the magician... a good looking guy who was easy to work with. And Mark insisted that I bring his secretary along to make sure everything was 'copasetic'. Understanding that Korean men, as in many Asian and Middle Eastern countries, look down on their women, the secretary asked me if she could helm the business meetings with the Korean backers. I didn't think too much about it and agreed. The Koreans were not too h, appy with that but the more I realized the way they were toward their women, the more I wanted Suzie to 'man' the meetings. I remember flying on Korean Airlines and entering the plane before take-off. It was like entering a cloud of cigarette smoke. Apparently Koreans can smoke whenever and wherever they like in their country and on their planes. Remember this was 1987. Getting off the plane and driving to the hotel, the scent that I smelled was not an unpleasant one then, but later on it became quite unpleasant. The scent... Kimchi, a traditional Korean fermented side dish make of vegetables, mostly cabbage, with a variety of seasonings. This dish kept the Koreans going for 500 years. It is a staple of Korean diet. But after a few days, the aroma does get to you. During rehearsals I had an interpreter. I needed to because when I auditioned the girls in there line who danced in all their shows, none of them spoke any English. These girls always did the first 30 or 40 minutes of the shows at the Sheraton. They were beautiful women and they all played the giant drums in the show. And I believe it is true that Korean women are the most beautiful women in the world. Interesting enough during the 3 weeks we had there I only saw 2 handsome Korean men, and one of them was doing a commercial at our hotel. And so I was allowed to use 8 of their 22 women and used 4 of their men in our show. For the opening I chose the overture to "High Spirits" one of my favorite Broadway overtures of all time. Now everynight after rehearsals there was nowhere to go to eat, so I went back to my room and ordered room service. They had a dish on the menu called Soba, which was stir-fried noodles and it was absolutely delicious. I'm not crazy about Japanese food and would probably be the last person on earth to say, "Let's go for Sushi!", but those noodles were fantastic. Working with the Korean dancers was a challenge, because I soon found out that they were not so different from my "Footlighters" divas, all seeing what the other ones were doing and how they were used in the show. It became evident that they had petty dealings with one another like jealousy, envy, etc. And trying to get them to understand my sense of humor I would often just 'faint' and fall on the floor after something went very wrong during rehearsals. Some of them began to get it, but others remained stern and quite serious. When we opened, I had some things made for the people in the show as opening gifts. I heard the Koreans loved baseball caps, so I had jackets with the name of the show on the back made and gave them to the Americans in the show, and had baseball caps with each of the Koreans' names on the caps and gave them to the others. Well, apparently no one has ever given them gifts like that, so they softened to me quite a bit. I wanted skimpier costumes for them to wear for the opening, so their legs would show, and they all fought me on that. They did do it for the opening, but when I saw the show 2 days later, they were much more covered up. Okay, they won on that request.

While we were in Seoul, there was a small section of the city called Itaiwon, where there was a Dunkin' Donuts, believe it or not. I loved Dunkin Donuts, so I went there often. And that was the area where they also sold those 'rip-off' athletic shoes dirt cheap. I would walk down the street and I would shout to them, "Six Dollar Reebok? Six Dollar Reebok?", and I would get sellers to sell me what appeared to be Reeboks for $6.00. Of course I knew they were fake. The only colors they had for men were white or black. On one afternoon I was asking for red shoes and they would laugh at me because in their own country men never wore red. But I did find one pair of shoes in my size that was in a very faint aqua shade, so I purchased them. They had a Reeboks label on them. Once I got back to the state, the first time I wore them and took them off, the insoles stuck to my socks and the insole underneath read "LA Gear". I find often that the treasures I find are not related to how much I pay for them, but are treasures nonetheless by the way I acquire them.

In 1991, I auditioned and danced in the MTV's 10th Anniversary Television Special. What was 'special' about this special was that Michael Jackson was the star, and Vince Paterson was the choreographer. I think there were about 45 dancers that were hired and we were put into smaller groups of eight, ten or twelve, each group doing different choreography. I was in the 'elder' group, as we wore long robes and didn't do very much dancing, just arm and body movements ... and I was the youngest of the elders, I think. On our very first rehearsal, and

I will never forget it, Vince was speaking to the entire dance ensemble. He was honoring the older dancers that were working as he was growing up, and he told everyone in the room to look at the elders, because that is the level of professionalism they should be striving toward ... and that we the elders deserved all their respect. I think he put it in better words, but we were all quite honored to be talked about with that esteem. Our first day on the set was the first time we saw Michael Jackson. He walked from one group of dancers to the other until he spoke to all of us, first introducing himself to us, then thanking us for doing the show. He proved to be a true gentleman, and I thought that was fantastic. I was so proud to be there. That was the show in which he introduced "Black or White", another one of his hits. To watch Michael work was like another course in dance education. His attention to detail, and just knowing what works for him was an amazing thing to watch. And Vince was wonderful with Michael. A nice combination that I'm sure made Vince proud of this work also. To be gratified in what we do in work, or play, in life... what could be more rewarding!

e

Another audition that I enjoyed was one for Kenny Ortega, the director/ choreographer of "Newsies", a musical film based on the New York City newsboy strike of 1899. I'm getting a little older now that I am 52, so I wasn't hired to dance with the younger dancers. Aside from dancing, we were also hired to work with the stunt coordinator Michael Vendrell, so once the real stunt people were hired he would know what to give them. Well, we worked with Michael for 2 weeks and we were told that we would be finished with the job. The stunt coordinator was so impressed with the way we picked up what he gave us to do, that he went to the producers and asked that we should do the stunt work instead of hiring the more expensive stunt people. They came down to watch our stunt rehearsals and lo and behold hired all of us for the stunt work. And Kenny used us also in the big number with all the dancers on the street.

Kenny was so great to work for and he must have liked what I did because a few years after "Newsies" he hired me to dance in a video film for the first opening of the first Wynn Hotel in Las Vegas, to be shown on their 90 foot screen. During the day the screen is just a huge waterfall, but at night they show these 8 minute videos while certain props or set pieces come out of the little lake that the screen sits in. Since I was featured as a detective in our film and there were only the two of us, the girl and I in it, I wanted to see it. So Dom and I made a reservation at the Wynn, the second night after they opened to the public. I paid $358 for that room for that night. We hadn't been to Vegas for several years, so I wanted to see some shows that we've missed. That night we saw "O" at the Bellagio right across the street, and saw the late show of "KA" at the MGM Grand. By the time I got back to the hotel the time was 1215am. I went to the desk to ask what time they were showing the film again that night. The man said, they stop showing them at midnight. Midnight? You mean I missed seeing my own video when that really was the only reason we came to Las Vegas!?! I felt very bad. Dom went up to bed, and I went to the casino. The few games I liked were Blackjack, Caribbean Poker, and Let It Ride. So I dejectedly sat down at the Let It Ride table. The dealer was this very sweet young black girl (I hate the expression of 'Afro-American' when I've been to Africa more often than anyone I know), who immediately saw the sad look on my face. When she asked what was wrong, I told her I came to see the videos on the outside screen and she asked, "Why, honey?" "Well, I was in one of them so I was curious." "Which one were you in?" "Ocean Club." "Don't tell me you were the detective, Lou Diamond?" "Yes, that was me." She immediately turned to the other dealers on the floor and shouted, "You won't believe this, but I got Lou Diamond at my table!" I asked how come she knew who I played. She told me that a week before the hotel opened, the dealers and other workers in the hotel were invited to a showing of the videos. She then said, "You were terrific, I enjoyed them so much... thanks!" Well her enthusiasm certainly made me feel like a million bucks. I was acknowledged for being a principal, after all I was told they auditioned thousands of people across the country for these videos before they hired me. I couldn't afford to spend another night there so I had to be content with the dealer's 'review'. Other friends saw the videos afterwards and said I looked great. Over the years since, I have learned that compliments from your friends should be a little tempered and not always trusted completely. After all, they are your friends.

160

Several years ago a good friend of ours, Phylis Felsot, came to a fund-raiser at The Group Rep, our Equity waiver theatre. Phylis owned a women's boutique called Le Chat in Manhattan Beach. At the theatre she won a raffle for a trip for two to Hawaii. The man she came with was Russell Tate, a very bright, intellectual gay man whom Dom and I have known for years. She felt obligated to ask him to go with her, which he could not do. Then she asked me. I said yes and even though we spent a week together traveling through Baja, and even roomed together there as well as on a riverboat boat trip in southern France, I didn't want to room with her again. So I used my Time Share at RCI and I happened to be right across the street from Phylis' hotel, at the time I believe it was an Outrigger. My hotel was the Waikiki Banyan. We tried to change our return from 7 nights to 5 nights, but we were told we had to stay for the total of the 7 nights. On about the 3rd night, we went for dinner and I even had a Hawaiian drink, as I usually don't drink alcohol unless it is a blended drink, since as I stated before I hate the taste of alcohol. So it must have been about 1am by the time I dropped off Phylis at her hotel. I went back to my hotel, and took my 2 Exedrin PM pills, which I have been doing nightly since Birl, one of the dancers on the Carol Burnett Show, told me that with them I would get a more peaceful sleep. I'm a very restless sleeper normally. The condo I had been given was terrific... I had a living room, then huge double doors into a bedroom, then another door into the bathroom and in the bathroom, another door to the commode. Well, after sleeping for about 2 hours, I got up to pee, and I am opening doors, closing doors, opening another door, and closing it, and finally after closing the last door, I opened my eyes and saw the number of my condo in big bold letters... '1501'. I look down and I am completely naked as I always sleep 'au naturale'. I look back up to the 1501 on the door and pray, "Please let this be a dream... PLEASE, LET THIS BE A DREAM!" It is not a dream and I look down the hall of the Waikiki Banyan Hotel & Condo, and there is nothing on the table opposite the elevators ... that is, no telephone in the hall. I am at the end of my hall, so the only door next to mine is the emergency exit door to the outside fire escape. It must be 330am and I am afraid to knock on any of the other room numbers. I don't go out the fire escape as I might get locked out of that door, 15 flights up. What to do? I decide I have to take the elevator down to the lobby. There are 4 elevators on one side of the hallway. The one that comes first is the first elevator of the 4. I enter and push the lobby button. In the upper corner of the elevator is a camera, which I wave to in case someone is in the security room manning the cameras. No such luck. The elevator moves at a super slow motion speed, or so it seems to me... 14... 14 and a half... 13... 13 and a half, and so on. The doors finally open to the lobby about what seems like 2 hours later and 'jewels' in hand I step to the L-shaped lobby desk where I am standing on the bottom of the T shaped counter. Surprisingly around the longer length of the counter toward the other end which is outside the lobby, if you understand that often Hawaii lobbies are inside/outside, the man behind the counter is taking care of an exiting family. Of course they cannot see that I am naked because I have the counter or desk covering my lower part of my body. All the while I am cupping my 'jewels' in my hand, and expecting that other people will be arriving down the elevators any second. I do realize that probably on the beach, there is so much nudity, but this is my nudity, so I particularly feel vulnerable. After another length of time that also seems interminable, the family leaves and the night desk man comes over to me and asks, "Can I help you?" "Yes, I am standing here butt naked as I've locked myself out of my room." He immediately leans over the desk to see that I have no clothes on and says quite calmly, "Please wait here, I'll be right back." Please wait here??? Where am I going to go??? He returns very quickly with a towel and a spare key to my room. I return to my room and find it difficult to go to sleep. That is the end of that story but not the end of the tale. When I returned back to California, I told my story to Lynn Cartwright at our theatre. This of course happened before her breakdown in NYC. After relating my feelings she said to me in her charming southern accent, "Well, Stan, that just goes to show you. You should never go to sleep with out something to wear. You never know when you might be involved in a fire or some emergency like that." No, Lynn, I don't think that is the moral of this story. I'm more inclined to think the moral is, "Never go to sleep alone!"

e

Every once in a while I accept a job teaching for other dance conventions. I was on the dance faculty of Danny Hoctor's Dance Conventions and traveled for several weeks over a two year period. I taught tap dancing. I remember how the faculty had to dance in the faculty show for all the convention students. The facility often would wax the floor so it would look great, but at the same time would make it extremely slippery in tap or ballet shoes. I've never fallen but sometimes I would be dancing 'very tightly' so as not to slip, consequently making the number less 'dancy' and more technical. We were in Myrtle Beach, South Carolina and the room was a huge convention center. While I was teaching, there was a large group of dancers near the stage making a tremendous amount of noise. I called out to one of the girls and after requesting them to be quiet several different times finally shouted, "You! You with the red shirt! Would you please leave the auditorium, your group is making so much noise it is impeding my class." Well what I didn't know was this person was the teacher that brought this huge group to the convention. I was not sorry for my outburst, so after Danny Hoctor's wife found out about it, I never was asked back to teach for them. I just do not understand why they wouldn't stand up for me in that situation... but I assume the adage, "Money talks and bullshit walks" came into play. Apparently dance teachers who bring their student to dance conventions are more important than the teachers teaching at those conventions. Another lesson perhaps.

e

On another occasion I was teaching at another dance affair at Disneyland in Orange County, this time NOT for Danny Hoctor. A good friend of mine, Madelyn Clark, who has a dance studio in North Hollywood was also teaching, so we made arrangements to drive down together. Now we taught ate the first day and had to teach early in the morning the following day so Madelyn and I decided we would share a cheap motel room instead of making the treck back and forth in each direction. So we did indeed find a very cheap motel with 2 beds and went to sleep. In the middle of the night I heard her shout, "Who's there? Who is that?" I opened my eyes and saw a dark figure in the room in silhouette with the light coming in from the window, and I added very butch-like, "Who is it? What are you doing here?" The meek voice responded while being very startled, "I'm sorry... I must have gotten in the wrong room." With that the man made a rapid exit through the same door in which he entered. It was a very exciting evening and something to talk about, but Madelyn and I were not hurt so it was an experience I'd like not to repeat. By the way, Madelyn and I are friends with no benefits... just thought I'd mention that.

e

In about 1993 during one of my travel group trips to the Western Caribbean, I met the pianist up in the lounge. He was a much older gentleman but very talented, and had worked on this particular ship for quite a while. I told him I was enjoying the trip, and he asked, "Why don't you come again and you can work as a dance host? They probably won't pay you anything, but at least you will get your trip free. And the work is easy. All you have to do is dance with a few ladies for an hour at night." I thought to myself, "An hour a night, and I get a 7-day cruise out of it? Why not?" So he told me to contact a woman named Tina when I returned to the states. Tina said they needed dance hosts very badly and she would keep me in mind. About 2 weeks later I got a call from Tina and we made arrangements for me to be a dance host on a Western Caribbean cruise for one week only. I wasn't doing anything at that time so it was like a vacation without having to pay for it. Let me tell you that my friend the pianist was wrong. One hour a night? Not by a long shot. Right after dinner I had to go to the lounge and begin work. It was like punching a time clock. I would have to go over to women who were sitting alone, women who were sitting with other women, and once I danced with them, they wanted more and more of my time. I even went to women who were not dancing but who were sitting with their husbands. I would ask them, "Would you care to dance?" They would invariably look at their husbands who would either give an affirmative nod or say, "Sure she would. Go ahead and dance with her." As soon as we got to the dance floor, they would always say words to the effect of, "Thank you so much for asking. I just love to dance, and my husband hates it." So I became sort of a hero of a type. But the hours were from around 7 to like 1130pm, and believe me, by that time at night I was 'shvitzing' ... sweating for people who don't know the slang Yiddish expression. A good workout but very much under-expected. There was one mysterious woman who approached me time and again to dance with her. She was pretty good but she would never tell me her name. I kept asking and she remained evasive saying things like, "I won't tell you my name because you might know me", or "I'll tell you my name when we leave the ship. I don't want anyone onboard to know I am here." The only thing I could get from her is that she was from Waco, Texas. Very mysterious indeed! So the last day as we were leaving I looked for her and found her, and she finally gave me her card with only her name on it. It wasn't until I got back to my home to look her up, and found she was an artist in Waco. I never honestly heard her name before, but since this was a Western Caribbean cruise and many of the clients were from Texas, it was possible that her name could have been known to them. So I believe that to me, the mystery was more interesting than the truth that came out of it at the end. But it did keep me going all week with wonder. Before that week was over, Tina contacted me and asked me if I could remain onboard for another few weeks. Apparently someone gave me a good report and she wanted to take advantage of it. I didn't have any other jobs immediately so I explained that I could only do it for one more week, as I had work commitments. I did not have work commitments but if I didn't get back to LA, I couldn't even look for a performing job. She thanked me very much and got me to stay for one more week and it was work but still fun. She did try getting me to stay after that, but I just couldn't. So that was my job as a dance host. I guess because of my professional dancing career and such, I was a better dance partner than most, but I don't think I want to do it again. Perhaps if I were to retire...

e

Perhaps... the word, 'perhaps', is probably in my opinion the most beautiful word in the English language. 'PERHAPS'. It makes your lips curl at the beginning with a wisp of air coming through them only to close lightly on the 'ps' with more air going out, and then it's gone... into the air. I've always loved the word ... 'perhaps' ... just another of my very strange thoughts.

e

My partner Dom came from a fairly large family. His mother Rose had four sons and one daughter. Out of the 4 sons, 2 were gay, Dom and his older brother Vito. There was one brother older than Vito, Richard, and the youngest was Franklin.

The only daughter was Lillian. Lillian was very much like her mother Rose, very 'spiritual' and pious. They went to church religiously and celebrated all the religious holidays. The family never ever talked about the relationship between Dom and me. Dom's brother Vito looked like a truck driver, and to look at him no one would ever suspect he was gay. Yet he designed curtains and redid upholstery for the stars. Some of his clients were Barbara Stanwyck and Nancy Sinatra Sr. to name just a couple. He became very close to his clients and to the day she died he maintained a very close relationship with Barbara. Vito was of course always friendly and warm to me.

I'm not sure myself how much of Vito or Dom's private life the rest of the family were aware of. Vito and I often talked about how 'square' they were. Vito loved to eat and he loved to cook Italian food. He was a bit overweight and developed Diabetes which Dom and I never knew until later in Vito's life. Vito had several friends but to my knowledge I'm unaware of any sexual relations that he had for any length of time. He

loved what is called 'rough trade' in gay slang. I'm sure he probably paid for it as well, but that's his business. Whatever anyone does outside of my awareness, that's fine with me as long as I don't hear anyone is hurt. Dom's mother Rose decided to move to California and spend her last years with her two favorite sons, Vito and Dom. She began living with Dom and me and that lasted for quite a while. And Rose would always say to me when Dom wasn't around, "When are you going to find yourself a girlfriend?" I'm sure that was her way of denying the situation. I would often retaliate by saying, "When Dom finds one, I will." I didn't want to be too rude... she must have known the situation because Dom and I had been living together since 1965. During the Carol Burnett days, I took up sewing with a sewing machine. I'm good at following directions, so as long as I didn't read ahead, I learned to make my own dance pants, because I used stretchable polyester, so if they didn't fit quite right, they could still stretch to my body. I even made a few polyester suits, but I feel my greatest accomplishment was making a dress for Rose that she loved so much, Dom buried her in it when she died. I always felt honored by that even though I never felt so close that I could speak honestly about our relationship to her.

e

Another of Vito's close friends in New York was Richard Granger. Richard had his own woman's clothing line that he designed years before. He also was Ginger Rogers' escort whenever Ginger went anywhere socially. So he felt very close to her. When she died Richard was very upset that she didn't leave him anything... she left it all to her mother and the church, I believe Christian Science. Anyway on one of our New York trips, Vito was there and he introduced Richard to both Dom and me. Now that Richard is in his later years, he had developed into a very 'needy' person. That is, he is alone and longs for the friendship of anyone who is able to give it to him. His friends of his age are mostly deceased and he certainly feels the loneliness. My Dom on the other hand has no patience for anything like that, so Richard made an immediate attachment to me. After all, I am a Pisces and am much more agreeable to people than Sagittarius Domenic. Richard was a very good friend of Ray Arnett who was Liberace's right hand man (was Liberace left handed?... a little joke here) and Ray was about

20 years older than I. Richard in talking to me about someone else, used to say things like, "Well, he's not OUR age", as if we were both the same age. It took him years to even begin to acknowledge that he was 'a couple of years' older than me. Now that several of Richard's contemporaries have passed on including Vito and Ray, he makes sure he calls me every day at least once, and sometimes two and three times a day. You see, years ago Vito's diabetes got so bad that he had to have some of his toes removed for circulation problems. It was only about 2 years after that that he died from the disease. So Richard's circle of friends is getting smaller and smaller. One of his best friends today is Patricia Clarkson, an actor whom I adore. She lives down the street from him and sees him quite often when she is not working and is in town. Now Richard knows how much I love her so oftentimes when I call, if she is at his apartment he will put her on the phone with me. I haven't met her yet, but hopefully will if we are at all in the same city at the same time. But I understand where Richard Granger is coming from so I try being as tolerant as I can through his lack of hearing, and the hacking cough that he continues to have during our conversations. I do love Richard and I feel for all the things he now misses. He unfortunately passed just recently, but I am proud to have been his friend for so very long. I think I am a good person.

e

By the way I danced in a group of 4 men on The Dean Martin Show that was choreographed by Ed Kerrigan (who Juliet Prowse nicknamed "Kitty Kerrigan" when they worked together) and the star of the number was Ginger Rogers. This was before I met Richard Granger so I couldn't talk to her about him. She was another dream to work with, and while we rehearsed she told us some stories about working with Fred Astaire. She told us, "Fred absolutely hated working with me. He picked up steps right away, and I had to rehearse much more than he did." And she went on to say it was a fluke that the two of them became such a fab dancing duo. She was thankful of course, but Fred never did make her feel too great. I found that to be an interesting observation.

e

While I was doing my first Broadway show, "High Spirits", I became pretty close to Kay Medford. We had friends in common and we lived around the corner from each other, so Kay often invited me to her apartment after she was finished with "Funny Girl" and I was finished with "High Spirits". She did smoke marijuana but I indulged very little since I didn't really care for it too much. Plus the fact that I never really thought it worked on me. To this day I have never purchased weed of any sort. Anyway, Kay invited me to a party that her show was throwing for Barbra Streisand. I remember going with the friends of Kay's and there was great food and everyone was drinking. I also remember when they rolled out this little cart with curtains between the first and second layers of the cart. And they rolled it up to Barbra and as soon as it stopped as if on cue, this little white curly haired dog stuck her head through the curtains, and that was the gift I suppose the show gave to her. She immediately took the dog and named her 'Sadie' from 'I'm Sadie, Sadie, Married Lady'. Soon afterwards, and you have to imagine her saying it with her New York accent, because I know you won't get it from what I'm writing, she said, "I can't believe it. When I first saw this dog, I knew this dog was mine... I just knew it. I looked at this dog and said this is my dog, I can't believe it. I love her!" I told you it loses a lot of the translation when it doesn't come from her mouth. I don't know Barbra... I never met Barbra... She doesn't even know I exist, but I wanted some sort of connection with her even for a split second, so as I was leaving I went by her table, and leaned down to kiss her on the cheek and told her I was a friend of Kay's and I wished her a Happy Birthday. For a second I'm sure I saw an expression on her face like, "Is this guy crazy?" Then I left. The only other time I was in near proximity to her was during a rehearsal of the first special she did titled, "My Name Is Barbra" in 1965. Our rehearsal pianist for "High Spirits" was Billy Goldenberg. He also wrote the dance music for the show. Billy developed into a fantastic composer conductor, arranger, and songwriter. We became close friends on HS and still maintain that friendship through all these years. We aren't in contact too often, but whenever we see each other we are like long lost family, and I truly love that with Billy. He has done so many things, but one of his famous scores is that of "Queen of the Stardust Ballroom". His credits are endless, but my favorite is the theme for the movie "Grasshopper" starring Jacqueline Bisset. Anyway, Billy wrote a song that Barbra was singing on her special, so he invited me to a rehearsal of that part of the special (I believe he wrote the song, and I know he was assistant musical director as well). She walked downstage supported by an entire orchestra and it was to be shot live. So during this rehearsal she started to sing one of the songs and in the middle she stopped and said that one of the instruments was not playing the right note. The conductor asked the musician in question what note he played, and he was playing what was written, but the conductor corrected his piece of music to the correct note. How anyone who is hearing an entire orchestra playing, can pick out one instrument that was playing one off-key note, I will never be able to figure out. But Barbra knew. I think that is probably why she seems to get a bad rap. She is a perfectionist and she really does know her business. I never forgot that afternoon and I don't think I ever will.

Billy Goldenberg, a couple of years ago, was involved with another version of "Ballroom" in the desert, so I got to see him there for the last time. Billy died a short while after and the world lost another hugely talented person, and I lost an enormously beloved friend. We can never spend enough time telling those we love how much they mean to us.

e

In between shows in New York I danced in "The Boyfriend" at Papermill Playhouse in Jersey. Sandy Duncan was in the show, and the star playing 'Polly' was none other than Barbara Cook. As well as being the Tango Boy in the show, the producers arranged for me to drive Barbara to the Theatre each night. So we became kind of like friends, and I was in awe. It is no secret that over the years Barbara has gotten very 'healthy' and this show was the beginning of her growth in that direction. But such a talent one would have to travel quite a ways to see another like her. After that show finished, I didn't see her for about 20 years or so. Finally she was going to appear out here in West Hollywood at Studio One, so Dom and I got tickets as soon as we could. After her performance there were several people waiting to see her in her dressing room. I waited patiently until the couple before me went in and I had to wait in the doorway. I was watching Barbara and while she was talking to the couple before me, she would look at me every once in a while and then go back to looking at them. Finally they left and she quizzically looked at me as I approached her. I started to say, "Barbara, I was your driver in "The Boyfriend" and was also the Tango... " I couldn't finish my sentence. She threw her hands in the air and screamed, "Oh shit, Stan... I remember you". She gave me the biggest hug, we chatted and I was again on that cloud nine that I strive to capture whenever possible. Another miracle of a moment that I have cherished in my not so long life! At least 'not so long' ... then... I miss her to this very day.

e

In the 90's I got a call from Pia Zadora. She was going to be doing a show in Florida called "The Shortest Rockette in the World" or a title similar to that, that Walter Painter was supposed to choreograph and possibly direct, and she asked me to coach her in tap. I was already teaching by that time so someone suggested she call me. I went with her to the David Lichine Studio in West Hollywood most of the time for our private classes. I found her to be an absolutely terrific girl, who never wanted to stop working. I had to tell her to take a break or she wouldn't take one. She told me that she was often thought of as a joke, but also said, "People forget that I was in the original "Fiddler On The Roof" as one of the daughters, and you don't get into a show like that for Jerry Robbins if you have no talent!" I found her delightful and talented. During our rehearsal time I was preparing to go to New York for one of my theatre tours so we would have to take like a week and a half off The day came for our last lesson before my trip, and she said, "Oh, wait a second. I forgot this was our last session until you return." She went to her driver and  asked how much cash he had, and he gave her $84.00. She immediately gave it to me and said, "Have a great time, Stan!" And she also gave me a picture of her and her children so I wouldn't forget her while I was away. Now I already got paid so this was like a little gift for my trip.

Well what I did was travel to Atlantic City for a day to see my half sister Denise, whom I also adore, and while there visited Steel Pier, which I used to frequent years before when we lived there. While there I found this booth that made t-shirts and sweatshirts with your own picture on it. So I had a couple of T-shirts made for the kids with the picture of them and their mom on it, and a sweatshirt with the same picture on it for Pia. When I returned she loved my gifts. And we finished our classes and I did hear that the show never came to fruition, but I really appreciated working with Pia Zadora anyway, and have nothing but respect for her as an artist as well as a terrific human being. She never got the credit she truly deserves.

e

I first met Alexandra Billings when she was a young boy named Scotty. Scotty's father was the musical director and teacher at LA Harbor College where I choreographed their summer musicals. Scotty was always coming to rehearsals and the shows, and I loved his mom, actually step- mom, Janet Billings. We, Mrs. Billings and I, were very good friends even to this day. Who knew then that Scotty would turn into this phenomenal actress and teacher who spearheads, or so it seems, the transgender community to acknowledgement for civil and moral rights. After my choreographic summers at Harbor were over, I didn't run into Scotty until years later when Don Grigware, a reviewer with whom I drive to see shows, asked me to go with him to see Alexandra Billings perform. I never put the 2 and 3 together before, so when Alexandra began talking about her early life and her father, Robert Billings, and the musicals at Harbor I woke up to the fact that this was indeed Scotty. After the show we waited to see her and when she saw me she immediately screamed my name and almost began to cry. I was one of the influential ones in her early life, and I was so sorry that I never realized how important a person she really is now. I hope even though I see her rarely, we will always have this special connection. By the way, if I never said so before, Alexandra Billings is one hell of a performer, whether seen in her own act or in the many roles she portrays on television and film. Recently she was one of the cast members of 'Transparency' starring Jeffrey Tambor. I am so impressed with the possibilities all children can achieve when they are allowed the freedom to become what they alone are meant to become.

e

I have another very good friend who is a reviewer and her name is Pat Taylor. She ran a vintage clothing shop in Burbank called Hubba Hubba, and unfortunately she was dealing with Fibromyalgia. Since I gave up smoking many years ago, whenever I see Pat at an opening, we both know that at intermission she will give me a cigarette to smoke, and that will last me until the next time I saw her, which sometimes was a couple of months later. You see, I used to smoke after sex, and now I smoke instead of sex, so I always thanked her for the 'good time'. She always said, "If you weren't gay I would go for you." As a matter of fact the following is a quote that she put in her column in The Tolucan Times. Although my name is not mentioned, she said everyone who knew us and saw us together knew who she was referring to. And this is a conversation that we definitly had. The following is from her column.

Savor life's sparkly gems!

I have a very dear and supportive friend with a heart of gold. I said to him, "If you weren't a gay man, we could've gotten together years ago." He amusingly answered, "If you were a gay man, we definitely would have!"

I file that under "Life's Little Precious Moments!"

I do love Pat but not in the way she might prefer. I have to be true to my body and mind. Fibromyalgia finally took Pat away from us. Whenever I see a show, watch a person smoke a cigarette, and even pass a vintage shop , it ALWAYS reminds me of Pat and our special relationship. Oh, no... they can't take that away from me.

Until a few years ago The Group Rep at the Lonny Chapman Theatre never had air conditioning. The theatre itself is on the ground floor, and being an Equity Waiver theatre, we only have 90 seats. Equity Waiver is not allowed under their rules to have more than 99 seats. We have a large rehearsal room on the second floor above the stage, plus a smaller room opposite that rehearsal space. Every summer our audiences would practically die from the heat as well as the actors... that came out very strangely. The audiences would not die from the actors, but both the audiences and the actors would do so from the heat. You understood me.

I remember when I played Jack, the husband in Neil Simon's "Broadway Bound" and we ran during the summer. The play took place in the winter, so besides wearing a 3 piece suit, I entered wearing a heavy overcoat, a hat, a scarf, and gloves. It was surely difficult to explain the sweat coming from my brow when in the play it was winter. So several years later after many unsuccessful attempts at getting air conditioning put into the theatre, someone had to initiate a fund raising effort for that purpose. I took on the burden and beginning with the membership and then extending the request to supporters of the GRT, I was able to get within $5000 of the $15000 cost to air condition the theatre downstairs. I went to the board and asked them if they would rename the larger rehearsal room upstairs in honor of any person who donated the final $5000. They okay'd my request and I was now on a hunt for the last of the money. I decided to call Bea Busch who was one of the original 13 members of The Lonny Chapman Group Repertory Theatre. She got back to me almost immediately and told me she would love to give the last $5000. I explained to her that the room upstairs was to be named with the name of the final donor. I asked if she wanted the name to be under Bea Busch or Bea Busch Wilcox, her married name. She said she would get back to me, which she did the following day. She said, "I want the room to be named the Stan Mazin Studio." I explained that it must be under her name. Believe me I have no ego large enough to want or need a space named for me. Bea said, "If you want the money, that is what I want. I know how much blood and sweat you've given for that theatre." I went to the board and they approved her request. I then called her back and asked, "Do you mind if we use your name on the studio sign since only members would be seeing it?" She allowed me to use her name and told me she wanted Bea Busch Wilcox on it. So now the sign above that room is, "The Stan Mazin Studio... Always for actors and seekers ... " (her expression not mine) ... "through the kind generosity of Bea Busch Wilcox." I am very proud of that sign especially since both Bea and her husband Clayton are both now gone. Now that Janet Wood has donated $10,000 to be used solely for the purpose of turning The Stan Mazin Studio into a little theatre, and it is now accomplished, the new name of the space is the Janet Wood/Stan Mazin Studio, and we are both very happy with that.

e

My partner Dom and I socially knew Ron Stephenson who cast "Murder, She Wrote". Not very close friends, but from time to time we would see him and his then partner Barry Cherin, whom I had a liaison with during my college days. At that time Ron was very good friends with John Petlock another close friend of mine, and he (Ron) often hired several of the members of The Group Rep for his show. When I got cast in "Broadway Bound" as Jack the husband I told him about it and his response was, "I sure won't miss you in that show! It's one of my favorite shows ever." Needless to say he never came to see our show, which was one of the best shows we've ever put on. I of course was hoping to get a shot at being cast in "Murder" even in a tiny role but that never happened. Another friend of mine told me that when he was asked why he never used my partner or me for his show, his response was, "They're dancers". It's too bad that some casting agents are so close-minded. I think we could have helped each other. Perhaps I am a bitter person inside, but to tell the truth, I have always been angry about that and about Ron. I never confronted him about it which if I were a better person I should have, but I've learned to live with it. It was not a big deal to him, but certainly to Dom and me. I would have felt better probably if he had seen me in the show and didn't care for my portrayal in "Broadway Bound". No, I take that back. It's no doubt better without his seeing me act... but it does still hurt to this day.

e

Bea and Clayton used to travel with me on my group trips. They were truly a joy to be with anytime and anywhere. And what good sports they were. Remember it was Bea who used to accompany me to the Adult films after our music rehearsals on the Carol Burnett Show on Thursday nights. Well on one particular group trip to London and Paris, the entire group went to see the show at Moulin Rouge. After the show, Bea and Clayton and I put the rest of the group on the bus to return to the hotel, and we three went to Pigalle, a questionable area of Paris, to see a sex show. We chose a place that looked fairly seedy enough, and then paid and went in. I believe we ordered some drinks as well. Fairly soon after we arrived the show began. A single woman came onstage and began touching herself. Well, this became quite erotic, until she reached, or at least acted as if she reached, her climax. This 10 minute act was followed by another woman, and after that one, two women came out and played with each other. They were all so beautiful, and between the lighting, the music, and the slow movements, it was quite tantalizing. Then a man and a woman came out and slowly began oral stimulation, followed by intercourse, and it was quite evident no one was faking the act. The couple was wearing what looked like the same wedding bands, and the three of us spoke of how great that would be for a married couple... if they were exhibitionists, getting paid to make love to their spouse. Well what happens with these acts is that they perform in one club, then immediately when they finish their 'act' they go to the club down the street, so they can be paid by going to 5, 6 or more clubs doing their act. Bea, Clayton, and I were so impressed with the quality of these acts that we decided to stay again, and sure enough, the same people returned for another set of acts. But this time, it was evident that this was the final performance of the evening for the married couple, because when they faked their orgasm, they did not fake their orgasm. Just at the right time, he exited his wife's love canal and we, the audience saw his explosion, which they usually don't do if they have more shows to do that night. It was all quite impressive as well as titillating.

Being a travel agent, I try giving my clients, and friends, an opportunity to go somewhere or see something that no other travel agent would ever show them, and something they would probably not do if they were traveling alone. But it is a chance for their curiosity to be satisfied, even at the expense of being revolted by an act. Sometimes it is good to find out even through disgust what might or might not be interesting to someone. And that curiosity is always interesting to me.

e

I remember on a trip to Bangkok with about 14 persons, mostly ladies, we were being driven to the hotel from the airport on our arrival. I was sitting next to our guide and asked her quietly if there was an area we should not go to with the group. She told me to avoid at all cost the Padding area. Now I've been told that that area was where they had sex shows and people for rent both for women and men. So when we arrived at the hotel, the guide went in to the hotel to pick up our room keys, and she told us to stay in the van until she returned. As soon as she left I turned to the group and explained that I wanted to offer them what no other travel agent I know would offer them. I asked who might be interested in seeing a sex show, but they would be very safe because I would be there with the group. Five of the ladies raised their hands and we made arrangements to meet in the lobby at 930pm that night. We rented a large taxi and proceeded to Padding. We walked around for a while, and every place was a little different. One of the clubs went so far as to have a 'menu' with pictures of the individual girls and the props they used in their specialty acts. Another was a 'boys club' where you could rent boys from the parading group of young Bangkok boys in their bathing suits. We decided to go to the club with the 'menu' out front. There we were the 6 of us, five of my ladies and myself We went in and were ushered to stools at the bar overlooking the stage. It was still very early and I was told that the men don't arrive to 'service' the girls until about midnight. As soon as we sat down and ordered drinks, one of the ladies, but not the ones who worked onstage there, approached one of my ladies and asked if she could buy the lady a drink. The ladies around her told the lady who was asking that she didn't want any more company, so the lady doing the asking left our group's company and they weren't bothered in that respect any more. There was a lady performing her act on the stage when we arrived. She had a paddle and she set up what looked like very lightweight bowling pins, and with the use of a paddle and a ball that she rolled on the floor proceeded to hit the ball with the paddle and knock as many pins down as she could. Did I mention the fact that she did this without using her hands, other than placing the paddle inside her female parts by hand? Can I ever look at bowling the same way now? When she was finished, the ladies jaws looked like the audience during 'Springtime for Hitler' in "The Producers". Another woman came out onto the stage, with a fishbowl and a goldfish swimming around in it. Somehow and I have no idea how, she ingested the live fish with much of the water in the bowl, without ingesting it down her throat. That alone was worth the price of admission. Then after doing a little gymnastic routine to music, placed herself over the bowl and proceeded to expel the water from her body, and finally expel the living fish which continued to swim in the bowl as before her act began. My jaw had dropped at this point. The acts went on and the final act that was performed was a woman who had a slew of sparklers that she lit and placed in every orifice of her body. Had this act ruined any expectation I would ever have on Fourth of July fireworks in the future? It was after this act that I was staring at the stage in awe when I received a sudden tap on the shoulder. Some of the ladies were there and said, "I think we can leave now." To me the show was just getting interesting. I couldn't imagine what they could possibly do to outdo what we had already seen. We were only there for about half an hour. We paid our bill and I took them back to our hotel. I'm sure they won't soon forget that evening.

e

After returning to the hotel, I ran into Dana Landers, one of my gay male travelers. I told him what we had seen and told him about the rent boy dub. He asked if I would possibly go back to the club and pick out a rent boy for him. I asked him to come along and he wanted me to surprise him. So being the good samaritan I am I said, "Sure". Off I went again to the Padding area of Bangkok to look for that boys club. I found it and went inside. While sitting there for at least half an hour, I counted about 22 boys that took turns on tiny platforms in the 4 corners of the room. All the boys were in bathing suits and each had a little label with a number on it. About every 2 minutes or so the boys would rotate to the next platform while new boys came onto the first platform. They would look a little like 'go-go' boys as they sort of danced on the platforms. I felt like King Farook sitting back and viewing the possible 'rentees' from the choices given. Dana told me he wanted a little more beef or muscle on his boy and hairy would be an asset, as most of the Thai boys are thin and hairless. The money in Thailand is the Baht. I forget what the value was but basically once you choose the boy, you give the number of the boy on his tag to the waiter or maitre'd. He brings the boy to your table and you talk or play charades (since most of them spoke no or little English) until you both agree on a price for him to leave the club. Once you decide, the club adds 300 baht to your bar bill (about $10 or $15 at that time) and you pay that and meet the boy at the entrance. I brought the boy back to our hotel and hand delivered him to Dana and told Dana what he would charge as well as what the taxi costs were, and the 300 baht to take him out of the club. After going with someone outside the club, the boys often come back to the club to make more money. I assume they had a great time since the following morning Dana thanked me profusely for choosing that particular boy. That ended my 'King Farook' days, but it was quite an experience. I'm much too shy to do something like that for myself but I love to have a mission, and since it wasn't for me, I can be as bold as the next person.

e

Since we're 'talking dirty', let me tell you about another 2 sex shows I took some friends to. While visiting Rio on a different tour, Jay Silverman and his wife, Janet Wood, an original member in GRT, decided they wanted to experience a sex show. So we made arrangements to go that night. We left the hotel about 10pm and hailed a taxi. Since most of the drivers speak no English, or at least at that time they didn't, I again played charades and with my broken Spanish, remember Brazil speaks Portuguese, I made a ring with my right index finger and thumb, and shoved my left index finger through it and kept saying, "Funcion. Funcion.", which I thought meant 'show'. Certainly that must be the universal sign for 'fucking', I thought. Well the driver seemed to understand what we wanted and he took us to a club. I told them to wait in the taxi and I would look inside to make sure it wasn't a different kind of show. When I opened the door, all I saw was a bunch of women dancing with each other on the dance floor. It looked like a lesbian club because there were no men that I could see. I went back to the taxi and told the man again, "Funcion, Funcion", and made the same gesture as before. He nodded his head, "Yes" and proceeded to mimic my hand gesture. He pointed at his watch and we all seemed to believe that the show would be later, so we went into the club. We were given a table right near the stage, and meanwhile the girls were dancing and going to their tables and talking. One of the girls passed our table and put her cigarettes on the end of our table, and Janet thought that had to be some sort of 'sign'. Anyway we all had at least one drink and we stayed there for about an hour or so. When nothing was happening we said we had better start to go, when all of a sudden, the music stopped, and the girls all left the stage empty. Then a guy came out from backstage and laid out a pretty large rug. We all thought, "This must be it". A man and woman came out and took off their underwear. They weren't particularly beautiful, but we weren't there to look at museum pieces. Never taking their eyes off the audience the woman bent down and gave the man head so he could get an erection. Once he had one, he entered her in one position and began humping away. They would stay in that position for about 45 seconds or so, never looking at each other and only staring out at the house, each in a different direction, and then change their position like clockwork and begin staring in another direction... all rehearsed but not enjoyed... not even a smile... just a clinical fuck. After their non related sex act was over, we decided that was it, and we left. I'm sure Janet and Jay's love making would have made more of a show, but they never invited me over to watch.

On another trip a few years later, Jay & Janet and I were again looking for another sex show, but this time we were in Barcelona. We found a show that advertised as a human circus, but were assured this was our type of show. So we finally got there and after a little wait the show began. The girls primarily were dressed in very slinky outfits like the animals they were portraying. One of the funniest bits was when the lion tamer, a pretty good looking man, was 'taming' 2 tigers. At one point he was on all fours facing the audience and the girls were on all fours facing away from us and they butted their asses into the sides of his face, making his lips 'purse'. It was one of the funniest visuals I've ever seen and that made us laugh through the rest of the show. The graphic sex acts weren't as visual as the one act in Rio or especially the beautiful love making in Paris. But I've also learned to take love where you find it... don't be blind it's... all around you... everywhere ... BUT WHERE???

e

In the early to mid 90's, not mine... but time's ... I began doing a little 'standing in' for TV shows like "Flying Blind" and "The George Carlin Show". In "Flying Blind" I stood in for Corey Parker, the lead opposite Tea Leoni. A 'stand-in' is the person who usually watches the actor go to their different marks on the stage, so when the laborious task of standing in for the cameras occurs, that is our job... to stand there in silence. Every once in a while when the star, or actor has to be someplace we get to read the lines. Needless to say this was my favorite part. The only time I was singled out in the show was when they asked me if I wanted to be the 'ooze man', which meant at one point I would have this oozing liquid coming from different parts of my body. Of course I accepted,, and was even given credit that week for being the 'Ooze Man'. On another occasion I remember I had a last minute inspiration to have liposuction done to my 'love handles'... I mean, I didn't think anyone should be that much in love. So I decided impulsively on having it done on a Saturday, not realizing how sore you are for almost a week afterward. On that Monday the scene I was standing in for had Corey and Tea crawling all over each other in bed, so when I had to do that with Tea's stand-in, I was sore as hell. .. I mean in great pain... I mean it must have felt like 'giving birth' pain. But I did survive, after all, dancers are used to pain, having to use 'new' muscles in different ways each time we are given a new dance number.

On "The George Carlin Show" I stood in for Alex Rocco. Now I believe Alex was like 6'2" or so, and I am only 5'10", but they let me stand in for him anyway. I must tell you that on every single show, before we began, George Carlin would go up to each table of extras on the bar set and introduce himself and welcome them to his show. That is something I've never forgotten. He was a real gentleman as well as a real gentle man. Now both he and Alex are gone. It's too bad that 'clock' can't be stopped whenever we want.

Not all stars are as gracious as George Carlin. I once danced in a show that starred Julia Louis-Dreyfus. As a matter of fact it was one of her own shows. We were in close quarters and it would have taken her 30 seconds to come to the dancers and welcome us. She had and still has a reputation of being a doll to work with. I'm not aware that she ever said hello to any of us, so I have never felt she was a warm person. Perhaps she is to the stars she works with, but I feel I can always tell what a person is like by the way they treat the 'underlings'. There is a huge difference between that behavior and the behavior of people like Carol Burnett, Betty Grable, Pia Zadora, Cheryl Ladd, and hundreds of others I've had the true pleasure of working with.

e

In 1995 Alan Johnson finally hired me again for Mel Brooks', "Dracula: Dead and Loving It". He hadn't hired me since the fiasco in "History of the World, Part I". I was partnered with a lovely English dancer named Anne McVey. Nothing out of the ordinary happened but we had a great time.

e

In 1997, my agent called me. In NYC we had open auditions for all the shows. Now in California we needed 'dance agents' to even find out about most auditions... a whole different ball game. Anyway he told me that there was an opportunity to work for one week for $200 and even though it was not under union scale, he thought we should know that if we did take this job, there was a possibility it might lead to a better job. Well, I wasn't getting any younger and no one was breaking down my door for a job, so I decided along with some other good union people to do the job. We worked for an English choreographer named Lynne Hockney. I suppose because we were professional dancers working below minimum, the entire project was a little 'hush-hush'. But I was working with great dancers... Kris Andersson, Bobbie Bates, Aaron Cash, Anne Fletcher (alias 'Mama'), Ed Forsyth, Andie Hicks, Scott Hislop, Lisa Ratzin, and Julene Renee. We were only told that we were doing the number to be put on video and shown to the director to see if he wanted to use the number. In a way, even the choreographer was auditioning. Well, we did the number and waited. In just about a week or so, I was called and told the director James Cameron loved the number and wanted to hire all of us. You guessed it, the film was "Titanic". Now if people aren't too familiar with the movie, they might ask if we danced in the ballroom sequence. There was no dancing in the ballroom sequence! We danced Irish style dancing in steerage, when Leonardo di Caprio asked Kate Winslet to go downstairs with him to see a 'real party'. So we flew to San Diego and were picked up by a van and taken to the new sound stages south of Rosarito Beach in Baja. On the first trip when we arrived on location we were greeted by our choreographer, Lynne Hockney. The first words out of her mouth after telling us to please listen as this was important was, "If anyone

182

asks you to go into the tank, tell them you don't go into the tank, you are a dancer!" She went on to say that the 'tank' was the stage that was filled with water, and since they didn't give the $40 a day extras proper breaks, everyone who was in the tank got sick... either stomach illness, eye infections, throat infections, diarrhea, and lots of other health problems. They then took us to the makeup and costume stage. In front was an all white van with a red cross on it, and it looked vintage, so I assumed it was for the set. But in many chairs near the ambulance were seated all these extras who looked like death since they had the melted wax covering their eyebrows, beards, eyelashes, and hair and hats. These were the bodies used in one of the final scenes where the boats were going through the bodies looking for survivors. Only these extras were truly sick and waiting for that same ancient ambulance to drive them to the hospital, while it picked up other extras from the hospital and took them back to the set. So it was a constant relay of extras to and from the hospital, mostly because the production crew would not give them bathroom breaks.

In our first rehearsal on the stage, in the 'steerage' stage, that is, we stood around a lot watching the principals. It was so interesting especially watching Leonardo. He smoked like mad, and if one didn't know who he was, he would be standing a little 'fey' smoking every chance he got. I was told he played a lot of pranks on the other principals. But when he worked, he certainly knew his business. At one point one of the extras was supposed to spill a glass of wine (water) on Kate Winslet. Now James Cameron already had a reputation that he isn't too cordial with actors other than the real principals. There was so much noise and commotion that is was difficult for us to even know what was being said. Well, James Cameron said to someone close to the extra and Kate, "When I say ACTION ... " and went on turning his head to another person. Well the extra heard the word 'Action' and he spilled the drink as he thought he was supposed to. James Cameron let out more 4 letter words than I thought existed, plus some. "You stupid asshole... you son-of-a-bitch... I didn't say 'Action'! I was giving directions!" The poor $40 a day player felt like crap after being bawled out in front of everyone. It really isn't necessary to belittle people working for you to make your point. I never felt that, and if I ever do anything like that I hope someone stops me short.

The housing they gave us was wonderful. We were each given our own condominium, which was at least 1 or 2 bedrooms with full kitchens. The condo building was just 1 block from Puerto Nuevo, commonly called Lobster Village, or the "Lobster Capital of Baja", because every restaurant specialized in local lobsters, boiled, broiled, and even deep fried. They are also pan-fried in lard, so the meat stays soft and tender.

After the first week we were off for a few days, so most of us came home. The next time we were there I drove my car, so I would have it there. Once we returned we were given another day off after a few more days at work. On this day off five of us including Bobbie Bates, Scott Hislop, and Andie Hicks and an extra who I believe wrote a travel guide, got into my car and we spent the day in Ensenada. We just relaxed, ate, drank and drove home relatively early but it was still very dark. I'm driving on the toll way, which is their expressway.

The road is a split highway with 2 lanes in each direction and in between is a center median of grass about 10 feet wide that has a huge dip in the middle of it. I repeat, it is pitch black outside with no moon. I'm cruising about 60 to 65 miles an hour and all of a sudden I see approaching my car what looks like the outline of an all black truck with no lights at all. It seemed to be approaching me but that is because my speed was so fast and he was traveling about 3 miles an hour and there was no moon that night so I came upon him very quickly. To prevent an immediate crash, I jerked the wheel to the left since we were both in the right lane. My car began to skid and I then turned the wheel to the right so my car wouldn't roll into the center ravine. In turning the wheel abruptly to the right my car was in a 360 degree spin to the right in front of the slow moving truck and my car ultimately rolled into the right ravine. We had crashed and the truck without any lights kept on going without even stopping. Once I realized we were all okay at that moment, since my car stayed upright, I tried after a few minutes to drive it out of the ravine. It would not even budge so I got out of the car and looked at the left rear wheel, and the entire wheel was lying parallel to the road, when the normal position of a car wheel is perpendicular to the road. My whole axle broke so there was no way my car was moving. I was just so grateful that that we were alive. The extra who was with us said he was going to flag down a bus, which he did with Scott and Andie. Bobbie stayed with me. We had to call the Mexican Authority who handled the tollway. We had no idea what the number was so Bobbie and I walked across the freeway and found a bar nearby and got the number from them. We called and very quickly the Mexican police came. Now I have heard horrific stories about how the Mexican police treat Americans, but I have to tell you they were absolutely wonderful to me. They arranged for my car to be towed to a nearby station, and they made sure we were taken back to our condominium south of Rosarito Beach. And because I paid whatever the small toll fee was for the use of the tollway, I was not charged anything... so our only inconvenience besides our aches and bruises was that I didn't have the use of my car. It took several days, but I was insured at that time by AAA Auto Insurance. Triple A made arrangements for my car to be towed all the way to San Diego, where they could examine the car. Within days they gave me a $15,500 check as they said my car was totaled. I will never complain about the cost of auto insurance again.

During our last week of shooting, we were finally beginning to shoot our number, on a stage that was constantly filled with the smoke they used for the scene. Remember this was the steerage part of the ship, below. The extras were complaining that they weren't being given bathroom breaks. There had to be at least 200 to 300 extras, plus the ten of us dancers, and at one point the Second Assistant Director (2nd AD.) made an announcement to all the extras. Basically he shouted through his megaphone that they were not to leave the set until they were told, or they would be reprimanded very harshly if they did. By this time I had had it with the production and how they treated the extras. I had nothing to lose as I was on a principal contract. I started shouting back at the AD. in an even tone and as I continued talking I got louder and louder hoping that James Cameron himself would hear me. I started by saying, "Excuse me. If you want the extras to listen to you, they should be treated with respect." Then the more I got into it the more excited I became. "They've been working their asses off for you and not even been given pee breaks. You wouldn't treat animals this way. How dare you treat people like this." It didn't seem to last too long but the 2nd AD. did allow them to take breaks after that. I have no idea if James Cameron ever heard what I said. All I know is that for days after that, many of the extras that I never even met were coming up to me and thanking me for speaking out for them. So they made me feel like I did a good thing... like I was some sort of hero. I do believe everyone would enjoy being a hero... at least I do.

As an added addendum, when "Titanic" finally came out on DVD, I had to watch that part of the movie frame by frame in order to see myself I was wearing a brown bowler hat and layered clothing so I looked even 35 pounds heavier than normal. I did see myself walking across the camera with a woman behind 2 guys who were arm wrestling... and again dancing (but could only see that part of the film frame by frame)... then saw my face partially hidden by a pole behind Leonardo while he was talking to Kate after her dance. So I couldn't actually say I starred in "Titanic"... but our names are in the credits... and they were listed at the end, long after Kraft Services... after the hundreds of stunt people... and right before the music credits. They didn't even put us up with the performers. But I did see my name, so in that small respect, I am a happy camper! And the residual checks don't hurt, even though I am strangely making more residual money from "Blues Brothers" than from "Titanic". Have you heard of 'Creative Accounting' perhaps?

e

"Between Christmas and New Year's" is an independent film that Stefan Lysenko wrote and directed. Stefan was one of my sons when we were both in "Broadway Bound" at GRT. He is a great actor and full of nervous energy that worked well with the roles I've seen him play. He asked me to be in this project and I said yes. I was paired with Dom Morra, a good singer and actor and friend whom Dom, my partner and I have known for years. We were playing an older gay couple who were song and dance men, so it was  great fun. We were able to camp around, and the song we sang was one that Dom wrote himself The film was a very dark film starring James Phillips as an almost suicidal man who lived in this apartment of eccentrics. I don't believe anything big ever came from the film, but it was still great fun to work with Dom Morra and Stefan Lysenko again. And part of the movie that was shot took place in Mae West's apartment on Rossmore in Hollywood. That was exciting!

Speaking of Mae West, I heard that even though she was an older person, she made herself have sex with all the muscle men in her act. And she really did take milk baths. No matter what is said about her, there was and still is no person in show business who was so ahead of her time with respect to her self written dialogue and her own unique personality. I only saw her once in person, and that was when Dom and I went to an 'English Music Hall' show in Santa Monica, when she was in the audience. Our friend Byron Webster was 'Mr. Chairman', the emcee sitting in the upper booth running the show. It's too bad that both Mae and Byron are gone now, as well as English Music Hall... a form of old English entertainment that we see all too seldom.

e

"The Beverly Hillbilies" was another film I got to dance in during the early 90's. This film was memorable mostly because we had lots of free time standing around, and during this free time, one of the dancers, Charles McGowan, taught those of us who tapped and wanted to learn it, the 'Moses Supposes' number that Donald O'Connor and Gene Kelly did in "Singin' In The Rain".

It was great fun, and the ones that tried learning it were besides myself, Anushka Jones (the wife of Birl), Birl Jonns (a dancer from the Carol Burnett Show), Beverly Polcyn (one of the oldest and cutest 'personalities' in show biz), Victoria Stevens (who on one of our London Theatre Tours wound up dancing on one of our tables at our New Years Eve party), Joan Pierce, Randi Pareira, and I believe John Woodruff. We had fun learning it but don't ask me now... I have a memory that works at the moment, but nothing permanent. That is why I was such a good dancer on television ... 'easy in, and easier out'. I would often have to really think when someone asked what the dance number was that we did the prior week on Burnett. 'Easy in, easy out'. It kind of works for other stimuli also.

e

The end of the 90's and into the next century found me working on several other films including "Wild, Wild, West", "Mrs. Harris" (a TV movie), "An American Carol" (where I played a 'singing' professor), and "The Wedding Planner", among others. "The Wedding Planner" starring Jennifer Lopez was directed by Adam Shankman, his first directorial film, I believe. We did a number with lots of dancers in front of what was like an outdoor drive-in screen. On our first rehearsal, I remember Adam talking to us and telling us now that he was the director, the number would definitely be in the final cut of the movie. I also remember him explaining how 'well' the co-star Mathew McConaughey was built. Adam had such a great sense of humor, and was absolutely another joy to work with. Now remember I was born in 1939, so I'm no spring chicken in the year 2001 when we made this film. My dance partner was Andie Hicks, and there were several lifts in the number. I'm so sorry she couldn't lift me, so I had to lift her, normally not a difficult task, but at 60 years of age (or so), difficult. But we endured and I'm proud to have gotten through with it, as I am at any dancing job at this age. But in the end, once the film was released, unfortunately there was no outdoor dance number. Producers have a lot more say than directors, and I'm sure Adam learned that the hard way.

e

There is a family in Luxor, Egypt that basically 'adopted' me. Whenever you are in Egypt you may find that the Egyptians you talk to are very anxious for you to visit their families. They want a connection with foreigners so that the foreigners might take a special interest in

them, and ultimately help them out financially. I don't find this is a bad thing, because they are genuinely a very good people and they have so much less than we do. So I did allow this to happen to me. And I do feel I got something out of it also. It was on my second or third trip to Egypt when I took a little walk on the dock in front of the boats in Luxor one evening. On this trip before getting on the boat for our Nile trip from Luxor, I booked the group into the Sonesta St George Hotel for 3 nights prior. Two uniformed men were talking behind me, and as they tend to do, began talking with me. So I continued walking with them. They told me they worked for security and were going to the office not far from there, and asked if I want to come in which I did. It was very near. I never at all felt unsafe. When we got to their office, they sat me down while they took care of some business and their boss, or whoever oversees them, came in. He spoke broken English and they introduced me. His name is Tayib, a very good looking man with a small mustache. They ultimately left and Tayib said I could sit there longer. I enjoyed being in a location that tourists never see. He was doing his business and every so often he would glance over to me, which to me, showed a slight interest. After a short while I said I should probably get back to the hotel. He walked me to the door walking very close behind me and we made an arrangement to go for coffee and sheesha (water pipe) the following night. The strange part is when I met him he said that once I see him to follow him not too closely but at a distance far enough so I wouldn't lose him. When we arrived at the sheesha cafe, which was a very local spot apparently, he explained that as one of the security bosses, he was not supposed to have any relations with tourists... business only. So again I felt very special. .. strange, but special. Tayib wanted me to meet his family and he lived in a small village just on the western side of the Nile. So he gave me directions, and told me to take the local ferry across, and it was only a 10 to 15 minute walk from there. The following day I took advantage of this adventure, first by taking the local ferry. The cost for locals was 25 piestras or one quarter of an Egyptian pounds, which converted to about 4 or 5 cents at that time. The ferry is a double deck boat and I sat in the upper deck with no roof, which gave a fantastic view of the Nile as we crossed.

Now when I am in Egypt I made a decision early on that I would wear a galabia, which is a type of 'mumu' the men wear, so I was dressed in my galabia. I hate to wear anything on my head like a scarf or hat, so the Egyptians see this gringo face in this galabia and doors fling open to me. People want to talk to me, and I love that. And almost everywhere I

go I am stopped and spoken to. But I was a man on a mission, which I love to have, so once I got off the boat on the other side of the Nile, I began my little trek. First I walked up a street to a traffic light and made a right turn. After walking the length of another 2 blocks, I was told to turn left onto a cornfield. About 200 more feet there was a dirt road to my right with went through the village. The road was filled with straw, chickens, mules, and I had to watch where I walked. Following the instructions into the village I came across his home. I was greeted by some of his family, as he seemed to be making an entrance at a little later time. But he must have told them about me as they seemed very happy to receive me. His home is much nicer than those surrounding his. And in the front of his home and part of his home are 2 tiny stores, one selling flour and sugar, and one selling other things like dry cooking foods. When Tayib came downstairs he showed me around, and when we were alone he didn't hesitate to touch my shoulder or arm to make contact. Going inside the outer doors, we come into a patio area with the bare ground as the floor. Then we went into a 'reception' room with large tables and benches where they ate and 'entertained'. He brought me into another room outside the kitchen which you might call a living room, where there was a 10 inch black and white television. His family consisted of his mother and father, a much younger brother Gabor about 12 years old, and an even younger sister Marwa about 8 years old, 2 other sisters who were older than Gabor but younger than Tayib, and his wife, a beautiful Egyptian woman who seemed to be extremely shy. Marhaba, one of his sisters was deaf and no one other than Gabor and Tayib spoke any English. And he had one other sister who was already married and to this day I never met. The reason why so many of third world countries have so many children born with birth defects is through generations of in-breeding, with members of their own family. Also, the respect for their

190

parents is absolute. But Egypt is an ancient civilization consequently the men's attention is less so with their women, especially their wives.

Another interesting thing about the Egyptian culture is that as the family grows, the wives come to their husband's family homes after marriage, and so the daughters leave their own homes when they wed. Consequently if a home has many boys, they keep adding rooms to the home, so you see that most of the homes in Egypt are not finished buildings, but still look like they are under construction, and in a way, they are, even though they may stay in that condition for years. I've also heard that in Cairo, the owner of an apartment building is taxed quite highly once the building is finished, thus almost all the buildings at that time still looked like they were under construction as well.

Going back to my first Egyptian home visit, Tayib then brought me upstairs to the outer roof where we could see all the land his family owned. He was very proud to show me the fields of sugar cane, corn, and other agricultural products that they sell in their stores in the front of their house. He explained that even though he was a 'boss' of security, he didn't make good money so they had to sell their products as additional income. His family all took turns in the stores. By this time he was becoming very 'comfortable' touching me, and I was pretty flattered. When we were in a bedroom upstairs and he knew his family was watching the TV, he would grab me and rub his body against mine, and that was that. Even though he had his wife downstairs, he was free to 'explore' with his own private tourist. Nothing more happened so I didn't object at all. I had some sugar cane, and a soda, then left to join the other tourists in my group for dinner. That night I followed Tayib again to the Sheesha cafe. The following day I took a walk and happened to pass an appliance shop, which looked more like a factory than a shop. They had a brand new 19" color television that they were selling for what converted to $219. I'm an American, and I figured that I could be a millionaire $219 later. So I bought the TV, got a taxi, and somehow found their house after several attempts in the cab. To get to the other side the taxi had to take a bridge which was about 10 miles out of the way. Well when I arrived at their home, we took the TV out and the family couldn't believe it. Tayib was sleeping since he gets up later in the afternoon as he works until very late at night. He set the TV up and I wish you could see the family's faces when they finally saw the color in the TV... as well as the size. They couldn't do enough for me with their 'thank you's' and shaking my hands and kissing my cheeks. It was as if I gave them a house. And I can't tell you the feeling I got from their response to my little gift. I never thought $219 would bring me such gratitude and satisfaction.

e

I decided then that I would make another journey to Egypt in about 6 months but this time alone, which I did. By this time Tayib's wife had their first son, Mohamed. As I said before almost every male Egyptian has the name 'Mohamed' somewhere in his name. Little Mohamed was born with a cleft palate and it was so sad to see. He needed $300 for an operation which the cost of which he did not have. Of course I came to the rescue... specially after the response from the television gift. Marhaba would greet me, by kissing both my hands, and thanking me again for the TV, in her silent voice of course. Another 6 months went by and I organized another group tour back to Egypt and saw that the baby's operation had been quite successful. And now, the family insisted that I bring my travelers to their home which I have done on every group trip I've made to Egypt. I did give them one other little gift. The 'reception' room with the large tables, had a dirt floor covered with rugs and the walls were just cement, not painted and not colorful. We Americans like things painted and finished and whatever, so I gave him another $200 and when I returned on another trip, the floor had linoleum on it and the walls were painted a beautiful tan color to within 2 feet of the ceiling and the ceiling was now painted a beautiful blue with stars overhead. It was really a wonderful reception room now. By the way, I always encouraged my travelers to bring something to the family whether it's just candy, or cookies, or something, so that was another reason my adopted family loved me to bring people to their home. I still never ever got the feeling that I was 'buying' their friendship. The only people who would ever say that are people who would be afraid to go to Egypt in the first place... the ones who warn you that it isn't safe.

Through the years I cannot tell a lie... Tayib and I did have a more than casual relationship, but it wasn't so much to be overboard. Sometimes during my visits we didn't even get the chance to be intimate. But I loved knowing what we already shared.

e

I'd like to explain that by the time I began traveling to Egypt, the relationship I had with my partner Dom had become much less physical. So any 'excursion' I had into other intimacies made me feel much less guilty. And while I was back home in the states, hardly anything ever happened to me sexually. Although I may have felt like a whore at heart, having never really gone through a sexual enlightenment, I tried taking advantage of my travel life to enjoy the sexual ecstasies of life when I could get it. And so into my life enters another of my special Egyptian friends, Kiery.

On yet another of my group trips to Egypt, our boat docks in Luxor where we are on the boat overnight this time. Having just had breakfast, I'm on the sunning deck of our boat overlooking the dock. People are arriving with luggage, and there seems to be a flurry of activity happening. While I'm looking around, there are several dock workers in orange jumpsuits, who I find out are gardeners and general maintenance crew for the docks. One of the crew keeps looking at me. So I stared back. He smiles... I smile. He does a little wave... I do a little wave. Signals me down with his hand. I nod and go downstairs off the ship and walk up to him. He is a very good looking man but has what appears to be a cataract in one of his eyes, and I doubt this is operable. We begin talking and he brings me to the room where they have their equipment. He is not shy about showing me that he is getting excited to see me, and he grabs my hand and puts it on his crotch. I don't object after not having any relations with anyone physically in quite a while. He unzips his jacket exposing his beautiful almost muscle bound upper body. I am not, nor have I ever been, interested in over muscular people. It just doesn't turn me on. But what does turn me on is any attention given to me, which Kiery certainly is doing. So we play around a little and when his cohorts enter we make arrangements to meet later in the afternoon. To me I was afraid Kiery was only interested in money, because when we met, we ate and he asked me to pay. I certainly understand that if Tayib doesn't even make enough to cover his son's operation, Kiery must certainly not be paid very much, so I didn't object to paying then, but I explained that I was also on a budget and he seemed more interested in me than money I couldn't afford to throw his way. Kiery, I learned, was an avid gym buff and lifted weights. Through the years the more I met with him, the less he 'worked out' so his body seemed to revolve into a body I enjoyed being with. And ultimately Kiery got married to a beautiful Egyptian girl and had a little girl. When I do still see him, we still try to become intimate, but sometimes that doesn't happen either. But both Kiery and Tayib still maintain special places in my heart... certainly in the Egyptian part of my heart. I'm not a nun ... I have had other dalliances but nothing as close to me as these two. Of course I always remember Hesham and Tarek, my first true friends in Egypt with whom I never shared sex. I know this is a country I will always return to for various reasons, some personal, and some for the absolute love of the people.

e

In 2003 I took a familiarization trip on a cruise from Saint Petersburg to Moscow in Russia. Since my grandparents on both sides were Russian, I thought it might be time. Sometimes the way it works out you are the only travel agent on a fam trip, because companies offer the trip often every week through a season. On this trip I was the one who was traveling alone. But while on the trip I met some very nice people, and continued a good friendship with two of them. They are lovely lady friends from England, and each are married but their spouses didn't come, so they shared a cabin. One is a woman named Victoria Lawrence, no relation to the one on Burnett Show, and the other is Maria, and for the life of me I cannot remember her last name. Anyway, on the boat near the end of the cruise, they have a tourist talent show, but not for regular talent like singers, etc. What they do is give groups of people a little 'script' of sorts that they can perform. So when they gave out the American script, I asked my English lady friends if they would help me with i t , and they did a lbeit reluctantly. It was  probably awful, but what it did do was bring the three of us together closer than we were before. On subsequent trips to London we would always make arrangements to see each other at least once during my trips since they live a ways away from the center of London. Between then and now Maria's husband, who used to work at the Transportation Museum in Covent Garden, has passed away. Victoria's husband works at the Colloseum as a physical therapist for the dancers in the company there. But both ladies still look great and they remain two of my closest friends in London. I do love to maintain those kinds of relationships. As for the Russian riverboat cruise itself, it was terrific. St. Petersburg is just an exquisite city, and The Hermitage Museum ... breathtaking; although I am really more cosmopolitan in my likes and dislikes, so I do prefer Moscow because it reminded me more of New York. On the boat I became friends with several of the boys and girls working there, and they even invited me to a birthday party for one of the girls. So when I arrived in their 'green room' (as it were), the rest of the boat's staff was quite surprised to see a tourist there. But immediately I was surrounded by some of the crew I had already befriended. That close connection with the working people on a tour is what I crave. It makes me feel so special. An interesting thing that happened which also relates to the following year, is that before getting to Moscow, I felt a little 'Onion Domed Out', meaning I've seen so many onion-domed churches that I didn't feel I had to see any more of them. So when we got to the last town to see another church, I let the group go there while I took a walk. I saw several locals heading toward a street not far away so I followed them. Low and behold we come to a huge flea market, where not one person spoke any English. I wanted as I usually do under these circumstances to have some communication with someone there, so I came across a cart of shoes, and between sign language and

hand language chose a pair of black athletic shoes that I purchased for what came to in USD $16. At the end of the transaction I asked to take a picture of the salesman. I showed it to him on my camera and he seemed excited. I left the flea market

and went to join the group at the church with my new purchase. And that was what I thought would be the end of it. Well, I enjoyed that trip so much that a year later I repeated the cruise in reverse, but only got a small handful of people to come with me, which included Johanna Marowitz, Tony Barberio, Lynn Kidder, Carolyn MacMullen, and Carl and Adrienne Short. It's still difficult to get a group of people who want to go to a specific place on specific dates. Everyone has their own lives to deal with. At any rate since I knew I was going back to do the same Russian river cruise, I took the picture of the shoe salesman and blew it up to 8 ½ x 11. The first stop after Moscow was this little town, I believe it was Uglich, known more for it's watches than anything else.

So the group went to the church and I went to the flea market. I thought I would remember where the shoe cart was, but it wasn't where I expected it to be. So I took out the picture I had enlarged and began showing it to the other salesmen and sales ladies, who were amazed that they knew the man in the photo. So as  they pointed and led me in the direction of where the man was selling his shoes, they joined me like I was the Pied Piper to see his expression I suppose when I found him. What can I say, when I saw him he didn't seem to recognize me but I immediately showed him the photo and gave it to him and he was ecstatic. Thrilled beyond belief that a foreigner would take the time to bring him that enlargement when I didn't even know him. He just hugged me and everyone cheered. I felt like a hero... again. It always amazes me how these people who are much less fortunate than we are, can make me feel like a million dollars, just by my doing a little something extra for them. This is always an encouragement for me to always accept friendships from everyone whom I think will appreciate it. I suppose I'm really doing it selfishly because it makes me feel so good... and there can't be anything wrong with that.

e

One of my ballet teachers in California was a wonderful teacher named Sally Whelan. She used to be a soloist with the San Francisco Ballet. She taught many celebrities to dance including Mary Tyler Moore and Georgia Engel. Ironically enough she had a child, Carmen, with a degenerative disease that forced her to have very serious operations throughout her brief lifetime and prevented her from walking. Sally never deserved that. And with that disease children generally don't live beyond 8 or 9 years of age, but with Sally's love and complete attention, Carmen lived to be 13 years of age. At that point Carmen was 'sitting' in the back seat of Sally's car and in a full body cast after one of her operations. Sally heard a little 'click' type of sound, and when she turned, she found Carmen already gone, with a little stream of blood coming down her face. An absolutely terrible discovery! So naturally those of us who were close to her felt even more so for Sally.

Well after studying with her for several years, trying to get the technique down that I've always felt lacking in ballet, another of her birthdays was coming around. Some of her students and I decided we wanted to do something special. I came up with the idea of putting her on 'trial' for being too good a teacher and we had to put her in her place. We secretly flew her sister in from upper California as a surprise witness for the prosecution. I asked Onna White, the choreographer of "Oliver" and Lucille Ball's "Mame", to be the judge, thinking she was so 'ballsy' and she could be loud. I had worked on the 'Mame' number in the film so I felt I knew Onna well enough to ask. I also asked George Chakiris to be the prosecuting attorney. I wrote the script and it came out good enough for Sally's prank birthday trial. But strange as it seems when we rehearsed, Onna White was not loud or strong, and the more I encouraged her, I believe the more intimidated she got. But she did do the trial for us, as did George, and even though she wasn't as strong as I wanted her to be, she adored Sally and it was a coup to get them both in our little play. Sally was thrilled with it and very surprised to see her sister in the 'trial'. So we all felt we honored her well.

By the way, ever since George did this little bit for me, he claimed he wanted to come to Egypt on one of my tours with me. That never came to fruition as I used to go there around October into November and he told me he was always with his mother on her birthday at that time of year. It is possible that he may have been slightly afraid to go there anyway, but I'm hoping he'll change his mind in the future. By the way, George Chakiris now has a beautiful jewelry line... so besides being an Academy Awards actor and dancer, he is a very successful businessman. Check him out.

e

I've been a member of Lonny Chapman's Group Repertory Theatre, now called The Group Rep for over 48 years, and besides my playing the husband in "Broadway Bound", I was fortunate to play the role of David opposite my old girlfriend in George Furth's "Company" at our theatre. Lonny directed it and Dom, my partner, choreographed it. It was one of our successes. Neil Simon's "California Suite" was next when I played another 'David' to Renee Gorsey's 'Millie'. The show was directed by our own Robert Benedict, and I will never forget our very first rehearsal for this show. The director had just worked with one of the other actors in the play on a different scene, and when I walked in the first thing he told me was how great this other actor was, which I already knew as I knew how good an actor he was, and Robert was so sure he would win awards for his performance in the play. I mean, I didn't act a word of dialogue yet. We never even rehearsed, and he hit me with that. Well that certainly didn't inflate my ego doing my role. By the time the show opened, I don't want to say the other actor was forgotten, because he surely was a great actor as I stated. But Renee and I got lots of kudos for our scene, but truly ours was the funniest scene. It was the one where the husband wakes up and there's a hooker in his bed, and his wife is on her way up to the hotel suite... a very funny premise. So I was very pleased at what we did with that scene in "California Suite".

e

An interesting note about Renee Gorsey is that during the summer of 1964 (or was it the summer of 1966?), I did two shows at City Center in NYC. One was "Where's Charley?", the musical based on "Charley's Aunt" by Brandon Thomas, and the other was "How To Succeed In Business Without Really Trying", the show that made Robert Morse a star, by Abe Burrows. Well Renee was in "How To Succeed" on Broadway, and she was in this revival as well. We never really got close in the show, which starred Billy De Wolfe, but I got the chance to dance the 'Pirate Boy' solo, entering and dancing to open the

Pirate Ballet number for the TV show within the play. What a thrill to enter and dance to the center of the stage, only to have the audience erupt in applause as I did this 'knee-popping' step which brought me slowly downstage until I was practically on the apron. The show was choreographed by Hugh Lambert, Nancy Sinatra's (Jr) future husband. They were applauding at me, alone doing my 'thing', and the feeling was unimaginable! Now flash forward to 1986, and I am at our GRT weekly Monday night meeting. A new member comes in and sees me, and after the meeting she comes over to me and says, "I think I know you." After talking back and forth trying to remember where, we fell on the "How To Succeed" revival, and were happy to reunite. The following week she sees me sitting with Dom, my partner who joined the theatre by this time. She never put two and two together until we spoke afterwards. You see, she had a huge crush on Dom way back in New York also... but I got him! But Renee Gorsey remains to be one of my best friends since our reunion.

Marvin Chernoff wrote a monologue that a good friend of mine Arnold Weiss performed called "Chaim's Love Song". When it was turned into a play Larry Eisenberg asked me to play the lead role of Chaim Shotsky. I was onstage for the entire play, and my good friend Bix Barnaba helped me with learning the lines while we were vacationing with his wife Cindy Fancher and others in Costa Rica. It was a great role with a lot of emotion ... which is always a good thing for someone to tap.

e

While waiting around to act in plays, I've been doing lots of directing, some for productions at our theatre, and some for what we call projects. Projects are created for a showing at the GRT so that the artistic directors might be interested in putting these plays on as regular productions. I've often directed plays by Art Shulman, a pretty prolific playwright at our theatre. If they are not done at GRT, then oftentimes Art rents space like The Secret Rose, another small theatre in the NoHo area. The ones I directed of his that became productions are "God, Bring Me A Miracle", "The Lemonade Girl", "Career Day", "September 10", and "Unity", among others.

One of the last roles I played in a production at GRT was that of the grandfather in Clifford Odets' "Awake and Sing", which was a highly touted show. Larry Eisenberg again directed the show whose cast included among others Michele Bernath, Bobbie Gallo, Daniel Kaemon, Edgar Mastin and Patrick Burke. Michele has always been one of my close friends that I cherish. Nevertheless I seem to gravitate toward these older Jewish parts even though I'm not in the least religious. I enjoy acting so I will gladly take the work where it leads me.

e

I've always felt I would be great in commercials, but because my commercial agents don't send me out a lot, I don't get many auditions. There used to be an 'understood' rule that you must go out for at least 200 auditions in order to get one of them. So I guess if I lived to be about 200 years old I might be able to look forward to acting in a commercial. In the meantime I'm still available.

e

Marcus Cohen asked me if I were interested in working on a project called "Visiting Mr. Green" by Jeff Baron. Now Marcus is not a member of The Group Rep even though he appeared in "Awake and Sing" for us. Wouldn't you know it... the role he wanted me to play was the one Eli Wallach acted on Broadway... another aging Jewish man. It must be in the cards for me. I asked Linda Alznauer from our theatre to direct it, even though I could have done it. And I trusted her to do a good job. When she was president of the board, the men on the board gave her a little grief, so this was my way of telling her I appreciated her. We worked on the project and even though we could have been on the script, both Marcus and I decided we wanted to be off book. We did the project for the membership and the artistic directors chose it to open the upstairs studio (The Stan Mazin Studio) for our first upstairs production. We were very disappointed that we couldn't get the rights for the play until a year later. I tried finding out who was doing it in our area, because I only need 10 more weeks under Equity's jurisdiction to receive my pension from Equity. I couldn't find out so I am back where I began. But I am so happy to have done the part even for a project.

e

As an added feature to my resume, I can now add Broadway (or at least off Broadway) producer. I directed Bix in a one man show called "Given Em Hell, Harry" written by Samuel Gallu. He had come to me to ask me to direct. I explained that I normally am not crazy about one-person shows, so he said, "Why don't we work on a little part of it and see how it goes?" That was fine with me. I like Bix very much as an actor but didn't really know how we would get along with my directing him. Well we worked great together. He was wonderful and we even did it for The Group Rep as a production. Then we brought it to NYC and we played it at St. Lukes Theatre for Ed Gaines. Honestly Bix did most of the producing, but I did help.

e

Another show that I produced at the Harold Clurman Theatre on 42nd Street was another one man show called "Nijinsky Speaks" written and performed by Leonard Crofoot. I know Len as a wonderful dancer, and because of his size he also played 'Tom Thumb' in the original "Barnum" with Jim Dale on Broadway. His size was perfect for him to play that role because he is the same size as Vaslov Nijinsky. My partner Dom directed this version and Len was nothing short of fantastic. I collected $5000 from several of my friends, and $15000 from another woman to make a total of $50000. We were able to put it on for that amount at the Harold Clurman Theatre on Theatre Row on 42nd Street. John Simon came to our second and last preview and gave us a rave. Let me say that again. JOHN SIMON GAVE US A RAVE! I allowed Len's fiancé Robin Palanker (as of this writing, his wife) to make all the artistic decisions for the flyer and the pictured wall in the theatre, because she is a fantastic artist in her own right. The sad part is that we only had enough money to run a limited amount of time and we didn't make enough money to move to another theatre after our run. But the people who came really enjoyed the show. I could tell because before the show they just barely glanced at the photos on the wall, but after the show they gathered to really examine Leonard's photos with great interest. And a year after our show, there was another show that played Washington, DC, and John Simon reviewed that one as well. And in the review he wrote, "Please do not mix this show up with "Nijinsky Speaks", which played New York last year"... or at least similar words. He really liked us. And so here I am... a little Off-Broadway producer. Another hat... fine with me, but my closet is getting bigger and my wallet is not!

e

It was during the mid to late '90's that I joined a travel club called 'Network For Living Abroad'. It was run by a woman named Ruth Halcomb. Each month we would meet at a restaurant, usually one with specialized food from outside the US, like Chinese, Thai, Mexican, Indian, etc. The cost would include the meal, the taxes, and the tip. Ruth would have a speaker at each luncheon, usually speaking about the country whose food we were eating. It would be up to the speaker as to what direction his lecture would be based upon, that is, living in that country, or visiting that country, or just his or her trip to that country. Most of the time the lecture would come with a slideshow that would be presented on a screen that Ruth would supply. We would begin each meeting with a microphone that would go around the room so each person who wanted to could share their favorite travel places, or if they were taking a trip, they could announce where they were going so others could later give them advice on the country. So the purpose of the meeting was not just for people who wanted to 'live' there. Eventually Ruth moved to Santa Fe, New Mexico, and the club was taken over by another wonderful woman named Odette Ricasa.

The club became more of a travel-oriented club, but continued as before. I would attend as often as my work would allow. The luncheon locations would run from the east, Pamona to the west, Malibu, and from the north, Mission Hills to the south, Laguna. There are a lot of restaurants within that area. Our meeting are usually listed in the Los Angeles Times, so people could network with new people who joined us each month. I never did give a lecture because I always felt I never really paid too much attention, or at least I didn't feel I could remember all the names of the churches, temples, shrines, etc., that I've been to. And I would hate to feel stupid in any of those meetings. But I did learn a lot about different countries, and also the ones I didn't care for. Once you see the slideshows and realize the difficult living conditions abroad, even the temporary ones for tourists, I often decide all I really need is to look and listen to the lectures to decide, "I'm definitely not going there!". I've been through the rotten smell of the tanning factories in Morocco where you would have to roll up lumps of mint leaves and literally stuff them into your nostrils just to get through the inspection process. After going to one of those tanning places in Morocco, Egypt, or any other country that has the process, I literally could not go into a nice leather store for at least two to four months afterwards. I don't ever mind 'roughing it' during any side day trips, but at night I want to be spoiled and go back to my 4 or 5 star hotel or lodging. Living in a 1 star or less tent, does not do it for me. Call me a spoiled American and I wear that badge with pride, all the while respecting people who love to experience everything. I'm just not one of them.

e

The first hotel I ever took in London for my yearly group theatre tours was the Strand Palace on the Strand. It was very strange because the hotel had at that time very small rooms and even though two people who had twin beds on their reservation, mostly to save money on the room, the hotel gave them each their own tiny room with bath. Most were delighted because they didn't have to share their bathroom with the other person. They even gave Dom and me our own little rooms, which was strange with us, because we usually had one king bed. I believe the hotel was redone and they no longer do that. By the way, The Strand Palace had one of the best Carvery restaurants in London. A Carvery is one where they have a buffet and come around with carved prime rib not too unlike Lawry's in Los Angeles. The next 2 to 3 years I reserved The Kenilworth Hotel in Bloomsbury for the group, which was very near the British Museum. After that the Edwardian Group opened The Mountbatten Hotel right on Seven Dials, and we all loved that location because it was much closer to the theaters, and that is primarily why we go to London. We stayed there for many years until The Hampshire opened on Leicester Square. All the people who worked at The Mountbatten said we wouldn't come back to them after we stayed at The Hampshire, but that wasn't true. We stayed at The Hampshire for two years then returned again to The Mountbatten. Since then we go to either, depending on the best rate I can get. I liked the staff at The Mountbatten better, and it was considered a 4-star hotel. Some of the Concierge men were Paul Pugh, Michel, Zoltan, and Luis. The Hampshire is a 5-star hotel so they are much too formal for my liking. I don't really remember any of the concierge other than Paul Pugh who was moved there from The Mountbatten, then later left to work at the Savoy Hotel. He now has his own travel type business. Many of my travelers like that '5-star' treatment though.

Whenever I travel I like to make friends with the people who work at the hotels. I want to be called 'Stan', and not 'Mr. Mazin'. I don't know what it is exactly but I don't want to be considered a 'client' but more of a friend. On one of the first years I was taking my group to London, I became friendly with one of the concierge boys named Michael, a young character looking man who looked slightly Middle Eastern. Anyway we would go to either my room or a spare room  and sniff poppers and laugh. Poppers are a liquid that many people use during sex, but can also be used without sex like in discotheques while dancing. It produces about a 30 second high which leaves as easily as it comes on, and I don't consider it a drug, and since I don't do alcohol or other drugs I don't believe it 'leads' to drug behavior. And I am not condoning poppers, just explaining what it is for me. Dom was traveling with me and he didn't share the silly feelings I enjoyed from it. We never did anything sexual, Michael and I, which I would not have minded, but what I enjoyed with him was the closeness I felt by doing something so personal yet without any sex. And every time I come to London I go to the Kenilworth Hotel where he works just to say hello. We no longer indulge in the old habits. He is now happily married and has two girls, one 14 and the other 12. I like to keep old close acquaintances and friends very much. I don't know why, but whenever possible I try reconnecting with them.

In case I neglected to mention it before, every time we went to London for our 'after Christmas' London Theatre Tour, we were of course there for New Years Eve. So we would have our own New Years Eve party at the hotel in our own private room. We would have Champagne, wine, soft drinks, and hot and cold Hors 'd Oeuvres. It was usually a great time to look forward to. As it developed we began doing our own little show that we would do where anyone who wanted to would get up and tell a story, a joke, a poem, a song, or whatever they wanted to do. At one party some of the men rehearsed a number to Tom Jones' 'You Can

Leave Your Hat On' as a strip. Miriam Nelson would always create her own words to a regular song and it was always so original. Jane Kean would do her fabulous impressions and her husband Joe Hecht would

do part of his vaudeville or comic act. Logan Ramsey would always do some bit in which he would wind up taking off his shirt. Even people who were not in show business were encouraged to get up and do something... anything, just to be a part of the evening. For one of our parties Dom and I invited Diana Rigg after seeing her in a show she was acting in on the West End, and low and behold, she showed up. After seeing that everyone was participating in the show, she said, "I'd like to do something". She proceeded to recite what seemed to be a poem, but afterwards she told us it was really a love letter that Queen Elizabeth (or possibly another English Royal queen) wrote to her beloved. It was a thing of beauty. And before Diana left, she made sure she went to each and every table to say 'Goodnight' to everyone who was still there. She really is a remarkable person. Another talent gone too soon.

e

A very good actor friend of mine, Toni Sawyer, came with my group to London several years back, in either '05 or '06. While there we learned that Ian McKellen was going to be performing at the Old Vic as WidowTwankey in the pantomime Aladdin. It was sold out so Toni and I decided to go very early one matinee and wait for turned back tickets. We got to the Old Vic very early and no one was there but then untimately they let us in. Well fortunately two tickets were just returned and we got them. We had a lot of time to wait and Toni wanted to use the restroom, which was downstairs just outside the bar. So I escorted her downstairs. While waiting I saw a woman with two children sitting at a table in the corner of the bar, and the only other person in the room was none other than Kevin Spacey, sitting alone reading a newspaper. I recognized him immediately because he had one of his baseball or was it a golfing cap on his head. I wanted to say something to him because I have always admired his work, besides hearing rumors that he and I might share the same propensity for our sexual endeavors. So in a moment of madness I approached him and said, "Are you slumming?" I was trying to make a joke because I knew he was running the Old Vic at that time. Well, he turned to me lowering his newspaper and stared me down with a look of absolute detest and said very sternly separating each word he spoke, "What do you mean, Sir?" I was so taken back that I melted and said something like... "I'm sorry. I just wanted to say hello." Then immediately said, "I'm so sorry to bother you". And I walked away feeling so small and humiliated. I didn't even realize that at that time it was only about a week or two weeks before that Kevin Spacey was found in a public park in London in the middle of the night looking for his cell phone and was arrested. Had I known that, I certainly wouldn't have used the greeting I gave to him. I now understand why he must have been so sensitive. At any rate, I never ever forgot that lowly feeling, but Toni came out of the restroom and I still managed to enjoy Ian McKellen's performance in ''Aladdin''. But that was the one and only experience I had with one of my still favorite actors, Kevin Spacey.

On my last trip to London, I went by myself and chose not to bring anyone with me. And to save money I found what I thought was a charming boutique hotel right next to the Palace Theatre where Shaftsbury crosses Charing Cross. The location was probably the best location I've ever had in London, but my room was so small. "How small was it?" "It was so small that I had to get another room in order to brush my teeth in the morning." "It was so small I didn't have enough room to change my mind." Well, almost. The room had not one drawer or even a closet. There was a protruding rod from the wall that hangers could be put. There was a tiny desk on which sat a coffee machine that offered complimentary coffee or tea. Butted up against the chair was the bottom of the bed, with the other two sides touching the window on the long side, and the back wall on the short side. Alongside the only free side of the bed were about 1 ½ feet of space then a glass walled partition separating the toilet, sink, and shower, which were all brand new. The glass was frosted from the floor to about 5 feet above it. And since it was frosted, if two people shared (I have no idea how they could unless they had no wardrobe), one could see the other one sitting on the throne. Not very romantic if that is why you are in that room. The breakfast was not included but can be purchased ahead of time for under ten pounds. But the best thing about this little hotel is that every single day from 5pm to 8pm they had a complimentary cheese and wine in the little restaurant. This also included fruit and crackers, all sorts of wonderful breads, and pastry... and you could have as much as you wanted. Unfortunately for me, I am not a wine drinker so when I ordered orange juice I was given a huge glass of it, and could have even had more had I wanted. I advise anyone who wants to try this place out, come with an empty suitcase and with $100 to $150 you can go to Primark 3 blocks away on Oxford Street and buy yourself a week's wardrobe. So all in all, the room was tiny, the location was prime, and the price was under $125 plus VAT for a double bed. I could have saved a little money on a single bed, but I sleep restlessly. The hotel is the "Z" Hotel in SoHo and there is also another one on Piccadilly Circus. And I'm not even getting a cent for this endorsement.

e

On my first few trips to London I went to a bath house, which was very interesting to me. Everyone walks around with a towel wrapped around themselves except for the real exhibitionists who carry a towel over a shoulder. The first time I recall thinking, "How great is this place? Everyone comes who is interested in the same thing, meaning sex in one form or  another, and other than the price of admission, you don't have buy someone drinks or dinner, or even play the 'what are you into?' game.

They let you know pretty quickly. I certainly got a vicarious thrill just being there. The feeling was not unlike the story that a good friend Eddy PFeiffer told me when he was explaining why he would rather hire a hustler than invite someone for a date. In a date, he would have to buy dinner and drinks and then 'maybe' find out what that person is into either before the 'act' or during the act. He went on to explain that with a hustler, all your interests are requested before any financial agreement, and you already know you won't be disappointed. It made complete sense to me. Well, in a bath house it is very much like that but the cost is much lower. My only advice is to be careful with what you do, because bath houses are notorious for being like HIV and STD farms. I have to admit that almost every time I went to a bathhouse, nothing happened to me, other than perhaps someone giving me a bit of oral sex. But I got a kick out of just being a voyeur. I did not take my lack of sexual activity as a rejection... most of the times.

e

I want to tell you about an experience I had in Egypt when I truly found out how the Egyptian police treat their own people. I have two other friends, Mohamed (yes, another Mohamed) and Shaban, who used to have a souvenir shop just adjacent to Karnak Temple in Luxor. Mohamed actually had the shop and Shaban worked for him. And right in front of Karnak was the police inspection station. Well one night my friends made arrangements through their good friend Ali who drives a taxi, to pick me up near my hotel. We were going to pick up beer and go to Mohamed's house and eat and have the beer. One of the reasons I was invited was the fact that Egyptians cannot go into a liquor shop and purchase beer. But I can. So I went in and purchased half a dozen large bottles of Stella, a local brand. In the taxi were Ali, the driver, Mohamed, Shaban, a friend of theirs I just met, and me, dressed in my Egyptian galabia. We put the beer which was in a brown paper bag down by my feet. We had to go through the police inspection area at Karnak to get to Mohamed's house. When we stopped for the inspection to pass to the other side of a gate, an Egyptian policeman came up to the car with a flashlight. He began asking where we were going, and he saw that I was the only one in a galabia, and he obviously knew I was a tourist from my accent and my gringo face. He then proceeded to ask my Egyptian friends for their papers. Now the new person I just met had never been stopped by the police and he got quite angry very quickly. The policeman then flashed his lights down to the bag at my feet. He asked what that was and I told him that I was having a party for the Americans at the Sonesta St. George Hotel and I had to ask my Egyptian friends where to purchase the beer for the party. He then asked the new person what he did for a living, and the angry Egyptian said (in Arabic), "Read it! It's in my papers!" The shouting began and before we knew it, both he and Shaban who tried to stand up for him were pulled from the car and taken to a small building about 100 feet from us along with the beer I purchased that they confiscated. Even though Shaban worked in that shop nearby, the police paid no attention to any familiar faces. The officer then told us to proceed through the gate, which we did. We of course pulled over and waited once we went through the gate. I kept going back to the gate to explain that all this was my fault because I asked them to help me buy the beer and they kept saying, "Not to worry, get back to the car!" But every 15 minutes we waited I would go back and apologize again, only to be told again to go back to the car. Finally after one and a half hours, they released the two men and we started the car to go and I stopped them and jumped out of the car and ran back to the inspection station. I shouted words to the effect of, "You have my beer! If you are going to keep it I want my money!" And I put out my hand as if waiting for their payment. They kept asking me why I needed the beer. I continued to tell them it was for the Americans at the hotel and we all chipped in for the beer, so I demanded the money back or the beer. This argument lasted about 5 or so minutes and I finally told them to go check it out with the hotel if they didn't believe me. After leaving me for about 2 minutes, they came back with the bag of beer and I brought it back to the taxi with me. I knew they couldn't check with the hotel but I was quite angry and loud. This made me realize that their treatment with tourists is much more forgiving than with locals. And after getting back into the car, the others told me that this was not a special incident, and that their treatment of their own people is quite nasty. We then drove to Mohamed's house where my friends enjoyed my beer. .. I still hate the taste of beer. Only one time in Germany I had a 'veet' beer (I guess 'white' beer) and after the bartender crushed a lemon slice at the bottom of my glass did I find that I liked that. But I've tried duplicating it and haven't found the right combination that I liked yet. I did recently discover "Not Your Father's Root Beer" and that is beer but doesn't have that 'beer' taste. But I do like ginger beer.

e

One of my favorite parts that I have played at The Group Rep was a play called "411 Joseph" and was beautifully written by Frawley Becker and directed by Pat Willson. I played the father of two young boys, and every scene took place about 8 to 10 years later, so we all got to age gradually, as well as act a little older with every scene. I loved the play because one of the reviewers compared it to Neil Simon's "Broadway Bound", but found "411" even more compelling. And the director was wonderful to work with, allowing us to 'experiment' with our natural instincts, which most directors do not have the time to allow. When I am directing I like to be able to give the actors time to allow for this, but it really depends on how much time we have to rehearse. Oftentimes that is a gift we rarely get in small live theatre.

Dick De Benedictis is a good friend of mine who is also a terrific composer lyricist-book writer. One of his pieces is called "Bert n' Eddie", a musical about the relationship between Bert Williams, a black performer over the turn of the last century and Eddie Cantor, a song and dance man of years ago. It was Flo Ziegfeld who originally put the two of them together, and through a rocky beginning they maintained an extremely close relationship until their deaths. It was a wonderful premise for a musical and Dick asked me to direct and choreograph it for a first small production to be done at Pierce College in Woodland Hills. The year was 2005. The show has terrific numbers in it and such a heart. I think the relationship between these two men was well established in Dick's writing. We had very few people turn up for the auditions, so I felt I did the best I could under the circumstances. I was assisted by Michele Bernath, whom I asked to even dance in one of the numbers as a male dancer. I don't like being in any of my shows if I am watching it from the audience in order to make it the best show I can. We did the show and unfortunately couldn't get any large producers to see the show. I personally think it would be a fantastic musical for Broadway, even though it would have to be a large production with Ziegfeld numbers and all. We found fantastic people for the leads, Gerald James as Bert and Graham Fenton as Eddie. Graham auditioned for the chorus, but he has such a unique talent that we immediately cast him as Cantor. We couldn't have been luckier in the casting of the two leads. Flo was played by Bix Barnaba who was perfect in his portrayal, originally set for Dick Van Patten who had to bow out for health reasons. The show has a lovely mix of original songs by De Benedictis and the traditional Williams and Cantor numbers like 'Nobody', 'Yes Sir, That's My Baby', 'If You Knew Suzie', and 'Ma, She's Making Eyes At Me'. If this show got into the right hands it would not only be a huge entertainment but an education into the times as well. An investment of this magnitude is bound to reap huge rewards for some producer. Too bad it's just laying around now.

e

Several years ago a friend of mine, Johanna Marowitz, asked me to direct a one-woman show she had written about her experiences after being a victim of an apartment fire that she lived through. Johanna has been a loyal tap student of mine for years, but after the fire, she almost lost her life. She was in intensive care for a month, and was not expected to survive, but she is a survivor, and a proud one. She also happens to be a relatively good song writer, and I only wish the right people could hear some of her songs. So she wrote this piece on her recovery as a kind of therapy to her bravery under her circumstances. I thought it would be a difficult piece to direct as I'm not sure how the general public would accept this subject matter. She called it "Embraceable Hue" and I was proud of our work in it, both hers and mine. The show included one particular song which I think should be a classic that anyone could sing including Streisand, and she said she wrote it with me in mind ... very flattering. Early on I felt that Johanna had a crush on me, but I think she learned after a long time there was no future in it for her... at least not the way she would like. She has remained a loyal friend and even though she is stubborn when it comes to corrections in my tap class, she still continues to be her own person. I like that.

e

As I mentioned before I do have one sister. In truth I have two sisters, but my three year older sister did not want her name to be mentioned in my book. So I am accepting her request with hesitation. I hesitate because the one wonderful thing she has given to this earth is her only daughter who probably is the best person on earth that I know. Her daughter Adrienne was always more sensitive than any of us, consequently winding up in tears through her relationship with her mother so often so that as soon as she became of age she left her mother and moved to Florida. She got married and had one daughter herself before her divorce. And for years she would not even speak to her own mother. At my persistence she began speaking to her once a week after I told her that she shouldn't let her mother hurt her. "Don't let her get to you, Adrienne! She can't hurt you over the phone. Whatever she says just know you can always put the phone down... you have the power to protect yourself." So she does tolerate her now and even though her mother has not softened in her verbal attacks, Adrienne seems to at least be  able to handle them better. Adrienne truly is one of the dearest people on this planet, along with Denise, my half sister whose father we both shared. Denise is another person who deserves a break in her life... a decent hard working mother herself proudly raising a wonderful son, Joey, who is turning out to be a person anyone could be truly impressed to know. As for my older sister, she passed away early in 2020, and being the person she really was, there are no people who mourned her passing that I know of. I think it would be good to at least be aware of any memories people have of you when you leave this world. It may change or alter your behavior, which probably would be a good thing.

e

The Professional Dancers' Society, or PDS for short, is a non-profit corporation formed to serve the professional dancer, active and inactive. They used to have several activities to help raise money for the organization. We used to have a June Picnic, a fall ball, and a PDS Luncheon that usually took place in February. Well I have been a proud member of PDS for well over 30 years. But now because of our economy I suppose the only activity we have left is the PDS Luncheon. At these functions we usually had an honoree of acclaim. At the Fall Ball the honorees started out with usually 'Gypsies', or working dancers, or dancers who have done a lot of work as dancers. Some of these honorees were Bob Sidney, Joe Tremaine, Ed Balin, Miriam

Nelson, Lee Hale, Michael Kidd, Tony Charmoli, and Danny Daniels to name just a few. The Gypsy Award Luncheons' honorees generally were slightly more famous... I hate to say that because as a dancer I cannot really tell the difference between the Fall Ball honorees or the Luncheon honorees. You will see that some of the Luncheon honorees may not have been dancers themselves, but they had sho ws that hir ed dancers, thus were honored. Some of these were Hermes Pan, Louis DaPron, Donald

O'Connor, Sammy Davis Jr., Bob Hope, Cyd Charisse, Mitzi Gaynor, Gwen Verdon, June Allyson, Carol Burnett, Chita Rivera, Mary Tyler Moore, Leslie Caron, and so many many more who were also deserving of this honor. Well when Carl Jablonski became a board member in or about 1983 he suggested we institute the tradition of Broadway's Gypsy Robe and have our own "Gypsy Robe" to honor Hollywood Dancers. Ret Turner who worked with Bob Mackie designed and made the robe to be given out at the PDS Fall Ball. Hence we have been giving the robe out since 1983, and I was the recipient m 1999 following Randy Doney the year prior, and I gave the robe to Charlene Painter in 2000. And each recipient was to attach something of their own or of their life onto the robe so eventually it got heavier and heavier. I didn't want to add more weight to it so I just put a laminated photo of the Ernie Flatt dancers from the Carol Burnett Show, since that was such an important time in my life. I have to add that these recipients were really the dancers who worked in Hollywood so often. And I couldn't be more proud to have worn that robe. When I look back over this particular list of honorees, I see that many of them are no longer with us. We will all miss the likes of Casse Jaeger, Larri Thomas, Rudy Del Campo, Jack Mattis, Crystal Gaer, Alex Romero, and Bob Street, among the many who left us too soon. Every job... and every day... must be an opportunity to get more enjoyment out of life... and living...

My actor's body is in relatively good shape, but my dancer's body needed a lot of work. If a dancer is successful, and works often throughout his life, he uses and abuses his body by constant pushing, bending, stretching, pounding, and so much more that eventually parts of the body get worn out. The first parts of mine were my knees. On my right knee I had arthroscopic surgery. On my left knee I had arthroscopic surgery. On my left knee I had another arthroscopic surgery. On my left knee I had my third arthroscopic surgery. After

that I tried other procedures. First I tried a series of about 20 shots around my knee area, and that had to be repeated a few times. When that didn't work I tried Prolotherapy, where they inject a fluid directly into your knee from the side usually to try to create more of a cushion behind your kneecap. When that didn't work I went to my doctor who replaced my two hips. He told me I should have a full knee replacement. I looked into the computer for new procedures instead of a complete knee replacement and found a procedure called MAKOplasty.

With this procedure only the bad portions of the knee are resurfaced so a knee replacement isn't necessary, however you must be a candidate for such a surgery. So I again looked to the internet and found a doctor with the Orth group at the Good Samaritan Hospital, and had x-rays done. This doctor told me that he could perform the Makoplasty but that in his opinion I really needed a knee replacement. I didn't want a doctor to do the 'mako' that really wanted to do a different procedure because if anything at all went wrong I don't want a doctor to tell me, "I told you so". So after again searching the internet, I found a doctor who specializes in 'mako' up in Carmichael, about 15 miles northeast of Sacramento. I sent him the x-rays this last doctor did and Dr. Paul Sasaura in Carmichael, the MAKOplasty specialist, said in his opinion he thought I would be a candidate for the procedure. So I planned everything out this way. I drove up to Carmichael on a Monday morning at 6am and checked myself into a cheap motel. I drove to the hospital to have my MRI of my left knee at 3pm, which they told me would only be about half an hour. I then made my 4pm appointment with Dr. Sasaura in his offices which were right next door to the hospital. I was then free to have dinner, go back to my motel and watch TV then sleep. Early the following morning, which was a Tuesday, I drove to the hospital, parked in their lot, and checked in for my surgery which happened later that early afternoon. You have to stay in the hospital overnight for this procedure. The following morning Dr. Sasaura came to see me. He said, "You know I've done thousands of these procedures." I said that that was the reason I chose him. He then added, "But yours was only the sixth one I've ever done like that." I told him I'm happy I didn't know sooner but was very glad it was over. In spite of that, he was very optimistic about the success of my operation. Both he and the hospital wanted me to stay in Carmichael for several days in a hotel at my own expense. I didn't have to see him for 2 more

weeks, so I was taken downstairs. I ordered a taxi and as soon as the nurse saw me getting into the taxi she went back inside. I gave the drive a ten-dollar bill and said, "This will probably be the fastest $10 you've ever made. Take me to that car" and I pointed to my car. Now remember my operation was on my left knee. Other than the inconvenience of getting in, out, in, and finally out of my car (I had to stop for gas closer to home), I was not in much pain being drugged of course, but not enough to prohibit my driving, in my opinion. So I drove the six and a half hour drive home where my real healing began with the help of my dogs, Reggie, Katie, their pups Ivy & Adam, and cats. Animals are a much better healer than a TV in a cheap motel

almost 400 miles from home. Two weeks later I went back for my checkup accompanied by two of my best friends, Bix and Sandra. And we made a full day of it. After my checkup in Carmichael, I drove us to San Francisco where we had Chinese food in the same restaurant that Obama ate at a couple of months before. We of course drove home the same night. I had my third and final checkup with Dr. Sasaura three weeks later, and I'm doing fine. And even if something should happen to my left knee, MAKOplasty does not prohibit me from getting a full knee replacement in the future. I 'done good!'.

e

I've also had hip problems which I have also taken care of The first hip I had to have replaced was my right hip. The only really interesting thing I remember about that surgery is that I apparently heal very quickly. I had to wear a catheter for several days and I remember that the day before the catheter came out I had a P.D.S. formal function I had to attend, which I did. And it brought me a very special feeling when, while speaking with some friends, I was able to pee, without making a personal judgement about them... just this very warm and comforting feeling. And they never even knew it. My left hip was operated two years later and some friends kept telling me to tell my doctor that he should operate in front of my hip. I told them that if my doctor normally did thousands of hips with the rear cut, I wasn't about to have him experiment on me. My first operation was quite a success and Dr. Richard Feldman did the same with my left hip. I often wonder if I really needed that second hip done, or did I just want to have that 'warm and comforting feeling'. Come to think of it, I think the catheter was from another operation… nevertheless again?

e

Before my hips I had a problem with my urethra. I would get up 30 times each night with my bladder full, go to the toilet and then, 'drip, drip, drip' and never be able to empty my bladder. So my doctor suggested a daily drug which would prevent that. I asked what other options I had because I hate taking drugs, with all the experience I had with my younger sister. He told me he could perform a 'rota-rooter' operation but it would prevent me from producing sperm. I didn't think I would be having children at that age, when he added, "But there is a 5% possibility you may be impotent." I thought, "5%. That means 95% that I won't be impotent". So I decided to have the operation and what do you know? I got that 'warm and comforting feeling' all over again... at least for a few days.

e

I am not what you would call a 'method' actor... not by a long shot. I've always felt that like religion, some people need it and some do not. I suppose my 'method' relies on the words, the meaning, and the communication between what I see and what the director sees, and the space, if any, in between. The 'reality' must come from the person, and if for some reason he cannot act 'real', I think that is when the training must enter his world. I do understand that everyone's 'reality' is not the same, but I've always felt pretty good since I am a Pisces and I feel like I can adapt to almost every situation. I certainly am not trying to become an acting teacher here, I just want people to understand me a little better.

And my feelings about age and getting older don't sit well with me, either. I look in the mirror over the years and cannot believe that the time has not only gone by, but at this point in my life, and I suppose the lives of many people my age and older, it seems to be passing faster and faster. So I try filling it with as many experiences as possible without allowing them to hurt me. Being a dancer, or having been a dancer, my body means so much to me, and I cannot feel great about what age does to it. I can now accept the fact that I once loved my body, but the toll does not make me adore it now. Sometimes it's difficult to accept the inevitable. But I doubt there is a choice or alternative. My father died when he was a mere 46, and my grandfather died at 73, as a very old person. I'm older than that now. I am proud of my age... or at least my years. I'm proud of my accomplishments as much as I am also proud of my mistakes. I find myself proud and ashamed at the same time sometimes. But I am a survivor even if I haven't survived with the success I would have liked. I'm proud I have love for my friends, my animals, and even my survival. Speaking of animals, I am really sorry that life being what it is does not allow animals to stay longer with us in our lives. That is a very special kind of love that few people can attain. Love from animals is so pure and absolute. Having lived with my partner for 44 years, it may be a sad state of affairs but my most satisfying moments in my life were the ones when my dogs would just

218

sit and we would stare at each other. Those are the times I never want to end. Don't get me wrong. The feelings I had for Dom were wonderful in the beginning, but time alters those feelings with people. I don't think that happens with dogs.

I cannot finish any conversation about dogs unless I tell you about one dog whose life I saved, and in turn I feel he unlocked a love in me I never knew I had. That may sound strange but it really isn't. I mentioned Valerie Miller earlier... she starred as Velma in The Group Rep's production of "Chicago" which I choreographed. She is and always has been an animal lover. She somehow finds out when certain animals are going to be put down in certain animal shelters and puts their pictures on either Facebook or email to her friends in case they are able to save a life. She sent me a picture of a male English Cocker who was 8 years old and was going to be destroyed the following day. I saw the picture and had to drive to the West LA Pound to save his life. Gary came with me, and on the drive home, both Gary and Kyou sat in the rear seat of my car. Animals somehow always know. As soon as we got home, Kyou never left my side until I had to leave the house. There was a bond between us that I never realized even with all my other loves in the dog kingdom. At night I would be sitting in my reclining chair while watching the TV programs I had taped, and he would seat himself in the chair almost facing my chair, and rest his chin on the armrest of his chair which faced me, and he would just stare... Go to sleep... Open his eyes and stare again in adoration. I never got that attention from any other animal or human for that matter. Is it any wonder why this animal has stolen my heart so completely. Remember he was 8 years old when I got him. When he was about 13, which is a long time

for an English Cocker I am told, he was showing signs of cancer. I certainly did whatever I could for him, and I swore that if and when he began to show signs of pain, I would not let him suffer. After many months of treatment, Gary, who adored Kyou as

much as I did, came to me and told me it was time. The fact that Gary brought it up really showed me I was being too selfish trying to keep him with us as long as possible. After making an appointment we brought him to Dr. Lori Birr, our wonderful vet. Once in the private examining room, we put him on the table, gave him a couple of his favorite cookies, and we let him go... 'let him go'... words I have heard before. There honestly isn't a day that goes by that I don't think of Kyou. I know only true animal lovers could possibly understand a bond like this. I hope you are one of them.

I don't know whether anyone wants to understand this or not. But, after attending a Buddhist memorial, I was influenced into making a conscious decision about what will happen to me when I die. Mind you, this is a conscious choice I am making, and it doesn't really matter if it happens or not, but I have CHOSEN that this is what will happen to me, in my mind. As Will Rogers once said and I paraphrase, I want to be with the animals when I die... I CHOOSE to be with my dogs when I go. It may sound silly, but that is what I want to happen right now, while I am alive, to think about what will happen when I die. As soon as I began thinking about my decision, any doubt, fear, or trepidation about death, has disappeared from my being. I don't believe in speeding up my own demise, but I am looking forward to seeing my dogs again. And if animals have souls, which they must, if you have ever looked into their eyes, then that is my choice. It's a better choice than putting my soul in a box underground. I hope someone out there can understand, or at least accept that.

e

My life with Dom in the 44 years we had together has been nothing like it started out. Fresh love is something that two people can maintain if they are very special and I don't think I am that special. We had a special relationship that most people wouldn't quite understand. No one knows what goes on behind closed doors of any couple. But in time we had a kind of understanding. I think Dom realized that I wasn't looking for the same thing he was in a relationship, but he accepted me pretty much the way I would like and I certainly accepted him the way he seemed to evolve. When I think of the later years together I long for the way things were in the early years. Things change... people

change... times are never the same. Two people oftentimes evolve at different speeds and sometimes even in different directions. I felt from early into our relationship that Dom was a little envious probably because I was younger than he was, and it's a natural thing that I worked more than he did. When I got to be his age, which was almost 11 years older, things changed for me as well. And living together makes you really see things that you were blind to before. I know I genuinely love people, and Dom did also, but he never showed it quite the same as I did. I know many times along the years he would have been completely happy if we were at home alone with the doors locked and only our animals with us. As I grew I realized that that was not going to be enough for me. I'm sure that the separation that Dom and I developed throughout the years was my fault. And I suppose it began in the bedroom as most couples' problems begin. I mentioned early on that we both wanted to be the aggressive one in bed, and we both acquiesced to the passive side when we 'switched' sides of course. I am a Pisces so I do truly like diversity, but I'm also an honest person and I do get not 'bored' exactly, but more 'disinterested' with sex sometimes. And I think I was the one who began making excuses in the bedroom first. I can't be sorry for what I did a thousand years ago, or at least it seems like a thousand years ago, and I probably hurt Dom so much in doing that. Of course I loved him. I still love him. But not the way he grew as he got older. He became more rigid in his thoughts and deeds. He got crankier and less friendly to our friends and the people around us. Of course he did have his special friends that we both adored, and whose love he still cherished like Suzanne Lishon, Catherine Battistone, Deke and Diane Lightholder, Leyla and Craig Lighthizer, Russell Tate, Sharon Macias, and a horde of others including his other dancers. An interesting fact is that when he did shows, new dancers that did not know him hated the way he treated his dancers, but the ones who stayed realized that being a perfectionist was more important to him than the treatment he gave out to others. They soon realized that he knew what he was doing and how to make his shows look great. And many of the new people who did additional shows with him came to that realization as well, so in time, his working popularity did well for his reputation. I suppose Niccolo Machiavelli said it best... "The end justifies the means". I just don't think it has to be that way. I think I learned from him also, but I never treated my dancers poorly for the purpose of achieving perfection. At least if I did I was and am completely unaware, and I would hope that one of my close friends including the ones mentioned here would tell me. Domenic was in perfect health almost all his life... through my knee surgeries, my hip surgeries, my liposuction, my hernia operations, my hair transplants (yes I am taking everything off here), and all of my quirky cravings and emotional and erratic compulsive behavior. The only thing we never shared was a three way in bed. I don't know, I never wanted it with him. I suppose I wanted to at least have a part of my personal life kept personal. Perhaps if we did have a three way we might have continued our sexual activity with each other a bit longer. It works for some people I know... whom I know. But that light slowly went out years ago. And as I have written I have continued to wander. And I know that Dom has also, and I often still think that is my fault. But strangely I was happy when I heard he was 'getting it' on the outside, I suppose because somehow it eased my guilt.

e

Dom's doctor wanted him to have a stress test. Up to this point I thought he was in excellent health, other than sometimes waking up in the middle of the night screaming with the pain of a charley horse in his legs. I would always get up to bring him his magnesium pills and it would always take a while to work as I tried massaging his legs until he fell asleep. Now when I think back I begin to think he might have been protecting me from any bad news he might have had. So he made an appointment to take that stress test. The following morning after the test he couldn't get out of bed because his legs hurt him so much. His doctor called and told him he had to see a specialist in blood circulation. After making the appointment and finally seeing the new doctor, the doctor told him, "Mr. Salinaro, I don't know how to tell you this but you need to have stints put into both of your legs to help your circulation." And so it was done, at Saint Joseph's Hospital in Burbank. The stint was put in his right leg, but his left leg presented a further complication. He needed a vein replacement in that leg as his veins in that leg were too far gone. So the doctor performed the surgery and he came home. After a few weeks his left leg again began to really bother him to the point that he couldn't walk. So the 'butcher' as I call him had to go in and do part of the left leg surgery again. Dom wasn't the same after that. He apparently caught that disease people get in hospitals that affect your organs. They call it Staphylococcus Aureus, or in layman's terms a 'Staph Infection', which apparently you can only get in hospitals. And that was the beginning of the end. Dom slowly began losing his ability to walk, and finally had to be in a wheelchair. Try to imagine what it would be like for an athlete who worked with his legs and arms, to slowly lose that ability.

Dom wanted to take one last trip before he was completely immobile. I arranged a riverboat cruise from Venice to Cremona, where they make the violins, outside of Milan. The year was 2008. I dreaded the trip because Dom wasn't really walking well, but how could I refuse his last request for a tour with me, even with him hardly being able to use a walker. It was so difficult. I remember that Johanna Marowitz, Marlene Dalton, Bobbie Bates, and Linda Montana, Monty's daughter, with other travelers as well. Our cabin was relatively close to the part of the boat that we boarded so it was great for day trips for Dom, but the dining room was at the other end of the boat, so it was a long walk for him to go to eat, and he tired easily. He didn't have a wheelchair at that time, but we should have rented one against his wishes to look like a 'cripple' as he put it. And he couldn't hold his bladder for long so he carried a portable hospital urinal in the bag he brought everywhere. One time after everyone was already seated and Dom and I were walking down the corridor to the dining room, his pants literally dropped from his waist because he forgot to tie them. I was angry with him and he said, "Don't worry! It's nothing these people haven't seen before." He was already excusing his condition. And my final straw came when we were having dinner and at our table and Linda was sitting right next to him, and during dinner he took out the urinal and peed under his napkin. I tried to speak to him afterwards and he just said, "Nobody saw me!", angrily. "But they could smell it!" I shouted. I was torn between being a care giver for Dom and trying to make my friends and clients have an enjoyable vacation. It was truly hell for me. Looking back, I know it was more of a hell for Dom. But at least he went, and he knew that was the last time he would be traveling abroad. It's funny but after we returned from Europe, while sitting watching television, he suddenly asked, "Why don't we get married?" I said, "What?" He responded, "Why not get married? We've waited long enough." "Dom, we're together for 44 years. Why now? What for? What would we be proving?" "I don't know. I was just thinking. I guess after all these years we don't really need it, do we?" And then we left it alone. And we never mentioned it again. I really don't mind that we didn't get married. If we did, I think Dom's family would be fighting me for half of the house. As it is now, they can't touch it since it is in my name.

e

Dom's illness was devastating. I remember a tragic moment some time after we returned from Italy when we were in the kitchen and he told me he had to go to the toilet, and he began walking there and 6 feet from where we were sitting he screamed out of shame because he went in his pants and made a complete mess of everything in and out of his pants. In panic I hollered, "Jesus Christ, Dom, couldn't you hold it a few more seconds?" I never ever was able to accept my shame for saying such an unfeeling remark to this handicapped person who was my lover, my hero, my world, for so many years, whether or not we shared sex together. Here I was still working even at my age, but he was becoming more and more wheelchair-bound. It got to the point that I had to lift him out of the bed and lower him into his chair. Then when he had to go to the bathroom I would wheel him to the toilet and lift him to put him down and lift him back when he was through. He never wanted me to wipe his ass because even though he was weak his arms still worked. This illness not only affects the organs, but the mind as well. If it was not the direct result of the staph infection, then his mind went because he knew he was losing his ability to function, and that left him like a bitter very old man. I would sit in my recliner and he would sit either at the far end of the couch or sit in his wheelchair at that end and we would watch television together. Then the extended visits to the hospital, then the recovery 'rehab' places, then back home. And this round robin went on for months... hospital, rehab, home, hospital, rehab, home and so on. The last time he went in I got a call from the hospital and they told me he just went into a coma. After seeing him, and not being able to do anything, the doctor there said I had to make a decision, because they told me he was not coming out of the coma. I went home and prayed in my own way that whatever happens would be the best thing for Dom, either he would have another temporary recovery, or not. Any Staph Infection like his slowly shuts down the organs of your body and Dom's heart, his liver, and his bladder were all failing. The hospital called me the next morning and said his condition was getting worse, and now his breathing was making him gag and he was still comatose. I rushed back and not knowing what to do I called Franklin, his brother in Connecticut. Franklin said, "Stan, you have to be strong. You have to do the same thing we did for our mother when she went. You have 'to let him go'." Let him go... let him go? How can I do that after we're together 44 years? How can I 'let him go' when he was that giant part of my life, a relationship that no one could ever possibly understand. How can I 'let him go' when I feel I'm losing a huge part of my own life. How can I 'LET **ME** GO'??? Domenic, I should have been a better lover to you. I should have told you more times than I did that "I love you". I should have said less, and loved you more. No I don't believe I could have loved you more, I just should have let you know that I did love you more.

e

Dom had already prearranged for his own cremation. A week later I had to go to New York for my Theatre Tour group. While there I rented a car and drove up to Waterbury Connecticut to visit his remaining family. There were two brothers, Richard and Franklin and their wives. I knew they wanted to hear the details. So I went and as I was telling them, of course I was crying. I explained, "There would never be another person who took better care of Dom and who could have loved him more". The family always seemed 'nice' to me, but these were very religious people and they came from the mother of all mothers, so I never could feel a true part of the family until Dom and I were free from them.

e

Dom had $200,000 in stocks and I tried to find out who were the beneficiaries. A lot of that money came from the sale of the house we had in Studio City. I wanted a larger house and Dom really didn't. I found a house in Van Nuys (the area is now called Sherman Oaks) and brought Dom to see it. He didn't usually like change. He wasn't thrilled with the house and said, "Well, if we changed the kitchen, opened up the front porch and make it into the living room, and extend the bedroom as much as we can, it wouldn't be too bad." I told him I would

put both our names on the deed if he split the $20,000 deposit with me. He said, "You're the one who wants to move. I'm not putting any money into this house." He was right. I was the one who wanted to move. So I bought the house in March of 1978, and

had work done on it until we could move in the end of October. We sold the other house so he had quite a bit of money that he would not have had had I not bought this house. He put no money into the renovations and the 'stupid' financial arrangement I had with him was that he would pay me only $450 a month and I would take care of all the house expenses, mortgage and taxes and insurance. I loved the house so I did it. In all the years until he died he never offered a raise in the $450 a month payment to me, and he knew during that time there were lots of times I was really struggling. I put myself into that financial hell so I cannot blame anyone but myself. After Dom died, I offered Gary Warmee the second bedroom if he wanted it, and told him I would only charge him $450 a month. Gary used to take care of Dom when he was sick while I had my group travel… and he also stayed at the house to take care of the animals when both Dom and I traveled with the group. Gary had gotten attached to an all black cat Dom and I called 'Mr. B', having just seen a special on George Balanchine when this cat came into our lives. So I told Gary I would put a doggie door in the wall and change the lock on the door so he would have lots of privacy in the front bedroom. I knew that Gary was a very private person. Gary told me he didn't want the bedroom, so I offered the garage which has no bathroom but told him if he wanted to sleep there I would only charge him $400 a month and he could have complete access to the house. He accepted and that is the present deal. Although I am still struggling financially, I feel secure in knowing at least I have someone around the house to take care of the animals, and clean the house. Gary wanted to do all this. I do believe he has a special need to be in charge of the running of the house, which really helps me and gives me the freedom to live my life. If I had to do everything Gary is doing, I wouldn't be able to even go to many auditions (as if I had many to go to) or have the time to spend with my friends. By the way, all those things Gary is now doing, I used to have to do most of them when Dom was here. So it's kind of perfect for me because I have someone to take care of the things I prefer not to have to take care of. It's like being married but there's no sex involved. I am a happy camper!

e

Bringing you back to the financial situation after Dom's death, I couldn't find out about Dom's stocks until getting a death certificate, and because of a botched communication between the mortuary and the doctor writing the death certificate, I couldn't get one until three weeks later. Dom's stocks were split up with his family getting three fourths of his two hundred grand and my receiving one quarter of it. Apparently Dom on his last visit to Connecticut before leaving us told each of his brothers he was leaving them $100,00 each. He must not have been thinking right because he only had $200,000 and I was a beneficiary also. After finding all this out I wrote the families a letter explaining that if it were not for our selling of the Studio City house he wouldn't have that money, and all I wanted was the money that he made from that house that we had for almost 10 years. The family of course rejected my plea. Another disadvantage arose over his will. I had a newer will and even sent a copy to his family so they could see that if I died before he did, he would get almost everything I had, and

I also have family that I should have left things to, but that was to no avail. Dom had a will he had made in 1988, after we were together for 23 years. We had talked about a new will a couple of years before he died and I thought he had made one, but he never wanted to talk about it, so I assumed (never assume) it was a done deal. Well in this old will, he left me very little. His checking and savings accounts were to go to his family, and his stocks were to be split as he directed in his beneficiary statement with that company. He left me his furniture, except for 4 things... one mantle clock, the picture of a man and a deer with a halo around it that was sitting on the wall above his French desk, his French desk, and the baker's rack that sits in the corner of our living room. I called the family to ask how they wanted those 4 things. They told me to send the mantle clock and the picture as it was their mother's favorite, and they couldn't take the desk or the bakers rack at this time. So I immediately had them shipped off to them. I was truly pissed at Dom for not valuing the time we had together in respect to his will. Even after only 23 years, I was certain we meant more to each other. And his not creating a new will was an absolute slap in my face. Perhaps that was his way of getting back at me for obviously hurting him the way I did. At any rate, a few days after they received the picture and clock I got a call from Franklin, the younger brother. He was very quiet on the phone and asked, "Stan, do you remember the china with the blue onion pattern?" "Yes, of course, Dom and I used it every day, and I'm still using it." "It's the china that Vito gave us many years ago ." Vito remember was Dom's older brother who died of Diabetes. Franklin responded, "I know. We've been talking and... we would like to keep it in the family." I was awestruck. For a second I couldn't speak. Then, "Okay, Franklin I will send it out to you right away." The next day I took all the pieces in a box and brought the box to Box City to have them wrapped individually and sent in a large box to Connecticut. The cost was $671 and I took that amount out of Dom's checking account and then sent them a check for the balances of his savings and checking accounts. Fuck them! That is the last time I will ever communicate with them. I couldn't care less now about his family if they all died. I was so hurt! I guess it is true... death really brings out the truth in people.

e

When I got Dom's ashes, I put them on the mantle for a few days. Finally I decided to spread them on the lawn in the front and back yards, and I was so angry at him that I was ready to then move out of the house... but I like the house so I'm still here. And whether or not Dom liked the house, he is still here too! Is that subtle revenge?

e

I decided a few years ago to go to Cuba before there is a Starbucks or McDonald's on every corner, so I organized a little group and 14 of us went. Among my traveler friends were Neile Adams, Jim Smith, Linda Montana, Marlene Dalton, and Edith Fields, another working actress. Of several new people on this trip I also met Liz Miller and Yvonne Kalman. Yvonne is the daughter of noted composer Emmerich or Imre Kalman. Yyonne has a fantastic 12 bedroom villa in Puerto Vallarta that she rents out, and from the looks of her site and the views from every bedroom, it looks like a paradise for anyone interested in that area. Going to Havana is like traveling into the past. The cars are all 50's automobiles and are in exquisite condition. The people are very friendly and even though we had to go with a group, once we were there we could go anywhere we wanted on our own. The assumption is that you cannot travel by yourself in Cuba, but that assumption is wrong. At least we were never bothered by any government officials, warning us not enter a certain area. So the trip was really educational on many levels. We stayed at the Melia Cohiba Hotel, and it was lovely. We were warned about staying at the Nacional which is Havana's most well known hotel, but when we visited there I spoke to a guest who told me their rooms were small and 'musty'. But the hotel itself including the grounds is beautiful. And you must take a visit to their bars and lounges, with all the

pictures of the celebrities and politicians whose visits they captured on camera. Even Neile who may be a little 'spoiled' loved our trip and our hotel. I only used the expression 'spoiled' because she looks like a little princess to me. I adore her and she's traveled many places throughout the world with me, and she is fun to travel with. I remember one year she was my dancing partner for one of the Share shows, and afterwards she sent me a gorgeous picture of the two of us, when I had her in a deep dip, and the lighting was so dim that we were mostly in silhouette with only our outline highly lit. I still have that picture on my coffee table in my living room... one of my treasures.

I have several friends who are reviewers. Two of them I feel much closer to than the others. In the last few years I've been driving one or both of them to see shows in and around the Los Angeles area. But honestly, we have gone south as far as Escondido to the Lawrence Welk Resort, the San Diego Globe Theatre, and the La Jolla Playhouse, and as far north as the Sacramento Music Circus to see shows. Now I understand that the reviewers do not get any remuneration for their reviews, and I don't get any for my driving, but I get the opportunity to see a lot more shows than I could ever afford to see on my own, so I don't complain. If we do go very far from this area, I will accept extra money for gas, but in and around this area, it is 'expected' that I will pay for the gas. And the one thing I really do not appreciate with any reviewer, and many do not have this quality, is the sense of 'entitlement' that some of them carry around with them. I suppose that 'entitlement' is in lieu of not getting paid for their services. My personal feeling whether I am right or wrong is that if you don't like what you do, given the benefits of your job, don't complain or carry an attitude with you that may come across as being snobbish or selfish. A close reviewer friend of mine goes as far as putting food in his bag at opening night parties whenever he can, I suppose as 'payment' for reviewing the shows. I find that very demeaning and I try walking away whenever I suspect he is doing that. I could use extra food in my larder as well but would never ever stoop to that level. He doesn't even realize it but the people around him are watching him take the food from the buffets and parties. And he is the only person I've ever seen do that, unless at the end of the parties when the hosts would say, "Please, help yourselves to something to take home. We don't have space for the leftovers." I know how embarrassed I get and can't believe that someone doing that doesn't feel at least a little humiliated. But that insensitivity is the quality I abhor in any person. And yet, this particular person never means harm to anyone. I've tried letting him know how I feel, but my words fall on deaf ears. Acceptance is the learning curve to this story, and acceptance is the word for every single relationship whether personal or general that we must acknowledge in order to receive the friendship or love of any other person. And so, I must learn to accept without letting it bother me. Perhaps I will get there someday. I still even at this age have so much to learn.

e

As I've mentioned many times before, my favorite place of travel is Egypt. I haven't been there since 2010, so I decided to take a famiilarization trip so I can let people know how safe they will be when they go there. After flying from Cairo to Luxor early in the morning, it was decided we would go to Karnak Temple on the way to our boat. This first morning in Luxor presented fantastic coincidences which boosted my ego and also allowed for me to contact some people I didn't think I could. When we got to Karnak Temple I decided not to go into the temple which I had visited countless times before. I knew a Mohamed who used to have a bazaar right adjacent to the temple, and he and Shaban were involved in the Taxi incident with the Egyptian police at Karnak which I described before. So when we were dropped off at Karnak, I told the guide I would meet them on their way out of the temple. I began to walk passed the shops to see if anyone looked familiar to me. The first shopkeeper came out and asked, "Can I help you find something?" I knew he thought I just might want to buy something, but I had a different agenda. "Actually," I responded, "I was really looking for a shopkeeper named Mohamed who used to have a person working there named 'Shaban'". "I know them" he responded. "Shaban is my cousin." Now I know that in every third world country everyone there claims they are the cousins of whomever it is you are looking for. But this man said, "Wait, I will call him", whereupon he dialed and put Shaban on the phone with me. I spoke to him and he was renewing something about his car with the government so he wasn't sure he could come to the temple before I left, but he would try. Now I hadn't seen Shaban since that police incident at Karnak, and that was over 12 years ago, so I was looking forward to seeing him. I hung the phone up, and the same shopkeeper who called Shaban said, "And I think I know where Mohamed is. Just follow me." And so I followed him passed many of the souvenir bazaars until we got to one toward the rear end of the rows of shops. And there was Mohamed, my friend whom I hadn't seen since about 2006. Mohamed is a wonderfully observant and religious Muslim man. We greeted each other and I had tea with him as well as a cigarette that he offered. I stayed there for about 45 minutes whereupon I felt I better get back to the other bazaar which overlooked the exit so I could recognize my group on their way out of Karnak Temple. While sitting there and talking with this shopkeeper I decided to have him order a gold and silver cartouche since the price of $45 seemed fair to me and he told me he would have it back before half an hour. I wanted to thank him for getting me in touch with my long lost friends, so the cartouche purchase was an easy way of doing this. While I waited patiently for the cartouche as well as the arrival of Shaban, I turned down the offer for coffee or tea by the young lad who took over the shop while the owner rode by bike to get my cartouche. When I saw our guide and some of the people returning, neither Shaban nor my cartouche had arrived. Suddenly the owner came peddling up with the cartouche. I had in hieroglyphics printed the name 'Mazin' since I had others with 'Stan' on them, I chose to let the group leave and was going to go to the boat by taxi and wait a few more minutes in the hopes that Shaban would show up. Well all the guide said to us before he left was that our boat, 'Nile Goddess', was near the bridge which was very far passed Luxor. While waiting for Shaban who was never able to get there, I told the Taxi-Beer-Karnak Police story to Abdu, the bazaar owner who led me to Shaban and Mohamed. The taxi driver that he had arranged was very late in picking me up but finally arrived. While driving to the boat, the shopkeeper decided to come with us to make sure I was delivered to the boat safely, so he sat in the front seat and I sat as a passenger in the back. He was telling the driver the story I had told him, and after just a few minutes the driver turned to me and said, "I am Ali!" Well Ali was the driver in that same incident, and I didn't recognize him. I was thrilled to see him since I told everyone that story. So we began looking for the boat near the bridge which as I already knew was quite far. We went to one boat dock and asked the policeman there if the Nile Goddess was there and he told us it was, so they pulled into the lot and I paid them and got out of the car and they drove off. Well as I'm walking toward the first boat there which was titled Nile Odyssey, I hear "Stan Mazin" very loudly, and saw a man who was obviously working for the boat, so I assumed they changed the boat on me and since he knew my name, I was probably the last person to check in. He then added, "I'm Kiery's brother!" Well, I had made arrangements to see Kiery, a friend from Luxor that day at 2:30pm in town. I said, "I can't believe it. I will be traveling on the same boat that you are working on, and I'm supposed to meet your brother at 2:30pm today." He brought me into the reception lobby and when I went up to the desk, the man at reception couldn't find me in their roster, or any other American group. So even though the officer outside said my boat was there, it was not, and he probably mistook Nile Odyssey for Nile Goddess. And so the time was running late and we still didn't know where my boat was. The man behind the desk tried finding out with little luck, but in the lobby sitting there was a taxi driver who said he may be able to find it, so I hired yet another taxi driver and we proceeded further this time on the far side of the bridge. We came to the Viking dock and that policemen said, "Yes, the Nile Goddess was there." I told the taxi man not to drive off until I definitely knew my boat was there. I paid him, my boat was there, and the second taxi driver finally left. I was thankful to find Mohamed, and at least speak to Shaban, and again meet Ali, the taxi driver of the incident with the beer at the Karnak police check point... and to top it all off accidentally meeting Kiery's brother Adli at the wrong boat but at the right time... four incidents that brought me even closer to the Egypt I love.

e

But even before I left for this last Egypt trip one day I was driving in Studio City to pick up Don Grigware, my reviewer friend that I attend most of the shows with, and all of a sudden this tremendous shattering noise came from the window on my drivers side... like an explosion, all the glass shattered all over me and all over my side of the car. I immediately pulled over and felt my left side up and down to check that I hadn't been shot. I know sometimes when something like that instantly happens a person goes into shock and doesn't realize he's been hit by something. Once I felt that I was not injured I dialed '911' and had to wait a bit. I explained to the operator what happened and she put the police department on the phone. I asked if I had to wait for them since I had an appointment, and they said, "As long as you aren't hurt, go to your appointment and go to a police station to make a report afterward." I did just that. My window of course was falling apart as I drove but I was afraid to touch any of the glass inside the car in case the police wanted to take pictures. So after my meeting with the reviewer I dropped the reviewer off and went to the North Hollywood Police Station to make my report. The officer was very nice and took care of me. He told me that since they couldn't find a shell in the car, it was probably a bee bee gun that shattered the window and bounced off the glass. On my way to another of my friends I made arrangements for an auto glass place to come to my house the following morning. When I think that my life could have been over in a second, I feel very grateful to be alive. Of course, I very often feel that way anyway. Dealing with one's life is a choice, and I intend to make the most of it whenever I'm able.

By the way, my living conditions have changed. In 2019 after a big birthday, I felt I had to have some sort of change to my life to 'goose it up' a little. So began looking for a new house, on my own, primarily through Zillow. Every house I looked at around half a million dollars was crap... a small fixer upper. But out of the blue, I saw pictures of this beautiful home that was only about $250000. The pictures were great and I had no idea why this seemed so cheap. When I went to the house I found out it was a 'manufactured home' in a 'manufactured park'. What that means is it is a mobile home that is in the ground, rather than on jacks. It was 2500 square feet, 3 bedrooms, 2 1/2 baths, and had a multiple patios around the house connected by a walkway. The house sits on a bluff, so I have no one in front of me on 3 sides. And the 300 degree view is absolutely fantastic. I found out after I bought the house that the owner of the park built this home for himself about 35 years ago. If this view were attached to a regular home, it would have to be valued at over 4 million dollars. I never in my life thought I would ever have a view like this, but now I do. The reason the price is so low is that I now own the house, but I will never own the land, so I lease the land from the gated park. If it were a house with this view,

I could never afford the mortgage payments, but I CAN afford the land payments. I am thrilled to get up every morning to see the view, which seems to change every 10 minutes. Even at night I see the lights of the valley, and it is thrilling for me. I cannot tell you what this has done for my life, but I absolutely love it here. Even my cats who were inside/outside cats in my other domain, love to be indoors here, and they never even try to get out. With the multiple patios, it will make a great party house when I get around to it. I ABSOLUTELY LOVE MY LIFE!!! I'm driving for Lyft every day, which I love... I'm directing, writing, and acting for the GTR... which I love I will soon be teaching tap again but only once a week to keep my mind in shape... and I am beginning to organize group trips for next year already. My life is more than full... it is overflowing!!!

I've always thought about the idea of being interviewed. Speaking freely is something I'm not really used to, but I thought it might be in an interesting idea to have me interviewed by myself So I think Stanley Howard Mazin (SHM) will interview Stan Mazin (SM) now... Here we go...

SHM

When you were young did you ever think you might wind up in show business?

SM

Never! Although my father loved to sing around the house, no one in my family ever was in show business in any capacity. And growing up, I never thought I had any talent. I was such a shy kid, and I was always under the impression that on the very loud and forward people in the world would ever 'make it', particularly in show business.

SHM

You've had a relatively successful career as a dancer. Are you sorry that you are not dancing now?

SM

Dancing was always a joy for me. Oftentimes I really couldn't believe I was getting paid for doing something I enjoyed so much. But the body doesn't lie, and it tells you when it's time to hang up your tutu. And unfortunately since I cannot even attempt to do the things I used to, even though in my mind I still feel that I should be able to, my body dictates what I can and can't do. And it constantly reminds me that I am older now. I look at the dancers today and think, "Thank God I don't have to do those things again". Actually in my day we never even attempted the things they are doing today dance wise. And I honestly have no idea where the time has gone. It's like I woke up and found myself 'old', even though I don't think I think 'old'. Does that make sense?

SHM

Of course it does. But that's what led you to acting, isn't it?

SM

Actually, in my mind, I've always felt that dancing was acting, and I even try to instill in my students that belief So in fact, I was acting before I was 'acting' without the dance. And I really do enjoy that. And again, having explained my feeling about acting, it doesn't seem a chore to me, and when it does, perhaps I'll do something else. I am a Pisces after all.

SHM

You mean you're multi-talented.

SM

I don't want to have an ego that admits that, so I'll just say I'm multi-faceted. I enjoy versatility so can probably be satisfied with doing other things as long as no one judges me against the professionals who do those same other things. I'm not really a good competitor, and I generally don't like to be judged, but let's face it. Everyone wants approval. So I suppose I just like to be appreciated, which I'm sure is normal. I think I can be called a 'Jack of all trades... master of none', although I like to think that I can be considered master of some. But that's probably my ego speaking.

SHM

Speaking of ego, while you were growing up were you aware of your good looks?

SM

Actually I never thought about it until I got to high school and college, when some friends told me they thought I looked like Louis Jordan the French actor and sounded like Tony Curtis. The Louis Jordan part I loved because once I looked him up, I thought, "Wow, what a good looking dude!" So of course I was flattered. As for the Tony Curtis part, he was from Brooklyn I think, and my accent seems to be from South Philly, but I suppose they are talking about the quality of my voice and not the accent. Tony Curtis... that's fine with me. And speaking of looks and age, a very funny thing happened a few months ago... at least I was proud of the humor of my response.

I received an email from someone who offered me a massage with a 'happy ending'. Now we all know what that means, and I honestly had a couple of those offers when I was younger and more handsome... but at this age??? My response was, "I so appreciate the offer... but at my age... a 'happy ending' is when I can get off the massage table, unassisted! What I thought was even funnier is that the recipient of my answer didn't even get my humor. The response was ... "Oh... okay... but are you still interested in the massage?" Needless to say I did not accept the offer, although I still have 'happy endings' from time to time. After all, I'm not dead yet."

SHM

Have you had in your career any truly embarrassing moments?

SM

Well, I don't know about my professional career, but while I was working my way through college, or was it high school, there is a memory that I can never forget. I was working as a busboy at Remo's Italian Restaurant on Sunny Isles in Miami Beach. In the bar there was a jukebox that only had opera numbers in it. I was serving some water to a large table when one of the ladies remarked about the song that was coming over the intercom. "Oh, listen!", she said. "That's 'Un Bel Di'. I just love that song." I leaned forward to her and said, "I'm sorry to correct you, but that's 'One Fine Day'. It's from "Madame Butterfly". I finished serving the water, and even though she looked at me strangely, I walked away rather smugly, while thinking, here I am a lowly busboy and I got to correct a really knowledgeable person... "'Un Bel Di' ... 'One... Fine... Day'... ". I never returned to that table again. I was humiliated and remembered that moment for the rest of my life. There were two other occasions years later that caused me some embarrassment and both of them were because of this reviewer friend I have named Don Grigware. Don loves to take pictures of the stars with him wherever we go. Consequently I became his photographer. Well, on one occasion during the Christmas Holidays we went to the Laguna Playhouse to see their Holiday show. They had these 2 huge Nutcrackers one on each side of the stage. Don kept saying, "I would love to get a picture with me and the Nutcracker for my Holiday card for next year". So while everyone was leaving the theatre, Don said, "Let's go!" and off we went onto the stage to take a picture or two. All of a sudden over the loudspeaker throughout the theatre came a booming voice saying, "Will you 2 gentleman please get off of the stage! GET OFF OF THE STAGE!" Everyone in the theatre who was still leaving turned to see what assholes were on the stage. Truly a humiliating experience. Don and I still laugh about that event. And he still was not finished embarrassing me on yet another occasion. We went to the Northridge Performing Arts Center to see another star and he wanted to go backstage but we didn't have a pass. He saw some people waiting around that seemed to have badges on them so he said "Let's follow them". Off we went backstage and while waiting in the long line I ran into several friends of mine in line like Carol Burnett costumer Bob Mackie and wonderful latino actor Sal Lopez who was there with his wife Urbani. I used to take ballet class and she and I were Sally Whelan's students. Anyway after waiting in line and greeting the people I knew, someone came up to us and said, "I'm sorry. You don't have a pass so you can't stay here". Don began arguing with them until we were escorted out in front of the entire line. I do not like it when someone else humiliates me like that. But Don was as embarrassed by that as I was. And we always remember those times. But I have to say that Don Grigware never meant any harm and he has never had a bad word to say about anyone personally. Did I mention that he is one of the best writers I've ever known? I do believe he is an innocent cherub, like many others I know.

SHM

I can imagine! But to change the subject a little, just for curiosity sake, where were you during 9-11?

SM

Actually, when we first saw the skyscrapers being attacked, I had a travel group and we were in Budapest. We heard about it and it was devastating but even if we were back home, there was really nothing at all that we could do. I know Janet Wood and her husband Jay Silverman were on the trip, and she told me that they had chosen out of respect for all the people who died in the World Trade Center, that they would forego the concert we were to attend that night. The rest of us went, and even though we felt absolutely helpless, I believe just having something to do in a way helped us to get through that day. I remember when we arrived in Prague a few days later, we stayed at the Ambassador Hotel on Wenceslas Square, which is not a square at all. I went into the elevator and one single woman came in. She asked, "Are you an American?" "Yes, I am". "Well, I'm an Australian, and we lost 67 people in the towers... but our hearts go out to you Americans."  My eyes tear up whenever I think of her words again, and again. Another of those moments I will never ever forget. I want to tell you another interesting story relating to the attack. My cousin Alan Levin who lives in south Jersey with his wife, Judy, often will take a day and visit us when I am bringing a group of people for my NYC Theatre Tour. He came alone once before 9-11. I had never met his niece, Alisha, and we made arrangements days before to go down to Wall Street where she was working. He came into town and it was raining. He said, "Let's not go to see her, it's raining. You'll meet her another time." I said, "Alan, I don't mind the rain. It's only water. Besides, how do you know when you'll see her again?" Two months after the attack Alan called me. He said, "I bet you won't remember what you said to me before we went down to see Alisha?" I responded, "No. What did I say?" He came back with, "Well it was raining so I didn't want to go but you said, 'How do you know when you'll see her again?'. Well that is the last time I saw her thankfully because of you." Her office moved to the World Trade Center, and everyone in her office got out including her. Rumor has it she went back for her cell phone. Alan continued, "The last time I saw her was when I was with you." I couldn't believe it. My cousin was thanking me for making him see his niece Alisha for what wound up being the last time. Let this be a lesson for everyone. Don't put off tomorrow what you can possibly do today.

SHM

What a horrific story!

SM

Well, if you've ever been to the WTC , the thought those buildings a block square ever coming down is so foreign to us. So I understand her not being able to even imagine that they would implode. A true tragedy...

SHM

Having read your book, I wondered if you think there was any woman who might have made you happy enough to marry?

SM

With my chosen life style, and I say chosen because in many cases especially in show business, a life style can be a choice, the only ones I came even close to were Maria Florentes , my former Flamenco teacher who has remained a close friend for over 55 years, Anita Murray my fantasy from my early high school years , and Judy Saul, my other girlfriend from Atlantic City High School who also has remained a close friend even though I hardly ever see her. Of course I've imagined marriage, but I know now that I wouldn't have wanted to ruin any woman's life, and it would have to be a very special person to tolerate my idiosyncrasies. So I really don't miss being married to a woman.

SHM

Do you have any regrets?

SM

My only regret is not being a father. I really think I would have been a good father... not a good husband, but a good father. My father was an only child, and I am an only male child in my family. So the end of the Mazin line stops with me. Is there Jewish guilt? Absolutely! But when I wanted a child or children, single men were not allowed to adopt children. Later in life, when we could, I never knew where my next month's mortgage payment was coming from, so I thought it was unfair to raise a child under those circumstances. I really respect the single men or gay couples who have taken that responsibility on. I wish I had been able to.

SHM

I want to thank you for sitting down with yourself and answering some of your own questions. Is there anything at all you'd like to say to the 'listeners', or in this case 'readers'?

SM

Only that life is too short, and should never be taken for granted. And no matter what anyone is experiencing in his or her life, no matter how awful or painful, time is a great healer, and life itself is too valuable to even think about giving it up. Things change and there is always a tomorrow in everyone's life, so look forward to the change. And if by some quirk of luck or talent you

are fortunate to have a good life, allow it to continue, and don't hurt anyone along the way... you can never make up for it. Make your life something you can be proud of. Only you can do that. Only you can truly appreciate that. "No man is an Island?" "Everyman is an island!" Don't waste yours!

LIST OF PHOTOS

EPILOGUE

So now you have it. Here are a slew of memories that make up only one person in this world of billions. I have learned that every one of us has his ownstories, memories, hopes and philosophies. Of course there is always more to be added, from both our past as well as our present and hope for the future. Notice that I used the word 'future' singularly, as even with billions, there is only one future. Imagine the possibility of discovering more lives who have lived... more experiences to have accumulated ... and even more to learn about life... and so much more. The mind boggles. And I hope that with each bit of knowledge we become more aware of, all of us, each and every one, become more tolerant of everything around us so that we can as a human species endure. And that is the only possibility for any future existence for humanity. Let's all give life a chance and not leave any more time for hate, bigotry, bias, or prejudice. Without hurting anyone else make the choice of being happy and accepting your life with all it's flaws. We are given our deck of cards at birth. Let's play the game of life as well as we can by taking advantage of our hand and by making the choice of happiness and sharing it with our friends, family and loved ones. The 'choice of happiness' is the best option of life that we have. Take full advantage of it and it will leave you with bliss, or the closest thing to it that you can imagine. Here's to your island! Here's to life!!!